THE CLOUDS

The Complete Greek Comedy
Edited by William Arrowsmith

Aristophanes

The Clouds

Translated by William Arrowsmith
with sketches by Thomas McClure

Ann Arbor
The University of Michigan Press

Published in the United States of America by
The University of Michigan Press and simultaneously
in Toronto, Canada, by Ambassador Books Limited

Library of Congress Catalog Card No. 62-7233

Manufactured in the United States of America
by The Haddon Craftsmen, Inc., Scranton, Pa.

Designed by George Lenox

FOR JOHN K. COLBY

who first taught me Greek

CONTENTS

Introduction

The Play

⸢The original version of *The Clouds* was presented in March, 423 B.C. at the Great Dionysia, where it disappointed Aristophanes' hopes by being placed third. The First Prize was awarded to the aging Kratinos for his final comedy, *Pytine* (or *The Wineflask*) and the runner-up was Ameipsias with his *Konnos*.[1] After the success of both *Acharnians* and *Knights,* this defeat must have been a bitter blow for Aristophanes. In *Knights* of the year before he had twitted Kratinos with being a doddering drunkard whose comic talents had decayed, and the drunkard had replied by confessing his drunkenness in a play of such comic verve and gaiety —accusing Aristophanes, for instance, of being a mere "Euripidaristophanizing" plagiarist—that he completely defeated his brash young critic. Worse yet, Ameipsias' *Konnos* was, like *The Clouds,* an attack on the sophistic movement, containing a Chorus of Sophists and, evidently, satirizing Sokrates by name. All this might not have mattered had *The Clouds* been a less ambitious play, but Aristophanes regarded it as by far the finest comedy of his career to date.[2]

Probably in the hope of getting a second hearing—if only from readers —he revised the play, and the version of *The Clouds* which we now possess is not the original of 423 B.C. but a revision carried out some three or four years later. According to the Scholiast, the revision was thorough and extensive changes were made, but the chief alterations affected three sections in particular: the *parabasis,* the *agon* between the two *Logoi,* and the finale, the burning of the Thinkery. The full extent of these changes cannot be ascertained. In the *parabasis,* the original choral anapests were replaced by a passage whose meter is unique in a

---

[1] Konnos was the name of Sokrates' music teacher, and it is likely that the play attacked the "New Music."
[2] *The Clouds,* 522: "convinced . . . that this play was the finest of my comedies . . ."

1

parabasis (a probable indication that the poet had no expectation of seeing the play restaged) and in which Aristophanes takes off the customary choral mask and speaks to his readers directly in the first person. To the *agon* was added the famous, passionate defense of the Old Education, a speech clearly designed, through its power of conviction and moral seriousness, to show Aristophanes' critics that what was at stake in this play was nothing less than the fate and future of civilized Athens. About the finale no such certainty is possible, though there is some small reason to believe that in the original version it was the god Hermes, rather than Strepsiades, who fired the Thinkery.

Even in its present form, revised for readers rather than for the stage, *The Clouds* is visibly a masterpiece, a play of wonderful, ragging satire, tilted so expertly toward the preposterous and the absurd that its effect is wholly and unmistakably comic. We have, in fact, almost a *reductio ad absurdum* of the satirical intent, satire become so *buffa* and burlesque that its characters and targets, by sheer exaggeration and incongruity, survive as directly comic. In short, a splendid play, beautifully sustained and shaped, and everywhere guided by Aristophanes' genius for comic distortion and his cunning of absurdity. If not the funniest play he ever wrote, it is certainly the cleverest: clever in construction and plot, clever in its exploitation of incongruities, clever in polemic and wit. Almost, perhaps, too clever for its own good. But for Aristophanes these very qualities of cleverness and wit were precisely what made *The Clouds* superior to his own previous work and that of his "cheap and vulgar rivals": for their slapstick of situation and crude horseplay he here substitutes the ludicrous slapstick of the intellect and the better horseplay of poetry and imagination. In its structure too *The Clouds* is an improvement. Unusually tight and coherent,[3] at least by Aristophanic standards, its action is all of a piece, a continuously unfolding plot, written to be performed by a small cast, and singlemindedly devoted to the pursuit of its quarry. If it lacks the miraculous violence and vigor of *The Knights* or the exuberance of *The Acharnians,* it makes up for those qualities by the greater clarity and economy of its design and the pure lyricism of its poetry. Until *The Birds,* there is nothing in Aristophanes to match the loveliness of the poetry here assigned to the Chorus of Clouds as it enters. In this play, for the first time, we catch a glimpse of that exquisite tension between slapstick and poetry, the obscene and the sublime, which was Aristophanes' major individual contribution to

[3] In my opinion the only major structural flaw in the play is the abrupt change in the role of the Chorus. At least I find a jar when the Clouds suddenly reveal that they are actually celestial *agents provocateurs* masking as the patrons of the Sophists.

comedy and which lies at the heart of his two greatest lyrical comedies, *The Birds* and *The Frogs*.

At first blush the improbable victim of *The Clouds* seems to be the philosopher Sokrates. But actually Aristophanes is deliberately exploiting Sokrates here as a convenient comic representative of the sophistic corruption which is the play's real subject. In the illustration of that corruption, Sokrates is nothing more than the poet's cipher, a curious catchpaw of those enormous cultural polarities (Old and New, Tradition and Innovation, Country and City, Peace and War, Poetry and Prose, Custom and Logic, etc.) which Aristophanes loved to elaborate and which he presented in play after play as locked in a life-and-death struggle for the soul of Athens. Whether Aristophanes privately believed that Sokrates was a sophist or presented him that way for its comic and preposterous effect, we shall never know. But for the purposes of the play, Sokrates is merely a genial polemical emblem of the sophistic movement—if that extraordinary simultaneous flowering of individual genius, crankery, "educationism," and fraud can be called a movement at all. For Aristophanes such distinctions are academic, and to his mind the sophists are a movement only because they are something worse, a conspiracy of charlatans and humbugs. Distinctions of doctrine and belief are totally disregarded. Jumbled together in ludicrous proximity and then stuffed into the mouth of Sokrates are the doctrines of Protagoras, the pre-Socratics generally, Anaxagoras, Diagoras, Gorgias, Prodikos, and perhaps Thrasymachos. It is grotesque—and hilarious. It is polemic on the grand scale, contemptuous of niceties, careless of reputations, unfair, Procrustean, and passionately loyal to its central perception. Addressed to, and exploiting, the average man's ridiculous stereotype of philosophy and science, it remains an honest and uncompromising play.

Grant Aristophanes his premises, and his logic is ruthlessly consistent. If Sokrates is a symbol of intellectual corruption and fraud, Strepsiades represents the Old Tradition in its corruption. Far from presenting Sokrates as the indispensable corrupter, Aristophanes shows that Strepsiades can be hoodwinked only because he had been corrupted *prior* to his enrollment in the Thinkery. All Sokrates does is to complete the process—or at least he tries to. But for Aristophanes the Sophists are merely symptoms of the general corruption, not its causes; they stand to education and the life of the mind exactly as Kleon stands to politics and Euripides to tragedy. If the Sophists are strong in being unprincipled, Strepsiades is weak because he is stupid and because the principles and values that might have protected him from his own stupidity have deteriorated. He is essentially only a denser Dikaiopolis become citified and decadent; in another context he might have been a peasant hero. But transplanted to Athens from the country, cursed with an expensive aristocratic marriage and a playboy son, he is an Awful Warning on the Perils of the City and the Evils of Imperialism. According to Aristophanes, the process of corruption began with Athenian imperialism and the war fought to maintain the empire. If imperialism brought with it tyranny, luxury, litigation, and the domination of political life by demagogic rhetoric, the war was destroying the very fabric of Athenian life by ravaging the countryside and forcing the evacuation of the country population into the city. There, cut off from the earth and uprooted from the context that gave it life and value, the Old Order had decayed, and with it were being destroyed all those traditions and virtues and decencies which, for a conservative countryman like Aristophanes, were synonymous with Athenian civilization itself. Strepsiades is his comic image of this corruption and Sokrates its aggravating symptom. If the causes were irremediable, he could at least struggle with the symptoms. And no quarter asked or given.

Aristophanes and Sokrates

Why did Aristophanes select Sokrates as his spokesman for the Sophists, and was he guilty of malicious slander and moral irresponsibility in so doing?

By now these two questions have become inextricably bound up with the fortunes of the play which is, ironically, more commonly read as a perverse adjunct to The Sokratic Problem than for its satire of the sophists. No definite answer is possible in the poor state of our evidence, but the questions cannot be shrugged off, and I offer the following considerations for what they may be worth.

1. Plato's charge against Aristophanes is the serious charge of moral irresponsibility. By circulating a distorted image of Sokrates, Aristophanes created, or abetted, those slanders which Plato believed led to Sokrates' death. The official indictment read: "Sokrates is a malefactor who meddles in the matters of the heavens and the earth below, who makes the Worse Argument appear the Better and teaches others to follow his example." And the Platonic Sokrates comments to the jury: "You yourselves have seen these very things in Aristophanes' comedy—a Sokrates who is carried around in a basket and asserts that he walks upon the

air and a great many other aburdities, of which I am completely ignorant." We *may,* if we wish, doubt Plato's interpretation, but presumably the charges are accurately reported, and the implication is clear: the slanders of *The Clouds,* directly or indirectly, created the formal accusation brought against Sokrates in 399 B.C.

2. But the evidence is partisan and polemical. Plato's account is that of a devoted disciple, not a reporter, and the prejudice of Platonists is almost religious.[4]

3. Sokrates' own reaction, if Plutarch can be trusted,[5] was not that he had been slandered but that he had been teased: "I am twitted in the theater as I would be at a drinking-party."

4. Nonetheless, judging from the available evidence, the caricature of Sokrates in *The Clouds* is so distorted that it cannot be called a caricature at all. Thus Sokrates refused payment, was not an atheist, had no Thinkery, and never held the doctrines which are here put into his mouth. Worse, he consistently attacked the Sophists and their doctrines. He does, however, admit in the *Apology* that in his earlier days he had dabbled in "scientific" research.

5. That Aristophanes could not have foretold the consequence of his "slanders" is irrelevant. Slander is slander.

6. Aristophanes' private opinion of Sokrates is also irrelevant. In Plato's *Symposium,* the two men are presented as being on friendly terms, but this does not entitle us to suppose that Aristophanes really admired Sokrates or thought his views anything but pernicious. If it does, then Aristophanes was a hypocrite as well as morally irresponsible.

7. If Aristophanes was really ignorant of Sokrates' beliefs, he is equally culpable. Ignorance is no excuse for slander. But Aristophanes was anything but an ignorant man, and his refusal to allow his Sokrates to make one statement that is recognizably Sokratic seems to me to indicate strategy rather than stupidity.

8. The distortions practiced upon Sokrates are typical and not exceptional. They are, for instance, completely of a piece with Aristophanes' systematic distortion of Euripides; if Euripides' words are quoted against him, they are invariably taken from their context and parodied by willful misunderstanding. But those who are angered by the spectacle of Sokrates mocked have never lifted a finger in defense of Euripides.[6]

---

[4] It has even been suggested that *The Clouds* failed to win First Prize because the audience recognized—and disliked—the distorted image of Sokrates. Given what happened to Sokrates, this seems excessively naive.

[5] *De educatione puerorum* xiv.

[6] As Speaker of the House Rayburn said in a different context: "It all depends on *whose* ox is gettin' gored."

9. In any case, the treatment of Sokrates is *not,* by Aristophanic standards, harsh or "pitiless satire," as Platonists claim. It is, in fact, surprisingly mild and impersonal. (The savage attack upon Kleon in *The Knights* is an instructive comparison.) Thus, apart from a couple of gibes at Sokrates' gait and general bathlessness, his personal life is strictly avoided. We hear nothing of the shrewish Xanthippe, nothing of the fashionable pederasty of the Socratic circle (or at least nothing that implicates Sokrates), nothing about Sokrates' midwife-mother (*cf.* the treatment meted out to Euripides' mother), etc. The charges are wholly professional: Sokrates is a humbug and a charlatan.

10. Aristophanes' "slanders" are, in some real sense, dictated by convention. Comedy is the heir of the early *komos,* and the *komos* was a convention whose essential attributes were invective and abuse. Which is to say merely that the Athenian comedian was not merely given license to be abusive, but that abuse was *expected* of him. And precisely because it was conventional, was expected, it could be discounted as conventional; and presumably those who were ragged were expected to take their ragging in good part—as Sokrates did, though Kleon (and Plato) did not. Needless to say, such a convention makes the notion of "moral irresponsibility" extremely hard to assess.

11. Sokrates is presented as preposterous and this strikes me as cool and deliberate strategy—doubtless sustained by malice and even a little contempt. There is, after all, a kind of humor—the kind of humor of the *komos,* I suspect—which contrives its fun out of a total inversion of the truth. Because the humor is conventional, the exaggeration is understood *as* exaggeration and the humorist's success consists in the very size and absurdity of the distortion. The comedy lies in the disparity between the known truth and the degree of distortion achieved. This explanation might be less acceptable if it were not for the fact that Aristophanes is, of all comedians, the master of the incongruous, and that the stunning distortion is everywhere his stock-in-trade.

12. If Aristophanes has not made Sokrates preposterous because the preposterousness was funny, he has done so out of dislike and the conviction that Sokrates was dangerous. In this he was probably mistaken, but Aristophanes was a man in the livery of an Idea, and if Sokrates is distorted or satirized in the service of that Idea, it is regrettable but not culpable. Ideas distort the world and those who serve them. Platonists should understand.

The texts which I have used as a basis of this translation are primarily those of Cantarella and Coulon, and I am, like every other translator of Aristophanes, indebted to B. B. Rogers' splendid notes and commentaries on individual passages. To both the University of California at Riverside and the University of Texas I owe my thanks for generous grants for the preparation of the manuscript. For help and encouragement and criticism, I am indebted to a great many people, but particularly to Douglass Parker and to my wife.

WILLIAM ARROWSMITH

Characters of the Play

STREPSIADES, *father of Pheidippides*
PHEIDIPPIDES, *a playboy*
XANTHIAS, *a slave*
STUDENTS OF SOKRATES
SOKRATES
CHORUS OF CLOUDS
KORYPHAIOS, *or Chorus Leader*
ARISTOPHANES
PHILOSOPHY
SOPHISTRY
PASIAS, *creditor of Strepsiades*
AMYNIAS, *creditor of Strepsiades*
CHAIREPHON, *disciple of Sokrates*

SLAVES, STUDENTS, WITNESSES, etc.

SCENE: *A street in Athens. On the left, the house of
Strepsiades,* an old farmer compelled by the war
to leave the country and take up residence in Athens;
on the right the tiny, grubby, ramshackle hovel
which houses Sokrates' Thinkery. On the extreme
left a statue of Poseidon. Before Strepsiades' house
stands a Herm, a bust of the god Hermes supported
by a square pillar; in front of Sokrates' house,
balancing the Herm, stands a potbellied stove with
a long tapering flue and a placard which reads:*
MODEL OF THE UNIVERSE ACCORDING TO THE CON-
VECTION PRINCIPLE.

*Two cots are placed before Strepsiades' house, one
occupied by Strepsiades himself, the other by
Pheidippides. Huddled on the ground nearby lie
several loudly snoring slaves. The time is just before
dawn.*

STREPSIADES

*Thrashing restlessly, then throwing off his blankets
and sitting bolt upright. He yawns.*

    Yaaaahhuuuuu.
    Great Zeus Almighty, what an endless monster
of a night it's been! Won't the daylight *ever* come?
I could have sworn I heard the roosters crowing hours
ago.
      And listen to those slaves. Still snoring away!
By god, things around here were a long sight different
in the good old days before this war! Drat
this stinking war anyway! It's ruined Athens.
Why, you can't even whip your own slaves any more
or they'll desert to the Spartans.*
                        Bah.

Pointing to Pheidippides.

                        And as for *him,*
that precious playboy son of mine, he's worse yet.
Look at him, stretched out there sleeping like a log
under five fat blankets, farting away.
                  —All right,
if that's the way you want it, boy, I'll snuggle down
and fart you back a burst or two.

*He burrows under the blankets for a moment, then
throws them off and sits up again.*

            DAMN!

I'm so bitten up by all these blasted bedbuggering debts
and bills and stable-fees, I can't catch a wink.

Turning on Pheidippides.

And all because of YOU!

Yes, you and your damned horses!
Gigs, rigs, nags, ponytails*. . . . Hell,
horses everywhere! Horses in your dreams!

But *me?*
I'm bankrupt, broke, ruined, waiting for the end of the month
when all these debts come due.

Savagely kicking Xanthias awake.

—You. You there,

light me a lamp and bring me my ledger.

*The slave rises, lights a flickering lamp, and brings
him the ledger.*

Now then,

I'll just run over this account of my debts and see
how much I owe.

Hmmmm.

Reading aloud.

TO PASIAS: *THE SUM OF THREE*

HUNDRED—
Three hundred to Pasias? What in god's name for?
Of course. I remember. That gelding I bought him. Idiot!
Better I should have gelded myself.

PHEIDIPPIDES

Shouting in his sleep.

PHILO,
YOU FOULED ME! KEEP IN YOUR OWN LANE!

STREPSIADES

That's it.

That's the horsey blight that has blasted me dead.
Even in his dreams he thinks he's winning the derby.

PHEIDIPPIDES

In his sleep.

HOW MANY LAPS FOR THE STEEPLECHASE?

STREPSIADES

Laps, is it?

A fat lot of laps you've driven your poor old man!

Resuming his accounting.

Let's see now. What's the next entry after Pasias?

Reading aloud.

> TO AMYNIAS: FOR GIG, BODY AND WHEELS INCLUDED,
> THE SUM OF—

PHEIDIPPIDES

In his sleep.

> ROLL THE HORSE IN THE DUST, TRAINER,
> AND THEN STABLE HIM.

STREPSIADES

You've rolled *me* out of house and
home, damn you!
I've lost two or three lawsuits on your account and now
the other creditors are clamoring for confiscation.

PHEIDIPPIDES

Waking up crossly.

Damn it, Dad,
why do you have to thrash around like this all night long?

STREPSIADES

Because there's a bumbailiff* in the mattress biting me,
that's why.

PHEIDIPPIDES

Oh, for god's sake, let me sleep, will you?

STREPSIADES

Go on, damn you, sleep! But I give you warning, boy.
Someday these debts will land on *your* head.

Pheidippides' only answer is a snore.

By god,
I hope that meddling matchmaker who prodded me on
to marry your mother dies a nasty death!
I used to be a farmer—the sweetest life on earth,
a lovely, moldy, unspruce, litter-jumbled life,
bursting with honeybees, bloated with sheep and olives.
And then, poor hick, what did I do but marry
your mother, a city girl, and niece of that Megakles
who was son and heir of old Blueblood Megakles* himself?
She was a pretty piece: Miss Megakles-de-luxe.
Well, so we got married and we clambered into bed—
me, a stink of wine-lees, fig-boxes, and wool-fat;
she, the whiff of spices, pure saffron, tonguekisses,
Luxury, High Prices, gourmandizing, goddess Lechery,
and every little elf, imp, and sprite of Intercourse.

13

But I'll say this for your mother: she was a worker.
Nothing slow about *her*. All day long she'd sit there
working away at her loom and shoving in the wool,
and then in bed at night she'd work on me
for more.
>   Expense meant nothing.
>   Clipped?
>   I was *shorn*.
"Madam," I said, "what do you think I am? A man
or a goat?

Suddenly the oil lamp sputters and goes out.

XANTHIAS
>   There's no oil left in the lamp.

STREPSIADES
>   Jackass!
And why in god's name did you light that guzzler of a lamp?
Come here and be whipped.

XANTHIAS
>   But why? What have *I* done?

STREPSIADES
Because you put in pot-bellied wicks, that's why.

He lunges at Xanthias who ducks away and dis-
appears into the house.

>   Anyway, when that darling brat of ours was born
to the missus and me, we immediately started squabbling
over his name. She, of course, wanted something fancy,
some upperclass, high-horse handle with *hippos** in it—
Xanth*ippos* or Char*ippos* or Kall*ippi*des—while I naturally
wanted to give him the fine old name of Pheidonides*
in honor of his thrifty grandfather. Well, we haggled
and at last agreed on a compromise name: Pheidippides.*
She used to gush over the baby: "Just imagine. Someday
he'll be an important man, just like his Uncle Megakles,
and drive in his purple robes up to the Akropolis."
And I'd put in: "Ha, drive his goats from the hills,
you mean, dressed like his dad in a filthy smock."
Well, needless to say, he paid no heed to me
and now he's ended up by squirting his dirty horse-pox
all over my money.

Anyway, after beating my brains
all night long, I think I've finally found a way,
the *only* way out, a wonderful little chink of a loophole.
Now if I can only shove him through it, I'm saved.
But first I've got to find some way of waking him up.
I wonder what's the nicest way to wake up.

Hmmmm.

Cooing in Pheidippides' ear.

Pheidippides.

Little Pheidippides.

PHEIDIPPIDES

Waking angrily.

Damn it, Dad, what *now?*

STREPSIADES

Give your Old Man a kiss. There, now your hand, son.

PHEIDIPPIDES

Look here, what's this all about?

STREPSIADES

Tell me, my boy,

are you *really* fond of your poor old father?

PHEIDIPPIDES

Sure, Dad.

I swear it. So help me Poseidon.

STREPSIADES

No, NOT THAT!

For god's sake, none of those horse-god oaths* of yours!
Poseidon indeed! That god's the cause of all my troubles.
But if you *really* love me, my boy, I beg you, implore you,
do what I ask.

Please.

PHEIDIPPIDES

Suspiciously.

Depends. What are you asking?

STREPSIADES

Reform yourself, boy. Change your whole way of life.
Follow my advice and make a new man of yourself.
A fresh Pheidippides.

PHEIDIPPIDES

But how?

STREPSIADES

First promise.

PHEIDIPPIDES

Reluctantly.

I promise.

So help me—Dionysos.

STREPSIADES

Good. Now then, look over there.
Do you see that dirty little hovel with the dinky door?

PHEIDIPPIDES
Yes. But what are you driving at, Dad?

STREPSIADES

Awesomely.

My boy,
that little hovel is the Thinkery. Intellectuals live there,
professors who will teach you—and what's more, *prove* it—
that the whole atmosphere is actually a Cosmical Oven*
and we're not really people but little bits of charcoal
blazing away. What's more—for a fee,* of course—
they offer a course called *The Technique of Winning Lawsuits.**
Honest or dishonest, it's all one.

PHEIDIPPIDES

Who are they?

STREPSIADES
Great Scholars. Scientists.

PHEIDIPPIDES

Fine. Who are they?

STREPSIADES

Er . . .

Gentlemen. Men of Learning.

PHEIDIPPIDES

Yes, but what are their *names?*

STREPSIADES
Why . . .

16

PHEIDIPPIDES

        Oh lord, I know those filthy charlatans you mean—
those frauds, those barefoot pedants with the look of death,
Chairephon and that humbug, Sokrates.

STREPSIADES

Scandalized.

        Here, here, boy.
Hush. For shame. Don't ever let me hear you talking
so disrespectfully. What's more, if you don't want
your poor Old Man to starve, you'd better go study there
and ditch your damn horses.

PHEIDIPPIDES

        By Dionysos, I *won't!*
Not on your life. I wouldn't go there if you bribed me
with every racehorse in Leogoras' stable!

STREPSIADES

        My dearest boy,
I implore you. *Please* go and study at the Thinkery.

PHEIDIPPIDES
Study *what?*

STREPSIADES

        I've heard that they teach two kinds of Logic.*
One of them is called Philosophical, or Moral, Logic—
whatever *that* may be. The other one is called
Sophistic, or Sokratic, Logic. Now, if you could learn
this second Logic, I wouldn't have to pay a penny
of all those debts you've saddled me with.

PHEIDIPPIDES

        Count me out.
I'd rather die. Why, those vampires would suck me dry.
They'd scrape the tan right off my face. How could I
face the fellows down at the track?

STREPSIADES

        Then, by Demeter,
you've had your last meal on me. Take your critturs
and pack out of this house and be damned to you!

PHEIDIPPIDES

won't let me go horseless for long. I'll go to him.
The hell with you.

Exit Pheidippides.

STREPSIADES

I'm down, but not for long.
First I'll say a little prayer to the gods, and then
I'll go and enroll at the Thinkery myself.

But whoa:
at my age the memory is bad, the intellect dull.
How could I ever master that hair-splitting logic?
Still, I have to go, so why am I dawdling here
instead of banging on the door?

He walks over to Sokrates' house and kicks at the
door.

—Hey, porter!

STUDENT

From within.

Go bang yourself.

Opening the door.

Who are you to kick our door?

STREPSIADES

Strepsiades, son of Pheidon. From Kikynna.

STUDENT

By god, the way you come here and kick in our door
I think your name should damn well be Stupidities.
Do you realize that you've just caused the miscarriage*
of a great scientific discovery?

STREPSIADES

Humbly apologetic.

Oh, please excuse me.
I didn't realize. You see, I come from the country.
But tell me, what discovery miscarried?

STUDENT

It's top secret.
Classified information. Access only to students.

STREPSIADES

You can tell *me* then. That's why I've come here,
to be a student at the Thinkery.

18

STUDENT

In that case, very well.
But remember, our researches are solemn mysteries.

Whispering.

Listen.

Just a minute ago Sokrates was questioning Chairephon
about the number of fleafeet a flea could broadjump.
You see, a flea happened to bite Chairephon on the eyebrow
and then vaulted across and landed on Sokrates' head.

STREPSIADES
How did he measure it?

STUDENT

A stroke of absolute genius.
First he melted some wax. Then he caught the flea,
dipped its tiny feet in the melted wax,
let it cool, and lo! little Persian bootees.
He slipped the bootees off and measured the distance.

STREPSIADES
Lord Zeus, what exquisite finesse of mind!

STUDENT
Elementary really. You haven't heard *anything* yet.
Would you like another sample?

STREPSIADES

Oh, I'd *like* that. Go on.

STUDENT
Well, it seems that Chairephon was asking Sokrates
which of two theories he held: that gnats tootled
through their mouths or, in reverse, through their tails.

STREPSIADES

Eagerly.

Gosh. Go on. What was his theory about the gnat?

STUDENT

Attend.

According to him, the intestinal tract of the gnat
is of puny proportions, and through this diminutive duct
the gastric gas of the gnat is forced under pressure
down to the rump. At that point the compressed gases,

as through a narrow valve, escape with a whoosh,
thereby causing the characteristic tootle or cry
of the flatulent gnat.

STREPSIADES

                              So the gnat has a bugle up its ass!
O thrice-blessèd mortals! What bowel-wisdom!
Why, the man who has mastered the ass of the gnat
could win an acquittal from any court!

STUDENT

                                        And you know,
just the other day he was cheated of an immense discovery
because of a lizard.

STREPSIADES

                        Cheated by a *lizard?* But how?

STUDENT

It happened at night, during the course of his researches on the orbit
of the moon. There he stood, gaping wide-mouthed
at the sky, when a lizard on the roof let loose on him.

STREPSIADES

Ha! A lizard crapping on Sokrates! That's rich.

STUDENT

And last night there was nothing in school to eat.

STREPSIADES

                                                    Goodness,
how did he ever manage your supper?

STUDENT

                                        A combination
of science and legerdemain.
                              He quickly sprinkled the table
with a fine film of powderlike ashes. Then,
deftly bending a skewer in the shape of a compass
he drew a vast arc along whose perimeter
the hook of his compass encountered somebody's cloak.
Quickly flicking his hand, he pulled back compass
and catch. He pawned the cloak; we ate the proceeds.

STREPSIADES

Why, Thales himself was an amateur compared to this!

Throw open the Thinkery! Unbolt the door
and let me see this wizard Sokrates in person.
Open up! I'm MAD for education!

*The ekkyklema is wheeled about to show the whole
interior court of Sokrates' Thinkery. High overhead
the crane supports Sokrates in his basket busily
scanning the heavens. Hanging on the walls of the
Thinkery are various charts, maps, instruments, etc.
In the center of the courtyard stand a number of
utterly pale, emaciated students deeply engaged in
a rapt contemplation of the ground.*

Great Herakles,
what kind of zoo is this?

STUDENT

What's so strange about it?
What do you take them for?

STREPSIADES

Spartan prisoners
from Pylos.* But why are they all staring at the ground?

STUDENT
They're engaged in geological research:* a survey
of the earth's strata.

STREPSIADES

Of course. Looking for truffles.

To one of the students.

—You there, don't strain yourself looking. I know
where they grow big and beautiful.

*Pointing to other students who are bent completely
double.*

Hey, and look there:
what are those fellows doing bent over like that?

STUDENT
Those are graduate students doing research on Hades.

STREPSIADES
On Hades? Then why are their asses scanning the skies?

STUDENT
Taking a minor in Astronomy.

To the students.

> —Quick, inside with you.
> Hurry, before the Master catches you.

STREPSIADES

> No, wait.
> Let them stay a little longer. I want to speak to them
> on a *private* matter.

STUDENT

> Impossible. The statutes clearly forbid
> overexposure to fresh air.

The students disappear through a door at the rear.
Strepsiades meanwhile is staring at the various maps
and instruments on the walls.

STREPSIADES

Pointing to a chart.

> In the name of heaven,
> what's *that*?

STUDENT

> That's for astronomy.

STREPSIADES

Pointing to surveying instruments.

> And what are those?

STUDENT
They're for geometry.

STREPSIADES

> Geometry? And what's that good for?

STUDENT
Surveying, of course.

STREPSIADES

> Surveying what? Lots?

STUDENT
No. The whole world.

STREPSIADES

> What a clever gadget!
> And as patriotic as it is useful.*

STUDENT

Pointing to a map.

Now then, over here
we have a map of the entire world. You see there?
That's Athens.

STREPSIADES

That, Athens? Don't be ridiculous.
Why, I can't see even a single lawcourt in session.*

STUDENT
Nonetheless, it's quite true. It really is Athens.

STREPSIADES
Then where are my neighbors of Kikynna?

STUDENT

Here they are.
And you see this island squeezed along the coast?
That's Euboia.

STREPSIADES

I know that place well enough.
Perikles squeezed it dry.* But where's Sparta?

STUDENT
Sparta? Right over here.

STREPSIADES

That's MUCH TOO CLOSE!
You'd be well advised to move it further away.

STUDENT
But that's utterly impossible.

STREPSIADES

You'll be sorry you didn't,
by god.

*For the first time Strepsiades catches sight of
Sokrates in his basket overhead.*

Look: who's that dangling up there in the basket?

STUDENT
Himself.

STREPSIADES
Who's Himself?

24

STUDENT

Sokrates.

STREPSIADES

SOKRATES!

Then call him down. Go on. Give a great big shout.

STUDENT

Hastily and apprehensively taking his leave.

Er . . . *you* call him. I'm a busy man.

Exit Student.

STREPSIADES

O Sokrates!

No answer from the basket.

Yoohoo, Sokrates!

SOKRATES

From a vast philosophical height.

Well, creature of a day?

STREPSIADES

What in the world are you doing up there?

SOKRATES

Ah, sir,
I walk upon the air and look down upon the sun
from a superior standpoint.

STREPSIADES

Well, I suppose it's better
that you sneer at the gods from a basket up in the air
than do it down here on the ground.

SOKRATES

Precisely. You see,
only by being suspended aloft, by dangling
my mind in the heavens and mingling my rare thought
with the ethereal air, could I ever achieve strict
scientific accuracy in my survey of the vast empyrean.
Had I pursued my inquiries from down there on the ground,
my data would be worthless. The earth, you see, pulls down
the delicate essence of thought to its own gross level.

As an afterthought.

Much the same thing happens with watercress.

STREPSIADES

Ecstatically bewildered.

You don't say?

Thought draws down . . . delicate essence . . . into watercress.
O dear little Sokrates, please come down. Lower away,
and teach me what I need to know!

Sokrates is slowly lowered earthwards.

SOKRATES

What subject?

STREPSIADES

Your course on public speaking and debating techniques.
You see, my creditors have become absolutely ferocious.
You should see how they're hounding me. What's more, Sokrates,
they're about to seize my belongings.

SOKRATES

How in the world
could you fall so deeply in debt without realizing it?

STREPSIADES

How?

A great, greedy horse-pox ate me up, that's how.
But that's why I want instruction in your second Logic,
you know the one—the get-away-without-paying argument.
I'll pay you *any* price you ask. I swear it.
By the gods.

SOKRATES

By the gods? The gods, my dear simple fellow,
are a mere expression coined by vulgar superstition.
We frown upon such coinage here.

STREPSIADES

What do *you* swear by?
Bars of iron, like the Byzantines?*

SOKRATES

Tell me, old man,
would you honestly like to learn the truth, the *real* truth,
about the gods?

STREPSIADES

By Zeus, I sure would. The *real* truth.

26

SOKRATES

And also be admitted to intercourse with their Serene Highnesses,
our goddesses, the Clouds?

STREPSIADES

Intercourse with *real* goddesses?
Oh yes, I'd *like* that.

SOKRATES

Very well. First, however,
you must take your seat upon the mystical couch.*

STREPSIADES

I'm sitting.

SOKRATES

And now we place this sacrificial wreath on your head.

STREPSIADES

A *sacrificial* wreath?
Hey, NO!
Please, Sokrates,
don't murder me like poor Athamas* in Sophokles' play!

SOKRATES

Athamas was saved. You must mean Phrixos.

STREPSIADES

Athamas,
Phrixos—so who's a critic? Dead is dead.

SOKRATES

Courage, gaffer. This is normal procedure, required
of all our initiates alike.

STREPSIADES

Yeah? What's in it for me?

SOKRATES

Sprinkling Strepsiades from head to toe with ritual
flour.

You shall be reborn, sir, as the perfect flower of orators,
a consummate, blathering, tinkling rascal.

STREPSIADES

That's no joke.
I'll be all flour the way you're powdering me.

SOKRATES

Silence!

Holy hush command your tongue. Listen to my prayer.

He stretches out his hands to heaven and prays.

O Lord God Immeasurable Ether, You who envelop the world!
O Translucent Ozone!

And you, O lightningthundered holy Clouds!
Great Majesties, arise!

Reveal yourselves to your Sophist's eyes.

STREPSIADES

Whoa, ladies, don't rain yet. Don't get me wet. Let me wrap up.

He wraps his head in his tunic.

What a damned fool! Coming without a hat.

SOKRATES

Come forth,
be manifest, majestic Clouds! Reveal your forms to me.
And whether on Olympos' snow your brooding eyrie lies,
or on the waves you weave the dance with Ocean's lovely daughters,
or dip your golden pitchers in the waters of the Nile,
or hover on Mount Mimas' snows, or over Lake Maiotis—
come forth, great Clouds!

Accept our prayers!

O hear us!

Amen.

From far off in the distance the Clouds are heard
singing. As they slowly approach Athens, the singing
increases steadily in volume as it rises in pitch.

CHORUS

Rise and soar
eternal Clouds!
Lift your loveliness of rain,
in sodden splendor come!
Soar from ocean's sullen swell,
rise higher to the peaks,
to the tall cliffs and trees!
Rise and soar,
while far below,
earth and shining harvest lie,
sound of god in river water,
blessèd ocean at its roar.

Arise!
For Ether's sleepless eye
now breaks with blazoned light!
Shake loose the rain,
immortal forms,
and walk upon the world!

A sustained burst of thunder is heard.

SOKRATES

O Clouds consummately blest, how clearly thy answer rumbles!

To Strepsiades.

—Did you hear that thunder crack, that *basso profundo* peal?

STREPSIADES

And how!

All hail your holyships! What a nasty jolt you gave me!
What a ratatat! You scared me so I've got to thunder too.

He breaks wind.

Sacrilege or not, I'VE GOT TO CRAP!

SOKRATES

Silence, boor!
No more of your smut. Leave filth like that to the comic stage.

A short low growl of thunder is heard.

Shhh.
Quiet.
The goddess swarm is stirring to its song.

CHORUS

Virgins of rain,
look on Pallas' shining earth,
this oil-anointed land,
country of Kekrops'
hero-breeding plain!
Holiness is here,
home of the mysteries,
whose unrevealable rites
sanctify the soul.
And here the gods have gifts.
Below the splendid gables go
processions of the blest,
and every season sees
its festivals, its crowns.

And early every Spring
Dionysos brings his joy,
the weaving of the dance,
the Muses and the flutes.

STREPSIADES
Holy Zeus, Sokrates, who were those ladies that sang
that solemn hymn? Were they heroines of mythology?

SOKRATES
                                                    No, old man.
Those were the Clouds of heaven, goddesses of men of leisure
and philosophers. To them we owe our repertoire of verbal talents:
our eloquence, intellect, fustian, casuistry, force, wit,
prodigious vocabulary, circumlocutory skill—

STREPSIADES
Suddenly carried away in cloudy inspiration.
                                        Then that's why
I suddenly tingled all over—as though I were carried up,
buoyant, exalted, swollen somehow with the flatus of philosophy:
a mist of verbal fluff, a sudden unsubstantial swelling,
a tumid bubble of wrangling words, a windbag of debate!
I seemed rent by lightning speech, ah, the thrust and parry
of opinion, of minds massively meeting . . .
                                        In short, Sokrates,
if I could see those ladies in person, I'd LOVE to.

SOKRATES
Then look over toward Parnes. I can see them settling down
ever so gently.

STREPSIADES
            Where?

SOKRATES
                There, a vast drifting swarm
nuzzling along through woods and valleys.

STREPSIADES
Rubbing his eyes.
                                        I wonder what's wrong.
I can't see them.

SOKRATES
            Look: just offstage.

STREPSIADES

Now I see them!

SOKRATES

You've got cataracts, friend, if you can't see them now.

Slowly and majestically, the Chorus of Clouds files
in and takes up its position in the orchestra.

STREPSIADES

Ooh, what venerable ladies! They take up all the space.

SOKRATES

And you actually mean to say that it's never occurred to you
that the Clouds of heaven were goddesses?

STREPSIADES

By Zeus, it's news to me.
I always used to think they were just fog and drizzle and mist.

SOKRATES

Clearly then you must also be ignorant of the fact that the Clouds
are also patrons of a varied group of gentlemen, comprising:
chiropractors, prophets, longhairs, quacks, fops, charlatans,
fairies, dithyrambic poets, scientists, dandies, astrologers,
and other men of leisure. And because all alike, without exception,
walk with their heads among the clouds and base their inspiration
on the murky Muse, the Clouds support them and feed them.

STREPSIADES

I see.
That's why they write*—
O downblow, dazed, of the sodden skies!
and
   Ho, tresses of the Typho-headed gale! Ho, puffcheek squalls!
or
   Spongy humus of the hyaline!
                              and
                        Hail, ye heaven-scudders,
sudden ospreys of the winds!
                     and
                        Come, ye wheeling cumuli,
ye clammy condensations, come!
                        And in return, these poets
gorge themselves on the flesh of the mullet and eat of the breast
of the thrush?

SOKRATES
And why not?

STREPSIADES
But what I want to know is this:
why, if these ladies are really Clouds, they look like women?
For honest clouds aren't women.

SOKRATES
Then what *do* they look like?

STREPSIADES
I don't know for sure. Well, they look like mashed-up fluff,
not at all like women. No, by Zeus. Women have . . . noses.

SOKRATES
Would you mind if I asked you a question or two?

STREPSIADES
Go right ahead.

SOKRATES
Haven't you sometimes seen a cloud that looked like a centaur?
Or a leopard perhaps? Or a wolf? Or a bull?

STREPSIADES
Often. So what?

SOKRATES
Well, the Clouds assume whatever shape they wish. Now suppose
they happened to meet some shaggy, hairy beast of a man—
Hieronymos, for instance; instantly they turn into wild centaurs
as a caricature of his lust.

STREPSIADES
I see. But what if they run into Simon,
that swindler of government funds?

SOKRATES
Presto, they turn into wolves
and catch his likeness to a T.

STREPSIADES
Oh, I see. And yesterday
because they met that coward Kleonymos, they turned into deer?

SOKRATES
Precisely. And just now, when they saw Kleisthenes in the audience,
they suddenly turned into women.

33

STREPSIADES

                             Welcome then, august Ladies!

Welcome, queens of heaven!

                           If ever you spoke to mortal man,

I implore you, speak to me!

A great burst of thunder.
Strepsiades cowers with fright.

KORYPHAIOS

                          Hail, superannuated man!

Hail, old birddog of culture!

To Sokrates.

                        And hail to you, O Sokrates,

high priest of poppycock!

                        Inform us what your wishes are.

For of all the polymaths on earth, it's you we most prefer—
you and Prodikos. Him we love for wisdom's sake, but you, sir,
for your swivel-eyes, your barefoot swagger down the street,
because you're poor on our account and terribly affected.

STREPSIADES

Name of Earth, what a voice! Solemn and holy and awful!

SOKRATES

These are the only gods there are. The rest are but figments.

STREPSIADES

Holy name of Earth! Olympian Zeus is a figment?

SOKRATES

Zeus?

       What Zeus?

              Nonsense.

                    There is no Zeus.

STREPSIADES

                             No Zeus?

Then *who* makes it rain? Answer me that.

SOKRATES

                        Why, the Clouds,

of course.

          What's more, the proof is incontrovertible.

                             For instance,

have you ever yet seen rain when you didn't see a cloud?
But if your hypothesis were correct, Zeus could drizzle from an empty
  sky

while the clouds were on vacation.

STREPSIADES

By Apollo, you're right. A pretty
proof.
And to think I always used to believe the rain was just Zeus
pissing through a sieve.
All right, *who* makes it thunder?
Brrr. I get goosebumps just saying it.

SOKRATES

The Clouds again,
of course. A simple process of Convection.

STREPSIADES

I admire you,
but I don't follow you.

SOKRATES

Listen. The Clouds are a saturate water-solution.
Tumescence in motion, of necessity, produces precipitation.
When these distended masses collide—*boom!*
Fulmination.

STREPSIADES

But who makes them move before they collide? Isn't that Zeus?

SOKRATES

Not Zeus, idiot. The Convection-principle!

STREPSIADES

Convection? That's a
new one.
Just think. So Zeus is out and convection-principle's in.
Tch, tch.
But wait: you haven't told me who makes it thunder.

SOKRATES

But I just *finished* telling you! The Clouds are water-packed;
they collide with each other and explode because of the pressure.

STREPSIADES

Yeah?
And what's your proof for *that?*

SOKRATES

Why, take yourself as example.
You know that meat-stew the vendors sell at the Panathenaia?
How it gives you the cramps and your stomach starts to rumble?

STREPSIADES

Yes.

by Apollo! I remember. What an awful feeing! You feel sick
and your belly churns and the fart rips loose like thunder.
First just a gurgle, *pappapax;* then louder, *pappaPAPAXapaX,*
and finally like thunder, *PAPAPAPAXAPAXAPPAPAXapap!*

SOKRATES
Precisely.
First think of the tiny fart that your intestines make.
Then consider the heavens: their infinite farting is thunder.
For thunder and farting are, in principle, one and the same.

STREPSIADES
Then where does lightning come from? And when it strikes
why is it that some men are killed and others aren't even touched?
Clearly it's *got* to be Zeus. He's behind it, blasting the liars
with bolts of lightning.

SOKRATES

Look, you idiotic Stone-Age relic,

if Zeus strikes the liars with lightning, then why on earth
is a man like Simon still alive? Or Kleonymos? Or Theoros?
They're liars ten times over.

But no. Instead of doing that,

he shatters his own shrines, blasts the holiest place names
in Homer and splinters the great oaks. And why, I ask you?
Have you ever heard of an oak tree committing perjury?

STREPSIADES

Say,

you know, you've got something there. But how do you explain
the lightning?

SOKRATES

Attend.

Illustrating his lecture by means of the potbellied-
stove Model of the Universe.

Let us hypothesize a current of arid air

ascending heavenwards. Now then, as this funnelled flatus
slowly invades the limp and dropsical sacks of the Clouds,
they, in turn, begin to belly and swell, distended with gas
like a child's balloon when inflated with air. Then, so prodigious
become the pressures within that the cloud-casings burst apart,
exploding with that celestial ratatat called thunder and thereby
releasing

36

the winds. These, in turn, whizz out at such incalculable velocities
that they catch on fire.

Result: lightning.

STREPSIADES

                        The very same thing that hap-
pened to me
at the great feast of Zeus!

                I was roasting myself a sausage
and forgot to slit the skin. Well, suddenly it bloated up
and SPLAT!

          —singed my eyebrows off and splattered my face with
guts.

CHORUS

—Ah, how he hungers after learning!

To Strepsiades.

                   —Sir, if you can pass our test,
we guarantee that you shall be

             —the cynosure of Hellas.
—Our requirements are these:

          —First, is your memory keen?
—Do you hanker for researching?

           —Are you subject to fatigue
from standing up or walking?

          —Does winter weather daunt you?
—Can you go without a meal?

          —Abstain from wine and exercise?
—And keep away from girls?

        —Last, do you solemnly swear
adherence to our code?

              —To wrangle

                —niggle

                   —haggle

                     —battle
—a loyal soldier of the Tongue, conducting yourself always
like a true philosopher.

STREPSIADES

              Ladies, if all you require
is hard work, insomnia, worry, endurance, and a stomach
that eats anything, why, have no fear. For I'm your man
and as hard as nails.

SOKRATES

And you promise to follow faithfully in my path,
acknowledging no other gods but mine, to wit, the Trinity—
GREAT CHAOS, THE CLOUDS, and BAMBOOZLE?

STREPSIADES

If I met

another god,
I'd cut him dead, so help me. Here and now I swear off
sacrifice and prayer forever.

KORYPHAIOS

Then, Sir, inform us boldly
what you wish. Providing you honor and revere the Clouds
and faithfully pursue the Philosophical Life, you shall not fail.

STREPSIADES

Ladies, I'll tell you.
My ambition is modest, a trifling favor.
Just let my muscular tongue outrace the whole of Hellas
by a hundred laps.

KORYPHAIOS

Sir, you may consider your wishes granted.
Never, from this time forth, shall any politician in Athens
introduce more bills than you.

STREPSIADES

But I don't want to be a Senator!
Listen, ladies: all I want is to escape the clutches
of my creditors.

KORYPHAIOS

Your wishes are modest; we grant them.
And now, Candidate, boldly commit yourself to the hands
of our ministers.

STREPSIADES

Ladies, you've convinced me completely. Anyway,
thanks to my thoroughbreds, my son, and my wife, I have no choice.

So I hereby bequeath you my body,
for better, dear girls, or worse.
You can shrink me by slow starvation;
or shrivel me dry with thirst.

You can freeze me or flay me skinless;
    thrash me as hard as you please.
Do any damn thing you've a mind to—
    my only conditions are these:

that when the ordeal is completed,
    a new Strepsiades rise,
renowned to the world as a WELSHER,
    famed as a TELLER OF LIES,

a CHEATER,
            a BASTARD,
                    a PHONEY,
                            a BUM,
SHYSTER,
        MOUTHPIECE,
                TINHORN,
                        SCUM,
STOOLIE,
        CON-MAN,
                WINDBAG,
                        PUNK,
OILY,
        GREASY,
                HYPOCRITE,
                        SKUNK,
DUNGHILL,
        SQUEALER,
                SLIPPERY SAM,
FAKER,
        DIDDLER,
                SWINDLER,
                        SHAM,
—or just plain Lickspittle.

And then, dear ladies, for all I care,
    Science can have the body,
to experiment, as it sees fit,
    or serve me up as salami.

Yes, you can serve me up as salami!

KORYPHAIOS

Ah, here's a ready spirit, undaunted, unafraid!

                                                     —Sir,

complete your course with us and you shall win a glory
that towers to heaven.

STREPSIADES

                             Could you be a little more specific?

KORYPHAIOS

You shall pass your entire existence up in the air, among us,
strolling about with your head in the Clouds. Your life
shall be the envy of all mankind.

STREPSIADES

                                    Ah, when shall I see that day?

KORYPHAIOS

Before long thousands of clients will stampede to your doors,
begging, pleading, imploring your service and advice
in all their lawsuits—many involving incredible sums.
I say no more.
                 —And now, Sokrates, take this old candidate
and test his worthiness to undergo the solemn rites of initiation.
Examine his mental powers; probe his mind and sift him.

SOKRATES

Now then, tell me something about yourself.
The information is essential if I'm to know
what strategies to employ against you.

STREPSIADES

                                       Strategies?
What do you think I am? A military objective?

SOKRATES

No. I'm merely attempting to ask a few questions.
First, is your memory keen?

STREPSIADES

                             Well, it is and it isn't.
If a man owes me money, I never seem to forget it.
But if I do the owing, I somehow never remember.

SOKRATES

Well, perhaps you have some talents for speaking?

STREPSIADES

No, no talent for talk. But for larceny, lots.

SOKRATES

But how can you possibly learn?

STREPSIADES

Don't you worry.
I'll manage somehow.

SOKRATES

But look: suppose I toss you
some tidbit of higher wisdom? Could you catch it
on the fly?

STREPSIADES

What do you take me for? A puppydog
snapping up wisdom?

SOKRATES

No, a beastly old ignoramus.
In fact, I'm afraid we'll have to whip our wisdom
into your hide.
Hmmm.
Tell me, suppose someone
gave you a thrashing, what would you do?

STREPSIADES

Why,
I'd take my thrashing. Then after a little while
I'd hunt up a witness, and then a little while later
I'd bring suit for Assault and Battery.

SOKRATES

All right, old man,
undress.

STREPSIADES

Undress? But why? Have I said something wrong?

SOKRATES

No, no. But we require all candidates for initiation
to strip naked.

STREPSIADES

But I'm not a burglar,* Sokrates.
Here, search me if you want.

SOKRATES

What do you think I am?
A policeman? This is a solemn philosophical initiation.
So stop your idiot blather and get undressed.

STREPSIADES

Starting to undress with extreme reluctance.

Oh, all right.
No, wait.

First answer me this. If I study very hard
and pay attention in class, which one of your students
will I look like?

SOKRATES

Why, you'll be the spitting image of—
Chairephon.

STREPSIADES

CHAIREPHON! But he's a walking cadaver.
I'll graduate a corpse.

He feverishly whisks his cloak back on.

SOKRATES

Damnation! Stop this stalling
and GET UNDRESSED!

*He pulls off Strepsiades' cloak and shoves him bodily
toward the black cavelike opening at the rear of
the Thinkery.*

Forward, Candidate!

STREPSIADES

NO! WAIT!
I'm scared. Brr, it's as dark as a snakepit down there.
Give me a honeycake to throw to the snakes, Sokrates,
or they'll eat me alive.

SOKRATES

Forward, fool. No hesitation now!

*Sokrates shoves Strepsiades before him into the
opening at the rear of the Thinkery. Then he rushes
back, snatches up Strepsiades' discarded cloak,
smiles, tucks it under his tunic, and vanishes into
the Thinkery.*

CHORUS

> Farewell, brave soul,
> and may your future gleam as bright
> as shines your courage now!
> May all good fortune come to you
> who, sunk in bitter age,
> in the somber twilight of your years,
> stride forth, undaunted, unafraid,
> toward that uttermost frontier of thought
> where wisdom lures you on,
> O pioneer!

*The Chorus turns sharply and faces the audience.
From the wing appears the poet, the bald Aristophanes; he strides forth and addresses the audience
directly.*

ARISTOPHANES*

Gentlemen, in the name of Dionysos to whom I owe my nurture as
     a poet,
I intend to confront you with my personal complaints, frankly
     and freely,
as a poet should.
                    My ambitions, of course, are very simply stated:
the First Prize and a reputation for talent and wit.
                                                 Accordingly,
firmly convinced that this audience was composed of men of taste,
and that this play, THE CLOUDS, was the finest of my comedies to
     date,
I submitted an earlier version, expecting your pleasure and approval.
It cost me enormous anguish and labor, and yet I was forced to with-
     draw,
ignobly defeated by cheap and vulgar rivals. My present reproaches,
needless to say, are aimed at those self-styled critics and wits
for whom this revision has been made.
                                       However, to the men of true
     taste
among you, I say this: I am, as always, your faithful friend,
and never will I willingly or knowingly abandon you or reproach you.
After all, I still remember that glorious day when the Judges—
men of whose extraordinary taste and discrimination it is a joy to
     speak—
awarded the First Prize to my youthful comedy, *The Banqueters*.
Now at that time, gentlemen, my Muse was the merest slip of a girl,
a tender virgin who could not—without outraging all propriety—

give birth. So I exposed her child, her maiden effort, and a stranger
rescued the foundling.* But it was you, gentlemen, whose generous
    patronage
nourished my offspring, and I have never since doubted those tokens
of your exquisite taste.

                And now, gentlemen, like Elektra in the play,*
a sister-comedy comes in search of you today, hoping to find
those same tokens of recognition. Let her so much as glimpse
a single curl from her brother's head, and she will know her own,
as I shall know the tokens of your approval.

                            She's a dainty play.
Observe, gentlemen, her natural modesty, the demureness of her dress,
with no dangling thong of leather,* red and thick at the tip,
to make the small boys snigger. Note too her delicate refinement—
her refusal to indulge in cheap cracks at the expense of baldness,
and the quiet dignity of her dancing, with nothing salacious about it.
Observe the absence of farcical slapstick and sensational situations.
Here you see no poor old man drubbing his opponents with a stick
in a futile attempt to hide the abysmal poverty of his verses.
Nor does she fling herself on stage with tragic torches blazing
and bloodcurdling fustian. No, gentlemen, my comedy comes to you
relying upon herself and her poetry.

                       This is what she is,
and I am the poet, her adoring father. Now I may be baldheaded
(as some of my competitors so tirelessly point out), but I am *not*
    vapid;
and it has never been *my* practice to serve you up some réchauffé
of stale and tired plots. No, my fictions are always fresh,
no two of them the least alike, and all of them uproariously funny.
Observe, moreover, gentlemen, that it was *I* who punched Kleon
in the paunch in his hour of pride; yet once I had him on the ground,
I refused to kick him.

                But consider my competitors; note their conduct
with poor Hyperbolos. Once they had him floored, they never stopped
grinding him down in the dirt—*plus* his mother into the bargain.
It was Eupolis, of course, who led the mass-attack upon Hyperbolos;
he gutted my KNIGHTS, botched it, and then dragged the resultant
    abortion
on stage—a stunning new plagiarism entitled (of *course*) THE
    PEDERAST.
Even as larceny, a complete flop: Eupolis wanted a dirty dance,*
so what did he do but introduce a drunken old hag to shake her hips?
Not that *she* was original either; he lifted her from an ancient play
by Phrynichos (who quite sensibly fed the old bitch to a sea monster).

So much for Eupolis.

  After him, Hermippos opened up on Hyperbolos,
and before long every imitator in town was after Hyperbolos' hide,
and every last one of them plagiarized my celebrated simile on the
 eels.*
I devoutly pray that those who like such stuff are bored to death
by mine. But as for you men of taste who enjoy your Aristophanes
and applaud his talent, why, posterity will endorse your judgment.

Exit Aristophanes.

CHORUS

    You, our king, we summon first.
    Omnipotence, in glory throned,
    look down upon our dances.
      O Zeus, be with us now!

    And you, steward of the sea,
    whose savage trident's power
    heaves the shattered world
    and pries the waters up,
      O Poseidon, hear our prayer!

    And you, O Father Ether,
    pure presence of Air,
    nourisher, sustainer,
      O Spirit, quicken us now!

    And you whose flaring horses blaze
    across the skies! O benison,
    splendor whose shining spills
    on earth, on heaven,
      O Light, illuminate us all!

KORYPHAIOS

Gentlemen, Critics, and Clever Fellows:
           YOUR ATTENTION
  PLEASE.
Because our agenda includes a few complaints and home truths,
we shall be blunt.
      WE ARE TIRED OF BEING IGNORED.
                   Of all
  the gods
to whom this city stands in debt for benefits conferred,
no god has brought more benefits than we. Yet we alone,
forsaken and forgotten gods, receive no sacrifice at all.

But surely we need not remind you of all our loving care,
the unsleeping devotion lavished, gentlemen, on your behalf?

For ex-
ample,
whenever you launch some exceptionally crack-brained project,
we promptly thunder our objection; we drizzle our displeasure.
Or look to recent history. Have you forgotten that black day
when a low tanner, a repulsive atheist nicknamed Paphlagon*
was running for election as General? And how we responded?
How we furrowed our beetling brows and rumbled with rage,
and *hard on the heels of the Levin rattled the steeds of Thunder?*
How the moon, in dudgeon, snuffed her flame amongst the rack,
and the sun in sullenness withdrew,* curling his blazing wick
back beneath his globe, refusing to shine if this Kleon
were elected?

So you elected—Kleon!

As native Athenians, gentlemen,
you are all familiar with that local brand of statesmanship
sometimes known as Blundering Through—the curious belief
which holds that, by virtue of some timely divine intervention,
all your most appalling political blunders will sooner or later
redound to the interest of Athens.

Whence the question arises:
why not make a good thing of this latest glaring example
of Blundering Through?

How?

By convicting this cormorant Kleon
of bribery and peculation. Then muzzle his omnivorous maw
and slap a yoke around his neck. Not only is such action
in perfect accord with your long tradition of Blundering Through,
but with one shrewd stroke all your bungling is redeemed
as statesmanship, manifestly furthering the noblest interests of Athens.

CHORUS

> O lord of Delos, you
> who haunt the cliffs and scarp,
> where the ridge of Kynthos rises,
>> *O Phoibos, be with us now!*

> And you of Ephesos, lady,
> glory of the shrine of gold
> where the Lydian women worship,
>> *O Artemis, come to the dance!*

And you, goddess on the hill,
mistress of this lovely land
beneath your aegis guarded,
  O Athene, be with us now!

And you, dancer of Delphoi,
runner upon the peaks, at dark
when the trailing torches flicker
and the whirling Maenads cry their joy,
  O Dionysos, dance with us now!

KORYPHAIOS

Our cluster of Clouds had gathered for the outing down to Athens
when we chanced to run into the Moon, who asked us to deliver
the following message on her behalf:

GREETINGS SALUTATIONS
  ETCET
TO ATHENS AND ALLIES STOP MY DEITY MORTALLY OF-
  FENDED
BY YOUR SCANDALOUS RUDENESS DESPITE MANY SUB-
  STANTIAL CONTRIBUTIONS
TO WELFARE OF ATHENS STOP AM WOMAN OF ACTIONS
  REPEAT ACTIONS
NOT WORDS
      (Signed)
        THE MOON.
            And the Moon has a point,
  gentlemen.
Thanks to her shining efforts on your behalf, your average savings
on lighting alone run more than a drachma a month. Why,
I can hear you now, instructing your slaves as you leave the house,
"No need to buy torches tonight, lad. The moonlight's lovely."
And moonlight is merely one of her many services. Nonetheless,
you brusquely refuse to devise an Accurate Lunar Calendar,
and your month is a consequent chaos,* a masterpiece of temporal
  confusion.
Worse still, when the gods come hungrily trudging home at night
and find they must do without their dinner because you celebrate
your festivals on the wrong day, it's the poor innocent Moon
who bears the brunt of their heavenly grumbling. What's more,
on the days when you ought to sacrifice to the gods, you're bustling
about holding trials or torturing some poor witness on the rack.

And conversely, no sooner do the gods fast or go into mourning
for Memnon or Sarpedon, than you Athenians start carousing
and boozing.
                    So be warned, gentlemen.
                                        Very recently the gods
stripped Hyperbolos of his seat* on the Commission for Public Fes-
    tivals
and Other Red-Letter Days—a measure designed to teach him
and all such Johnnies-Come-Lately a little respect for time.

*While the Chorus resumes its customary position,
the doors of the Thinkery are thrown open and
Sokrates appears.*

SOKRATES

Almighty Effluvium! Ozone and Chaos! Never
in all my days have I seen such peerless stupidity,
such a bungling, oblivious, brainless imbecile as this!
I no sooner teach him the merest snippets of science
than he suffers an attack of total amnesia. Still,
the Truth is my mistress and I obey.

*He goes to the Thinkery door and peers into the
darkness.*

                                        —Strepsiades,
        where are you?
                    Fetch your mattress and come outside.

*Strepsiades appears at the door, tugging at his
mattress.*

STREPSIADES
I can't come. The little bugs won't let me leave.

SOKRATES
Down with it, blockhead. Now your attention, please.

STREPSIADES
Ready.

SOKRATES
        To resume then, what particular discipline
in that vast array of choices offered by your ignorance
would you especially like to acquire? For instance,
would you prefer diction or rhythm or measures?

STREPSIADES

                                                   Measures.

Why, just the other day the flourman swindled me
of half a peck.

SOKRATES

                Not dry measures, dunderhead!
I want to know which *meter* you'd prefer to master—
trimeter or tetrameter.

STREPSIADES

                Well, I like the yard
as well as anything.

SOKRATES

                Rubbish. Palpable rubbish.

STREPSIADES

What would you like to bet that your trimeter isn't
exactly three feet?

SOKRATES

                Why, you illiterate numskull!
However, perhaps you'd do better with rhythm.

STREPSIADES

                                Rhythm?

Will rhythm buy the groceries?

SOKRATES

                        Sensitivity to rhythm
confers a certain ineluctable social *savoir-faire.*
Polite society will accept you if you can discriminate, say,
between the marital anapest and common dactylic—
sometimes vulgarly called finger-rhythm.*

STREPSIADES

                            Finger-rhythm?

I know *that.*

SOKRATES

        Define it then.

50

STREPSIADES

Extending his middle finger in an obscene gesture.

Why, it's tapping time

with *this* finger. Of course, when I was a boy

*Raising his phallus to the ready.**

I used to make rhythm with *this* one.

SOKRATES

Why, you lout!

STREPSIADES

But look, you goose, I don't want to learn this stuff.

SOKRATES

Then what *do* you want to learn?

STREPSIADES

Logic! Logic!

Teach me your Immoral Logic!

SOKRATES

But, my dear fellow,

one must begin by mastering the rudiments of language.
For instance, can you list me the male quadrupeds?

STREPSIADES

Pooh, I *would* be a damnfool if I didn't know *them*.
Listen: the ram, the buck, the stallion, the bull,
the duck—

SOKRATES

And now the females of the same quadrupeds.

STREPSIADES

Let's see: the ewe, the doe, the mare, the cow,
the duck—

SOKRATES

Stop right there. A gross solecism.

According to you, the word *duck* apparently applies
to both the male and female of the species.

STREPSIADES

Huh?

How do you mean?

SOKRATES

In *your* usage, they're both ducks.

52

STREPSIADES

Holy Poseidon, you're right! What should I have said?

SOKRATES

The male is a *duck;* the female's a *duchess.**

STREPSIADES

A *duchess?*

Bravo! Almighty Ozone, that's a good one!
For that little lesson, you can bring out your basket
and I'll fill it with seed.

SOKRATES

Oops. Another solecism.
You've made *basket* masculine, when it's feminine.*

STREPSIADES

What?

Basket is masculine? But why?

SOKRATES

Because the ending-*et*
is what in grammar we call a masculine termination.
Like the *-os* ending of *Kleonymos.*

STREPSIADES

Wait. I don't see.

SOKRATES

I repeat: *basket* and *Kleonymos* are masculine in form
and ending.

STREPSIADES

Kleonymos *masculine?* But *he's* feminine.
Form and ending. Queer as they come.

But look,

what *should* I call a basket?

SOKRATES

Why, a *baskette,* of course.
By analogy with *toilette.*

STREPSIADES

Baskette, eh?

SOKRATES

That's it.
Now you're talking Greek.

STREPSIADES

The *baskette* of *Kleonymette?*

SOKRATES

Precisely. Which brings us to the distinction between
men's names and women's names.

STREPSIADES

Oh, I know the female names.

SOKRATES

For example?

STREPSIADES

For example: Lysilla, Philinna, Demetria,
Kleitagora—

SOKRATES

And now recite some masculine names.

STREPSIADES

Easy. There's thousands of them. Like Philoxenos, Melesias,
Amynias—

SOKRATES

Stop, you nincompoop. I asked for men's names,
not women's names.

STREPSIADES

You mean those *aren't* men's names?

SOKRATES

Not men's names at all. A transparent confusion
between singular and plural. Suppose, for instance,
we drop the plural *s* from Amynias, what would we have?

STREPSIADES

Why, Amynia.*

SOKRATES

You see, by dropping the plural *s,*
you've made Amynias a singular woman.

STREPSIADES

                              Well, the draftdodger,
it serves him right. But why am I learning stuff
any damn fool knows?

SOKRATES

                    Fool, you flatter yourself.
However, lie down on your mattress and—

STREPSIADES

                              And what, Sokrates?

SOKRATES

And lucubrate upon your dilemma.

STREPSIADES

                         Please, no, Sokrates!
Anywhere but there. Couldn't I just go and lubricate
on the ground?

SOKRATES

               Permission refused.

STREPSIADES

                         Ohh, what a fate!
Those little bugs are sure to crucify me now.

*Strepsiades burrows under the infested sheepskins
on his mattress, while Sokrates chants encouragement.*

SOKRATES

                    First concentrate.
                    Then cerebrate.
                       Now concentrate again.

                    Then lucubrate.
                    Next, speculate
                       Now ruminate. And then,

                    if your mind gets stuck,
                    don't curse your luck.
                       Get up! Quick as a wink,

                    cut through the knot,
                    swift as a thought,
                       but THINK, Candidate, THINK!

Now hence, ye Syrops of Sleep! Come hither, O Pain!

STREPSIADES

Yooooooow! Yooooooow!

SOKRATES

Look here, what's biting you now?

STREPSIADES

Biting, you say?
THEY'RE MURDERING ME!
Out of the ticking
the bugs come creeping.
They're biting my ribs.
They're swilling my blood.
My balls are all sores.
My ass is a shambles.
THEY'RE MURDERING ME!

SOKRATES

There, there, old fellow. Don't take it so hard.

STREPSIADES

DON'T TAKE IT SO HARD?
When my money's gone?
When my skin's gone?
When my blood's gone?
And then what's more,
when I tried to hum
and forget these bites,
I DAMN NEAR DIED!

There is a brief interval of silence during which
Strepsiades hums and thrashes under his covers.
Then Sokrates picks up a sheepskin and peers under.

SOKRATES

Here, what's this? Have you stopped lucubrating?

STREPSIADES

Who, *me?*

By Poseidon, I *have not!*

SOKRATES

What thoughts have you had?

STREPSIADES

Only this: I've been thinking how much of me would be left
when the bugs got through.

SOKRATES

Bah! Consume you for an ass.

STREPSIADES

I *am* consumed.

SOKRATES

Courage, gaffer. We mustn't repine.
Pull back your covers and concentrate. What we need
is some clever quibbling subterfuge with which to frustrate
and fleece your creditors.

STREPSIADES

Who's fleecing *who*, Sokrates?
That's what I'd like to know.

Another brief silence follows.

SOKRATES

Hmmm. I wonder
what he's up to now? I'll just peek under the covers.

He lifts the sheepskin.

What's this? Asleep on the job, are you?

STREPSIADES

By Apollo,
I'm *not* sleeping!

SOKRATES

Any thoughts yet?

STREPSIADES

Not a thing.

SOKRATES

Surely you've found *something*.

STREPSIADES

Well, only this thing
I've got in my hand.

SOKRATES

Buffoon! Get back to your pallet
and cogitate.

STREPSIADES

But, Sokrates, what am I cogitating *about?*

SOKRATES

A moot question, friend, whose answer lies with you.
When *you* know what *you* want, kindly illuminate *me.*

STREPSIADES

But I've told you ten thousand times already, Sokrates.
It's my debts. I want to welsh on my debts.

SOKRATES

Splendid.

Then back to your pallet.

Strepsiades dutifully crawls under his sheepskin.

And now distill your mind
to its airiest essence, allowing the subtle elixirs of thought
to permeate and penetrate every pore of the problem.
Then Analyze, Refine, Synthesize, Define—

STREPSIADES

Frantically thrashing to escape the bugs.

OUCH!

SOKRATES

Stop fidgeting!
—However, in the case of a dilemma,
defer your inquiry briefly. When refreshed, return,
sift your conclusions and knead vigorously. Then mull
the results.

STREPSIADES

Suddenly illuminated.

Ooooh, Sokrates!

SOKRATES

Yes?

STREPSIADES

EUREKA!
I've got it. A glorious dodge for ditching my debts!

SOKRATES

Aha. Expatiate.

STREPSIADES

Well, just suppose—

SOKRATES

Supposing *what?*

STREPSIADES

Just suppose I rented one of those witchwomen from Thessaly*
and ordered her to charm down the moon from the sky. And then
I snatch up the moon and I pop her into a box,
and polish her face until she shines like a mirror.

SOKRATES

And what would you gain by that?

STREPSIADES

What would I gain?
Why, think what would happen if the moon never rose.
I wouldn't have to pay interest.

SOKRATES

No interest? But why?

STREPSIADES

Because interest falls due on the last day of the month,
before the New Moon, doesn't it?

SOKRATES

A superlative swindle!
Now then, let me propose a somewhat thornier case.
You are threatened, we assume, with a suit for five talents.
Problem: how do you quash the verdict?

STREPSIADES

How? *I* don't know.
I'd have to meditate on *that.*

SOKRATES

By all means meditate;
but beware of immuring your mind with excessive introspection.
Allow your intellect instead to sally forth upon her own,
as though you held a cockroach on a leash.

STREPSIADES

Suddenly illuminated.

Ooh, Sokrates, I've found a glorious bamboozle! I've got it!
Admit it, it's wonderful!

SOKRATES

Kindly expound it first.

STREPSIADES

Well, have you ever noticed in the druggists' shops
that beautiful stone, that transparent sort of glass
that makes things burn?

SOKRATES

A magnifying glass, you mean?

STREPSIADES

That's it. Well, suppose I'm holding one of these,
and while the court secretary is recording my case,
I stand way off, keeping the sun behind me,
and scorch out every word of the charges.*

SOKRATES

By the Graces,

a magnificent Bamboozle!

STREPSIADES

Whew, and am I glad

to get *that* suit quashed!

SOKRATES

Now then, try your teeth

on this little teaser.

STREPSIADES

Shoot.

SOKRATES

This time imagine
that you find yourself a defendant without a witness.
Your case is absolutely hopeless. Problem: to prevent
your opponent's suit from coming to trial.

STREPSIADES

Pooh,

nothing to it at all.

SOKRATES

Elaborate.

STREPSIADES

But it's a pushover,
Sokrates. While they were trying the case before mine,
I'd go hang myself.

60

SOKRATES

Preposterous!

STREPSIADES

It's *not* preposterous.
You can't sue a corpse.

SOKRATES

Poppycock. Palpable rubbish.
As your tutor, I hereby resign. And now, GET OUT!

STREPSIADES
You resign? But why?

Falling on his knees in supplication.

Oh, please. I implore you, Sokrates . . .

SOKRATES
But you forget everything as fast as you learn it, numskull!
Tell me, what was the first lesson?

Well, speak up.

STREPSIADES
Let me think.
The first lesson?
The *first* lesson?
Ummm. That whoozit you put seeds in!

For god's sake,
what *is* it called?

SOKRATES

Why, you blithering bungler!
You senile incompetent! You . . . you mooncalf! Clear out!

STREPSIADES
Sweet gods in heaven, what's to become of me now?
I'm a goner unless I master those sleights-of-tongue.

Falling on his knees before the Chorus.

O most gracious Clouds, please advise me. Tell me
what to do.

KORYPHAIOS

Our counsel, reverend sir, is this.
Have you a grown-up son perhaps? Then send him off
to study in your place.

STREPSIADES

It's true, ladies, I have a son,
but he's a gentleman, you see, with a true gentleman's
natural distaste for learning. So what can I do?

KORYPHAIOS
Is he the boss?

STREPSIADES

Well, he's a strapping, sturdy boy,
and there's a bit of eagle-blood on his mother's side.
Still, I'll go fetch him anyway. If he refuses
to learn his lessons, by god, he'll never set foot
in my house again!

To Sokrates.

—I won't be gone a moment.

Exit Strepsiades into his house.

CHORUS

Now, sir, you see
what blessings we,
    the Clouds, have brought to pass.

E.g. this fool-
ish, willing tool,
    this frantic, eager ass.

But seize your prey.
Avoid delay.
    No matter how well hooked,

your fish is not
fried fish till caught—
    and goose is better cooked.

*Exit Sokrates. Enter Strepsiades, dragging
Pheidippides.*

STREPSIADES
Out with you! By Condensation, you won't stay here!
Go cut your teeth on Megakles' money!

PHEIDIPPIDES

But Father,
what's the matter with you? Are you out of your head?
Almighty Zeus, you must be mad!

STREPSIADES

                          "Almighty Zeus!"
What musty rubbish! Imagine, a boy your age
still believing in Zeus!

PHEIDIPPIDES

                What's so damn funny?

STREPSIADES

It tickles me when the heads of toddlers like you
are still stuffed with such outdated notions. Now then,
listen to me and I'll tell you a secret or two
that might make an intelligent man of you yet.
But remember: you mustn't breathe a word of this.

PHEIDIPPIDES
A word of what?

STREPSIADES

              Didn't you just swear by Zeus?

PHEIDIPPIDES
I did.

STREPSIADES

    Now learn what Education can do for *you:*
Pheidippides, there is no Zeus.

PHEIDIPPIDES

                  There is no Zeus?

STREPSIADES

No Zeus. Convection-Principle's in power now.
Zeus has been banished.

PHEIDIPPIDES

            Drivel!

STREPSIADES

                Take my word for it,
it's absolutely true.

PHEIDIPPIDES

          Who says so?

STREPSIADES

              Sokrates.
And Chairephon too. The famous expert on fleafeet.

PHEIDIPPIDES
Are you so far gone on the road to complete insanity
you'd believe the word of those charlatans?

STREPSIADES
                                        Hush, boy.
For shame. I won't hear you speaking disrespectfully
of such eminent scientists and geniuses. And, what's more,
men of such fantastic frugality and Spartan thrift,
they regard baths, haircuts, and personal cleanliness generally
as an utter waste of time and money—whereas *you,*
dear boy, have taken me to the cleaner's so many times,
I'm damn near washed up. Come on, for your father's sake,
go and learn.

PHEIDIPPIDES
                    What do they teach that's worth knowing?

STREPSIADES
Worth knowing? Why, the accumulated wisdom of mankind.
For instance, what a blockhead and numskull you are.
Hmmm.
            Wait here. I'll be right back.
Strepsiades darts into his house.

PHEIDIPPIDES
                                Gods in heaven,
what should I do? My father's gone completely balmy.
Should I hale him into court on charges of insanity
or notify the undertakers?
*Strepsiades reappears with a pair of ducks. He holds
up first one and then the other.*

STREPSIADES
                        Now then, what's this called?

PHEIDIPPIDES
That? A duck.

STREPSIADES
                Excellent. Now what do you call this?

PHEIDIPPIDES
Why, another duck.

STREPSIADES
                        Another duck? You stupid boy.

From now on you must learn to call them by their right names.
This one is a duck; that one's a duchess.

PHEIDIPPIDES

A *duchess!*
So this is the glorious wisdom you've picked up
from those walking corpses!

STREPSIADES

Oh, there's lots more too,
but I'm so old everything I learn goes in one ear
and right out the other.

PHEIDIPPIDES

Ah. Doubtless that explains
how you lost your cloak.

STREPSIADES

I didn't lose it. I swapped it.
For thoughts.

PHEIDIPPIDES

And where have your sandals gone, you idiot?

STREPSIADES

In the words of Perikles himself when they asked him
where the money went: *Expended as required.*
*No comment.**
And now, inside with you, boy.
Humor me in this and you can make an ass of yourself
in any way you like. Ah, how well I remember those days
when you were six, and I had to humor your tantrums.
Why, the very first pay I ever drew as a juror
went to buy you a cart at the fair.

PHEIDIPPIDES

All right, Dad.
But someday you'll be sorry.

STREPSIADES

Ah, good dutiful boy.
—Hallo there, Sokrates!
Hey, Sokrates, come outside.
I've brought my son along—no damn thanks to him.

Enter Sokrates from the Thinkery.

SOKRATES

Why, he's still a baby. How could a toddler like this
possibly operate our Hanging Baskets?

PHEIDIPPIDES

As for you,
why don't you hang yourself and skip the basket?

STREPSIADES

Here,
for shame! You'd insult the Master?

SOKRATES

Imitating Pheidippides.

"Thkip the bathket."
Dear me, what adorable, childish prattle. And look
at those great sulking lower lips. How in the world
could this fumbling foetus ever master the arts
of Verdict-Quashing, False Witness, Innuendo,
and Character Assassination? On the other hand, however,
the case is not without precedent. *Even* Hyperbolos,*
after all, somehow mastered the tricks of the trade.
The fee, of course, was prodigious.

STREPSIADES

Now don't you worry,
Sokrates. The boy's a born philosopher. Yes, sir,
when he was just a mite of a shaver, *so* high,
he used to make the cleverest things you ever saw.
Why, there were dollhouses, sailboats, little pushcarts
from scraps of leather, and the sweetest little frogs
carved from fruit peel. He's a scholar, all right.
So tutor him in your two logics—traditional Philosophical Logic
and that flashy modern sophistic logic they call Immoral
because it's so wonderfully wicked. In any case,
if he can't master both logics, I insist that he learn
the Immoral Kind of argument.

SOKRATES

Philosophy and Sophistry*
will instruct your son in person. And now, gentlemen,
if you'll excuse me, I must leave.

STREPSIADES

But remember, Sokrates:
I want him able to make an utter mockery of the truth.

*Exit Sokrates. After his departure the doors of the
Thinkery are thrown open and Philosophy and
Sophistry are rolled forward in great gilded cages.
From the shoulders down, both are human; from the
neck up they are fighting-cocks.* Philosophy (or
the Traditional Logic) is a large, muscular
rooster, powerful but not heavy, expressing in
his movements that inward harmony and grace and
dignity which the Old Education was meant to produce; his plumage is so simple and dignified as
to seem almost dingy. Sophistry, by contrast, is
comparatively slight, with sloping shoulders, an emaciated pallor, an enormous tongue and a dis-
proportionately large phallus. His body is graceless
but extremely quick-moving; his every motion
expresses defiant belligerence, and his plumage
is brilliant to the point of flashiness. The debate
itself should be conducted at top speed with much
scratching and spurring. As the Attendants open the
cages, the fighters step out and circle each other
warily, jockeying for position.*

PHILOSOPHY

Front and center, you Feathered Impertinence.
Take your little bow before the audience.
You like to swagger.

SOPHISTRY

      Why, you Pompous Lump,
with all my heart. The bigger the crowd,
the better I'll rebut you.

PHILOSOPHY

      You'll rebut *me?*
Who are *you,* runt?

SOPHISTRY

    A Logic.

PHILOSOPHY

      You,
A Logic? Why, you cheap, stunted Loquacity!
You pipsqueak Palaver!

SOPHISTRY

                        I may be called
Mere Sophistry, but I'll chop you down
to size. I'll *refute* you.

PHILOSOPHY

                     Refute *me?* How?

SOPHISTRY

With unconventionality. With ultramodernity.
With unorthodox ideas.

PHILOSOPHY

                   For whose present vogue
we are indebted to this audience of imbeciles
and asses.

SOPHISTRY

       Asses? These sophisticated gentlemen?
These wits?

PHILOSOPHY

       I'll *invalidate* you.

SOPHISTRY

                  Invalidate *me?*
How, fossil?

PHILOSOPHY

       My arguments are Truth and Justice.

SOPHISTRY

Then I'll disarm you and defeat you, friend.
Your Justice doesn't exist.

PHILOSOPHY

             What? No Justice?
Preposterous!

SOPHISTRY

       Then show it to me. Where is it?

PHILOSOPHY

Where is Justice? Why, in the Lap of the Gods.

SOPHISTRY

In the Lap of the Gods? Then would you explain
how Zeus escaped punishment after he imprisoned
his father?* The inconsistency is glaring.

PHILOSOPHY

                                     Aaaagh.

What nauseating twaddle. It turns my stomach.

SOPHISTRY

Why, you Decrepitude! You Doddering Dotard!

PHILOSOPHY

                                       Why,

you Precocious Pederast! You Palpable Pervert!

SOPHISTRY

Pelt me with roses!

PHILOSOPHY

                    You Toadstool! O Cesspool!

SOPHISTRY

Wreath my hair with lilies!

PHILOSOPHY

                    Why, you Parricide!

SOPHISTRY

Shower me with gold! Look, don't you see
I welcome your abuse?

PHILOSOPHY

                  Welcome it, monster?
In my day we would have cringed with shame.

SOPHISTRY

Whereas *now* we're flattered. Times change.
The vices of your age are stylish today.

PHILOSOPHY

Repulsive Whippersnapper!

SOPHISTRY

                    Disgusting Fogy!

PHILOSOPHY

Because of *you* the schools of Athens
stand deserted; one whole generation
chaffers in the streets, gaping and idle.
Mark my words: someday this city
shall learn what you have made her men:
effeminates and fools.

SOPHISTRY

Ugh, you're squalid!

PHILOSOPHY

Whereas you've become a Dandy and a Fop!
But I remember your beggared beginnings,
playing as Telephos,* grubby and shifty,
tricked out in Euripidean rags and tatters
and cramming your wallet with moldy leavings
from Pandaletos' loaf.*

SOPHISTRY

What a prodigy of wisdom
was there!

PHILOSOPHY

And what a prodigy of madness here—
your madness, and madder still than you,
this maddened city which lets you live—
you, corrupter and destroyer of her youth!

SOPHISTRY

Throwing a wing about Pheidippides.

Why, you Hoary Fossil! This is one student
you'll never teach!

PHILOSOPHY

Pulling Pheidippides back.

Teach him I *shall*—
unless he's prepared to devote his career
exclusively to drivel.

SOPHISTRY

Bah, rave to yourself.
—Come here, boy.

PHILOSOPHY

You touch him at your peril.

KORYPHAIOS

Intervening.

Gentlemen, forego your wrangling and abuse,
and each present his arguments in turn.
Describe how *you* taught the men of the past,
and *you,* Sir, your New Education.

PHILOSOPHY

                                    I second
your proposal.

SOPHISTRY

                As do I.

KORYPHAIOS

                       Excellent.
Who will speak first?

SOPHISTRY

                  Let him begin.
I yield the floor. But when he's done,
I'll smother him beneath so huge
a driving hail of Modern Thought
and Latest Views, he cannot speak—
or if he does, my hornet words
and waspish wit will sting him so,
he'll never speak again.

CHORUS
—At last!
         —The Great Debate begins!
                        —Between these two
contending, clever speakers,
                —matched so fairly,
                       —who
will win, is anybody's guess.
                —Both are subtle,
—both facile, both witty,
             —both masters of rebuttal
—and abuse.
         —The stake? Wisdom.
                   —Wisdom is the prize.
—For her they fight.
         —For her their rival hackles rise.
—So listen well.
         —Upon their skill, the destinies of Language, Intellect, and Educated Athens hang.

KORYPHAIOS
To Philosophy.
Come, Sir, I summon you—you who conferred your crown of virtue
upon the Older Generation—to take the stand. Be bold; rise
and with clarion tongue tell us what you represent.

Gentlemen,

I propose to speak of the Old Education,* as it flourished once
beneath my tutelage, when Homespun Honesty, Plainspeaking, and
    Truth
were still honored and practiced, and throughout the schools of Athens
the regime of the three D's—DISCIPLINE, DECORUM, and
    DUTY—
enjoyed unchallenged supremaçy.

Our curriculum was Music and
    Gymnastic,
enforced by that rigorous discipline summed up in the old adage:
BOYS SHOULD BE SEEN BUT NOT HEARD. This was our
    cardinal rule,
and when the students, mustered by groups according to region,
were marched in squads to school, discipline and absolute silence
prevailed.

Ah, they were hardy, manly youngsters. Why,
even on winter mornings when the snow, like powdered chaff,
came sifting down, their only protection against the bitter weather
was a thin and scanty tunic. In the classes, posture was stressed
and the decencies firmly enforced: the students stood in rows,
rigidly at attention, while the master rehearsed them by rote,
over and over. The music itself was traditional and standard—
such familiar anthems and hymns as those, for instance, beginning
A Voice from Afar or *Hail, O Pallas, Destroyer!*—and the old modes
were strictly preserved in all their austere and simple beauty.
Clowning in class was sternly forbidden, and those who improvised
or indulged in those fantastic flourishes and trills so much in vogue
with the degenerate, effeminate school of Phrynis, were promptly
    thrashed
for subverting the Muses.

In the gymnasium too decorum was de-
    manded.
The boys were seated together, stripped to the skin, on the bare ground,
keeping their legs thrust forward, shyly screening their nakedness
from the gaze of the curious. Why, so modest were students then,
that when they rose, they carefully smoothed out the ground beneath
    them,
lest even a pair of naked buttocks leaving its trace in the sand
should draw the eyes of desire. Anointing with oil was forbidden
below the line of the navel, and consequently their genitals kept
their boyish bloom intact and the quincelike freshness of youth.
Toward their lovers their conduct was manly*: you didn't see *them*

73

mincing or strutting, or prostituting themselves with girlish voices
or coy, provocative glances.

At table courtesy and good manners
were compulsory. Not a boy of that generation would have dreamed
of taking so much as a radish or the merest pinch of parsley
before his elders had been served. Rich foods were prohibited,
raucous laughter or crossing their legs forbidden. . . .

SOPHISTRY

Ugh,
what musty, antiquated rubbish. It reeks of golden grasshoppers,
all gewgaws and decaying institutions!

PHILOSOPHY

Nonetheless, these were the pre-
cepts
on which I bred a generation of heroes, the men who fought
at Marathon.

To Sophistry

And what do *you* teach?

Modesty?

No, vanity and
softness,
and the naked beauty of the body muffled in swirling clothes,
gross and unmanly. Why, at Panathenaia now it sickens me
to see the boys dancing, ashamed of their own bodies, effetely
forgetting their duty to the goddess while they screen their nakedness
behind their shields.

Bah.

To Pheidippides.

No, young man, by your courage
I challenge you. Turn your back upon his blandishments of vice,
the rotten law courts and the cheap, corrupting softness of the baths.
Choose instead the Old, the Philosophical Education. Follow me
and from my lips acquire the virtues of a man:—

A sense of shame,
that decency and innocence of mind that shrinks from doing wrong.
To feel the true man's blaze of anger when his honor is provoked.
Deference toward one's elders; respect for one's father and mother.
To preserve intact, unsullied by disgrace or stained with wrong,
that image of Manliness and Modesty by which alone you live.
Purity:—to avoid the brothels and the low, salacious leer
of prostituted love—which, being bought, corrupts your manhood
and destroys your name. Toward your father scrupulous obedience;
to honor his declining years who spent his prime in rearing you.
Not to call him Dotard or Fogy—

Boy, if you follow his advice,
you'll finish by looking like one of Hippokrates' sissified sons.
They'll call *you* Mollycoddle Milksop.

PHILOSOPHY

Rubbish. I promise you,
not contentious disputations and the cheap, courtroom cant
of this flabby, subpoena-serving, shyster-jargoned de-generation,
but true athletic prowess, the vigor of contending manhood
in prime perfection of physique, muscular and hard, glowing
with health.

Ah, I can see you now, as through an idyl moving—
you with some companion of your age, modest and manly like you,
strolling by Akademe perhaps, or there among the olives,
sprinting side by side together, crowned with white reed,
breathing with every breath the ecstasy of Spring returning,
the sudden fragrance of the season's leisure, the smell of woodbine
and the catkins flung by the poplar, while touching overhead,
the leaves of the linden and plane rustle, in love, together.
So follow me, young man, and win perfection of physique. To wit—

Demonstrating each attribute individually.

BUILD, Stupendous.
COMPLEXION, Splendid.
SHOULDERS, Gigantic.
TONGUE, Petite.
BUTTOCKS, Brawny.
PECKER, Discreet.

But follow my opponent here, and your reward shall be, as follows:

BUILD, Effeminate.
COMPLEXION, Ghastly.
SHOULDERS, Hunched.
TONGUE, Enormous.
BUTTOCKS, Flabby.
PECKER, Preposterous!

(but thereby insuring you an enormous and devoted political following.)
What is worse, you shall learn to make a mockery of all morality,
systematically confounding good with evil and evil with good,
so plumped and pursy with villainy, sodomy, disgrace, and perversion,
you resemble ANTIMACHOS himself.

Depravity can sink no lower.

CHORUS

—Bravo!
        —What brilliance!
                —What finesse!
                        —*This* is wisdom
at its noble best!
                —Such Modesty,
                        —such Decorum
in every lovely word distilled!
                        —Ah, lucky they
—whose happy lives were lived
                        —beneath your dispensa-
tion,
                —by all the ancient virtues blessed!

To Sophistry.
                                —So, sir,
—despite your vaunted subtlety and wit,
                        —take care:
—Your rival's speech has scored.
                        —Some crushing *tour de force,*
—some master stroke,
                —is needed now.
                        —The stage is yours.

KORYPHAIOS
Unless your strategy is shrewdly planned and your attack ferocious,
then your cause is lost. We'll laugh you out of court.

SOPHISTRY
                                At last!
A few minutes more and I would have exploded from sheer impatience
to refute him and demolish his case.
                        Now then, I freely admit
that among men of learning I am—somewhat pejoratively—dubbed
the Sophistic, or Immoral, Logic. And why? Because I first
devised a Method for the Subversion of Established Social Beliefs
and the Undermining of Morality. Moreover, this little invention of
        mine,
this knack of taking what might appear to be the worse argument
and nonetheless winning my case, has, I might add, proved to be
an *extremely* lucrative source of income.
                        But observe, gentlemen,
how I refute his vaunted Education.

                                  Now then, in your curriculum
hot baths are sternly prohibited. But what grounds can you possibly adduce
for this condemnation of hot baths?

PHILOSOPHY

                                  What grounds can I adduce? Why,
they're thoroughly vicious. They make a man flabby and effeminate.

SOPHISTRY

You can stop right there, friend. I have you completely at my mercy.
Answer me this: which of the sons of Zeus was the most heroic?
Who suffered most? Performed the greatest labors?

PHILOSOPHY

                                  In my opinion,
the greatest hero who ever lived was Herakles.

SOPHISTRY

                                  Very well then.
But when we speak of the famous Baths of Herakles,* are we speaking
of hot baths or cold baths? Necessarily, sir, of hot baths.
Whence it clearly follows, by your own logic, that Herakles was
both flabby and effeminate.
                     Q.E.D.

PHILOSOPHY

                        Q.E.D.! This is the rubbish I mean!
This is the logical claptrap so much in fashion with the young!
This is what fills the baths and empties the gymnasiums!

SOPHISTRY

                                    Very well,
if you like, consider our national passion for politics and debating,
pastimes which you condemn and I approve. But surely, friend,
if politics were quite so vicious as you pretend, old Homer—*
our mentor on moral questions—would never have portrayed Nestor
and those other wise old men as politicians, would he? Surely
he would not.
                  Or take the question of education in oratory—
in my opinion desirable, in yours the reverse. As for Moderation and Decorum,
the very notions are absurd. In fact, two more preposterous
or pernicious prejudices, I find it hard to imagine. For example,

can you cite me *one* instance of that profit which a man enjoys
by exercising moderation? Refute me if you can.

PHILOSOPHY

                                                    Why, instances abound
Er . . . Peleus,* for example. His virtue won him a sword.

SOPHISTRY

                                                         A sword,
you say? What a charming little profit for the poor sucker!
Look at our Hyberbolos: nothing virtuous about *him,* god knows,
and yet, what with peddling lamps—plus a knack for swindling—
he piled up a huge profit. All cold cash. No swords for him.
No sir, Hyperbolos and swords just don't mix.*

PHILOSOPHY

                                                    Furthermore,
Peleus' chastity earned him the goddess Thetis for his wife.

SOPHISTRY

                                                         Precisely,
and what did she do? Promptly ditched him for being cold,
no passion for that all-night scrimmage between the sheets
that lusty women love.
                    Bah, you're obsolete.

To Pheidippides.

                                                    —Young man,
I advise you to ponder this life of Virtue with scrupulous care,
all that it implies, and all the pleasures of which its daily practice
must inevitably deprive you. Specifically, I might mention these:
Sex. Gambling. Gluttony. Guzzling. Carousing. Etcet.
And what on earth's the point of living, if you leach your life
of all its little joys?
                        Very well then, consider your natural needs.
Suppose, as a scholar of Virtue, you commit some minor peccadillo,
a little adultery, say, or seduction, and suddenly find yourself
caught in the act. What happens? You're ruined, you can't defend
     yourself
(since, of course, you haven't been taught). But follow me, my boy,
and obey your nature to the full; romp, play, and laugh
without a scruple in the world. Then if caught *in flagrante,*
you simply inform the poor cuckold that you're utterly innocent
and refer him to Zeus as your moral sanction. After all, didn't he,
a great and powerful god, succumb to the love of women?

Then how in the world can you, a man, an ordinary mortal,
be expected to surpass the greatest of gods in moral self-control?*
Clearly, you can't be.

PHILOSOPHY

　　　　　　　　　And suppose your pupil, by taking your advice,
is promptly convicted of adultery and sentenced to be publicly reamed
up the rectum with a radish?* How, Sir, would you save him from
　　　that?

SOPHISTRY

Why, what's the disgrace in being reamed with a radish?

PHILOSOPHY

Sir, I can conceive of nothing fouler than being buggered
by a radish.

SOPHISTRY

　　　　　　　And what would you have to say, my friend,
if I defeat you on this point too?

PHILOSOPHY

　　　　　　　　　　　　What *could* I say?
I could never speak again for shame.

SOPHISTRY

　　　　　　　　　　　　Very well then.
What sort of men are our lawyers?

PHILOSOPHY

Why, they're all Buggers.

SOPHISTRY

　　　　　　　Right!
What are our tragic poets then?

PHILOSOPHY

Why, they're Buggers too.

SOPHISTRY

　　　　　　　Right!
And what of our politicians, Sir?

PHILOSOPHY

Why, Buggers to a man.

SOPHISTRY

Right!

You see how stupidly you spoke?
And now look at our audience.
What about them?

PHILOSOPHY

I'm looking hard.

SOPHISTRY

And what do you see?

PHILOSOPHY

By heaven,

I see an enormous crowd of people,
and almost all of them Buggers.

Pointing to individuals in the audience.

See there? That man's a Bugger,
and that long-haired fop's a Bugger too.

SOPHISTRY

Then how do we stand, my friend?

PHILOSOPHY

I've been beaten by the Buggers.

Flinging his cloak to the audience.

O Buggers, catch my cloak
and welcome me among the Buggers!

*With a wild shriek Philosophy disappears into
his cage and is wheeled away into the Thinkery, just
as Sokrates comes out.*

SOKRATES

Well, what are your wishes? Will you take your son home,
or shall I instruct him in the Pettifogger's Art?

STREPSIADES

Teach him—

and flog him too. But remember: I want his tongue
honed down like a razor. Sharpen him on the left side
for piddling private suits, but grind him on the right
for Grand Occasions and Affairs of State.

SOKRATES

                              Sir,
you may depend upon me. I promise I'll send him home
a consummate little sophist.

PHEIDIPPIDES

                    God, what a picture of misery—
a nasty, pasty-faced, consummate little stinker!

Exeunt Sokrates and Pheidippides into the Thinkery.

KORYPHAIOS
Very well, go in.

To Strepsiades.

                    —You, Sir, shall live to regret your decision.

Exit Strepsiades into his own house, as the
Chorus turns sharply and faces the audience.

CHORUS

And now, Gentlemen of the Jury, a few brief words about the Prize
and the solid benefits you stand to gain by voting for *THE CLOUDS*—
as you certainly should anyway.

                              First of all, when the season sets
for Spring and plowing time has come, we guarantee each judge's fields
the top priority in rain. Let others wait. Furthermore,
for his vineyards and orchards, we promise, perfect growing-weather:
no drought shall touch them, no flooding rains destroy.

                                        However,
if some presuming mortal dares dishonor our divinity,
let him savor his punishment:

                              His acres, hard, dry, and barren,
shall see no harvesting. No wine, no fruit, shall ripen for *him.*
And when the olives sprout, and the season's green festoons
the vines, *his* shall wither, battered by our ratatat of rain.
And when he's busy baking bricks, we'll snuff his kiln with water
and smash his tiles with cannonades of hail. If he, his friend,
or relatives should celebrate a wedding, we'll send a DELUGE down
and drown the wedding night in rain!

                              By god, we'll make him say
he'd rather be roasting in Egypt than have voted wrong today!

Enter Strepsiades from his house, counting on
his fingers.

STREPSIADES

Five days, four days, three days, two days, and then
that one day of all the days of the month

I dread the most, that makes me fart with fear—
the last day of the month, Due date for debts,*
when every dun in town has solemnly sworn
to drag me into court and bankrupt me completely.
And when I plead with them to be more reasonable—
"But PLEASE, sir. Don't demand the whole sum now.
Take something on account. I'll pay you later."—
they snort they'll never see the day, curse me
for a filthy swindler and say they'll sue.

                                        Well,
let them. If Pheidippides has learned to talk,
I don't give a damn for them and their suits.

                                   Now then,
a little knock on the door and we'll have the answer.

He knocks on Sokrates' door and calls out.

        Porter!

               Hey, porter!

Sokrates opens the door.

SOKRATES

                  Ah, Strepsiades. Salutations.

STREPSIADES

Same to you, Sokrates.

He hands Sokrates a bag of flour.

                       Here. A token of my esteem.
Call it an honorarium.* Professors always get honorariums.

Snatching back the bag.

        But wait: has Pheidippides learned his rhetoric yet—
that swindling Rhetoric that performed for us just now?

SOKRATES

Taking the bag.

        He has mastered it.

STREPSIADES

                 O great goddess Bamboozle!

SOKRATES

Now, sir, you can evade any legal action you wish to.

STREPSIADES

Really? Even if I borrowed the money before witnesses?

SOKRATES

Before ten thousand of them. The more the merrier.

STREPSIADES

In parody.

>Then let my loud falsetto peal
>with gladsome paeans plangent!*
>Mourn, O ye lenders of money,
>weep, O principals! Gnash your teeth,
>O ye interests compounded.
>For lo, within mine halls
>a son hath risen,
>a son with burnish'd tongue,
>yea, with double edges lambent!
>Hail, O hero of my halls,
>who delivered my domicile,
>who fractur'd mine enemies
>and drowned a father's dolor!
>Ho, fetch forth mine son
>forthwith! O my son,
>debouch from mine abode!*
>O heed thy father, prithee!

*Pheidippides, the very image of "modern youth,"
slouches contemptuously out of the Thinkery.*

SOKRATES

Behold the man!

STREPSIADES

O joy! My boy!

SOKRATES

Take him and go.

STREPSIADES

O my son! O! O!
O! O! O! O!
Oh, how gladly I behold thy pasty face,
that negative and disputatious look! And see there,
how there blossoms on his lips our national rejoinder,
"Huh? G'wan!" How perfectly he is the rogue,
but looks the victim through and through. And on his face
that utter pallor, ah, that true Athenian look!
—All right, Son, you ruined me, so it's up to you
to save me.

PHEIDIPPIDES
>What's eating *you,* Dad?

STREPSIADES
>>>Your damn debts.
And the date. That's what. Your debts are due today.
Today's Dueday.*

PHEIDIPPIDES
>>Today's two days? Or two Duedays?
But how can one day be two days?

STREPSIADES
>>>How should *I* know?
It just *is!*
Resuming more calmly, patiently explaining.
>>Today's Dueday, son. *This* is the day
when creditor's are required by law to post their bond*
in court in order to obtain a summons against their debtors.
No bond, no summons.

PHEIDIPPIDES
>>>*Ergo,* they will forfeit their bond.
By definition, one day cannot be two days.

STREPSIADES
>>>It *can't* be?
But why not?

PHEIDIPPIDES
>>Because it's a logical impossibility, numskull.
If one day were two days, then *ipso facto* a woman
could be simultaneously a young girl and an old hag.
Which she can't be.

STREPSIADES
>>But it's the law!

PHEIDIPPIDES
>>>In that case,
I suspect the law on debt has been profoundly misinterpreted.

STREPSIADES
Misinterpreted? But how?

PHEIDIPPIDES

Enigmatically.

Old Solon loved the people.

STREPSIADES

And what in god's name has that got to do with the Duedate?

PHEIDIPPIDES

Solon's sympathies lay with the debtor, not with the creditor.

STREPSIADES

And so?

PHEIDIPPIDES

And so, when Solon promulgated his law on debt,
he carefully specified *two* distinct Duedates
for debts, not *one,* as the current interpretation has it.
Prima facie, a summons *could* be issued on either day,
though in practice this was impossible, since the creditor's bond
could be paid only on the second Duedate.

STREPSIADES

But why did Solon
set two Duedates?

PHEIDIPPIDES

Read between the lines, moron.
Solon intended that the debtor should present himself in court
on the first date and declare himself absolved of his debts
on the grounds of the creditor's failure to issue a summons.
He won by default. *If,* however, the debtor failed
to take advantage of the deliberate ambiguity of the law,
he had to account to his creditors in court the next day.
Not an attractive prospect.

STREPSIADES

But wait. If that's the law,
then how do you account for the glaring fact that the magistrates
actually demand that the creditor's bond be paid on the first day
and not on the second?

PHEIDIPPIDES

Precisely because they *are* magistrates.*
Ipso facto, their greed is magisterial and their gluttony
uncontrollable. And because they can't wait to get their fingers
in the pie, they have quietly connived among themselves

to set the Duedate back a day earlier. Their procedure,
of course, is utterly illegal.

STREPSIADES

Still perplexed.

                  Huh?

But suddenly illuminated.

                     Hey!

      Haw, that's good!

Turning to the audience.

           Well, numskulls, what are *you* gawking at?
Yes, *you* down there!

             You dumb sheep with the pigeon faces!
Cat's-paws for cleverer men! Any sophist's
suckers!

       O shysterbait!

              Generation of dupes!
Poor twerps, poor silly saps!

               O Audience of Asses,
you were born to be taken!

              —And now, gentlemen, a song.
A little ditty of my own, dedicated to me and my son,
offering us warmest congratulations on our success.

                      Ready,

    everybody?

Singing and dancing.

> *Oh, Strepsiades, Strepsiades,*
> *there's no one like Strepsiades!*
> *He went to school with Sokrates*
> *who taught him all his sophistries!*
> > *He's smarter than*
> > *Euripides,*
> > *for only he's,*
> > *yes, only he's*
> > *Pheidippides'*
> > *Old Man!*

      By god, if ever I heard a hit, that's it!

To Pheidippides.

      Once you finish off my creditors' suits, the whole town
will go green with envy of Strepsiades.

              And now, son,
I'm throwing a dinner in your honor. So let's go in.

Exeunt Strepsiades and Pheidippides into the house.
An instant later Pasias arrives, accompanied by
his Witness, with a summons against Strepsiades. A
notorious spendthrift, drunkard, and glutton, Pasias
is grotesquely fat. Essentially a good-natured
man, he has prepared himself for a difficult ordeal,
and comes equipped with a wine flask from which
he periodically fortifies himself.

PASIAS

Well,
what am I supposed to do? Throw my hard-earned money
down the drain?

Something in his own words reminds him that
he needs a drink, a stiff one.

Playboy Pasias, is it?
Nossiree.
Bah! Me and my great big heart! Soft-touch Pasias.
But I should have known. You've got to be a bastard.
Hard as nails.

He hardens himself with a drink.

If I'd sent him packing when he tried
to put the touch on me, I wouldn't be in this fix now.
What a mess!

To Witness.

I have to drag you around to stand witness,
and what's more, I'll make an enemy of Strepsiades for life.

He fortifies himself with still another drink.

Well, I'll sue him anyway.
Yessiree.
Athens expects it,
and I won't have it said that Pasias ever besmirched
the National Honor.*
Nossiree.

Shouting into the house.

—Strepsiades! I'm suing you!

STREPSIADES

Appearing at the door.

Somebody want me?

PASIAS

I do. Today's the Dueday.

STREPSIADES

To the audience.

Gentlemen, you're all witnesses: he distinctly mentioned
two days.

To Pasias.

—What are you suing me for?

PASIAS

What *for?* Why,
the money you borrowed from me to buy that horse.

STREPSIADES

Horse?
What horse? Everybody knows I'm allergic to horses.
Ask the audience.

PASIAS

By god, you swore you'd pay me!
You swore it by the gods.

STREPSIADES

Well, by god, now I swear
I won't. Anyway, that was before Pheidippides learned the Science
of Unanswerable Argument.

PASIAS

And *that's* why you won't pay me?

STREPSIADES

Can you think of a better reason? I'm entitled to some return
on his education, aren't I?

PASIAS

And you're prepared to perjure yourself
on an oath sworn by the gods?

STREPSIADES

By the gods?
What gods?

PASIAS

What gods?
Why, Zeus, Poseidon, and Hermes.

STREPSIADES

Damn right
I would. And what's more, I'd do it again. Gratis,
by god!
I *like* perjury.

PASIAS

Why, you barefaced swindler!
You damnable liar!

STREPSIADES

Prodding Pasias in the belly.

Boy, what blubber!
—You know,
that paunch of yours ought to make someone a mighty dandy
wineskin . . .

PASIAS

By god, that's the last straw!

STREPSIADES

Hmmmm. Yup,
five gallons, I'd guess offhand.

PASIAS

So help me Zeus!
So help me every god in heaven, you won't get away
with this!

STREPSIADES

You know, you and your silly gods tickle me.
Zeus is a joke to us Thinking Men.

PASIAS

By god, someday
you'll regret this.
Now then, for the last time,
will you pay me or won't you? Give me a straight answer
and I'll be off.

STREPSIADES

Don't you budge. I'll be right back
and bring you my final answer.

Strepsiades rushes into the house.

PASIAS

To his Witness.

I wonder what he's doing.
Do you think he'll pay me?

STREPSIADES

*Reappearing from the house; in his hands he
holds a large basket.*

Now where's that creditor of mine?

Holding up the basket in front of Pasias.

—All right, you, what's this?

PASIAS

That? A basket.

STREPSIADES

A *basket?*
And a stupid ignoramus like you has the nerve to come around
badgering me for money? By god, I wouldn't give a cent
to a man who can't even tell a basket from a baskette.

PASIAS

Then you won't pay me back?

STREPSIADES

Not if *I* know it.
Look here,
you Colossus of Lard, why don't you quietly melt away?
Beat it, Fatboy!

He threatens to beat him with his baskette.

PASIAS

I'm going. Yessiree. And by god,
if I don't post my bond with the magistrates right now,
my name's not Pasias.
Nossiree.

STREPSIADES

Tch tch. Poor Pasias.
You'll just lose your bond on top of all your other losses.
And, personally speaking, I wouldn't want to see you suffer
just because your grammar's bad.

Beating Pasias over the head with his baskette.

Remember?
Baskette!

90

*Exit Pasias at a run pursued by Strepsiades. An
instant later, hideous wails and shrieks are heard offstage, and these are followed by the pathetic
entrance of the notorious effeminate and gambler,
Amynias. He has just had an accident with his
chariot, and his entrance is a picture of misery: his
head is covered with blood, his clothes torn, and
his language, a delirious compound of tragic rhetoric
and a marked lisp, is almost unintelligible.*

AMYNIAS
Alackaday!

   Woe is me!

      Alas! Alas!

STREPSIADES

       Gods in heaven,
what a caterwauling!
    —Look, who *are* you?
        The way you whine
you sound like some poor blubbering god from a tragedy
by Karkinos.*

AMYNIAS

   Wouldst hear how I am hight? Know then:
a wretched wight in woe am I, Adversity
yclept.

STREPSIADES
  Then hit the road, Buster.

AMYNIAS

      O Funest Doom!
O Darkling Destiny!
     How fell the fate by which I fall,
ah, Pallas!
   O all unhors'd! O human haplessness
I am!

STREPSIADES
  I get it. You're an actor, and you want me to guess
what part you're practicing.
      Hmm.
       Must be a female role.
But of course!
    You're Alkmene in the play by Xenokles,
and you're mourning your brother . . .

AMYNIAS

You're *such* a tease,
you naughty man.
Now then, be a dear, and ask Pheidippides
to pay me my money. You see, I'm in the most frightful way.
You simply can't *imagine!*

STREPSIADES

Money? What money?

AMYNIAS

Why, the money
Pheidippides borrowed.

STREPSIADES

Hmmm. You *are* in a frightful way.
You simply can't *imagine.*

AMYNIAS

But I *can.* You see, on my way,
I was thrown from my chariot. Literally *hurled* into the air.
It was *too* awful.

STREPSIADES

It fits. You must have hurt your head.
That would explain that gibberish about money.

AMYNIAS

What's gibberish
about wanting my money?

STREPSIADES

Obvious case of delirium.
Brain damage too, I suspect.

AMYNIAS

Brain damage?

STREPSIADES

Yup.
You'll probably be queer the rest of your life. That's how
I see it.

AMYNIAS

Pay me my money, or I'll sue you! That's how
I see it.

STREPSIADES

     Is that so?

            All right, let me ask you a question.
I'm curious to know which theory on rainfall you prefer.
Now then, in your considered opinion, is the phenomenon of rain
best explained as a precipitation of *totally* fresh water,
or is it merely a case of the same old rainwater
in continuous re-use, slowly condensed by the Clouds
and then precipitated once more as rain?

AMYNIAS

                My *dear* fellow,

I really couldn't care less.

STREPSIADES

           Couldn't care less, eh?
And a sophomore like you, completely ignorant of Science,
thinks he's got the right to go around pestering people
to pay him money?

            Boy, some nerve!

AMYNIAS

            Look here,
if you're temporarily short of cash, then let me have
the interest.

STREPSIADES

     Interest? What the devil's interest?

AMYNIAS

                Why, interest
is nothing more than the tendency of a cash principal
to reproduce itself by increments over a period of time.
Very gradually, day after day, month after month,
the interest accrues and the principal grows.

STREPSIADES

              Dandy.
Then in your opinion there's more water in the ocean now
than last year? Is that right?

AMYNIAS

           But, of course, it isn't.
Oceans *can't* grow, you silly man. It's against the Law
of Nature.

STREPSIADES

        Then what about you, you unnatural bastard?
If the ocean, with all those rivers pouring into it,
doesn't grow, then who the hell are you to expect your money
to grow?

        And now CLEAR OUT! Go peddle your subpoenas
somewhere else.

*Amynias stands firm and Strepsiades calls out
to his slave.*

        —Bring me my horsewhip.

*The slave brings the whip and Strepsiades cracks
it threateningly at Amynias.*

AMYNIAS

Appealing in terror to the audience.

        —Gentlemen,

    you're my witnesses!

STREPSIADES

        Still here, are you?

He flicks Amynias with the whip.

        Giddeap!

    Gallop, you gelding!
        Gee!

*He flicks Amynias again with his whip, this time
in the rear.*

AMYNIAS

        A hit! A hit!

    A palpable hit!

STREPSIADES

Raising his phallus to the ready.

        Git, dammit, or I'll sunder your rump
    with my ram!

*With a wild whinny of fright, Amynias
rushes offstage.*

        Going, are you?

        A damned good thing.
And don't come back here nagging me about your money,
or I'll badger your bum!

        You'll get the ride of your life!

*Strepsiades re-enters the house to resume his inter-
rupted dinner with Pheidippides.*

CHORUS

Individually

—Such is wickedness,
                    —such its fatal fascina-
tion:
        —this senile amateur of fraud,
                            —by greed
    and guile obsessed,
                    —frantic to disown his debts
—(and,
        —such his luck,
                    —apparently
                            —succeed-
ing).
        —BUT please take note:
                            —soon,
                                —perhaps today,
—this poor man's Sokrates must learn his lesson,
—*viz.*
        —CRIME DOES NOT PAY.
                            —Dishonesty
comes home to roost.
                    —It's Poetic Retribution!
—But *now,* poor fish!
                    —he thinks he's sitting
                                —pretty.
—Success at last!
                —For hasn't his Pheidippides
become
        —so voluble a speaker,
                        —so specious
a sophist,
        —a shyster so vicious,
                        —that he's
now
        —ABSOLUTELY INVINCIBLE?
                            —So
he gloats.
            —But wait!
                    —Take note:
                            —the time will come—

Strepsiades howls in pain offstage.

—in fact, it's coming now—

—when poor Strepsiades

will wish to god

—Pheidippides were

—DUMB!

With a bellow of pain and teror, Strepsiades
plunges out of his house, hotly pursued by Pheidip-
pides with a murderous stick.

STREPSIADES
OOOUUUCH!!!

HALP!

For god's sake, help me!

Appealing to the Audience.

Friends!

Fellow-countrymen! Aunts! Uncles! Fathers! Brothers!
To the rescue!

He's beating me!

Help me!

Ouuch!

O my poor head!

Ooh, my jaw!

To Pheidippides.

—You great big bully,

Hit your own father, would you?

PHEIDIPPIDES

Gladly, Daddy.

STREPSIADES
You hear that? The big brute *admits* it.

PHEIDIPPIDES

Admit it? Hell,

I *proclaim* it.

STREPSIADES

You cheap Cutthroat!

You father-beating Bastard!

You Turd!

You . . . you . . . you—

PHEIDIPPIDES

Carry on. Don't you know

you're complimenting me?

STREPSIADES

Why, you . . . you . . . you Palpable Pervert!
You Pederast!

PHEIDIPPIDES

Roll me in roses, Daddy!

STREPSIADES

You Bugger!
Hit your own father, would you?

PHEIDIPPIDES

Damn right I would.
God knows, I had good justification.

STREPSIADES

Justification, you say?
Why, you Dunghill, what justification could there *ever* be
for hitting your own father?

PHEIDIPPIDES

Would a logical demonstration
convince you?

STREPSIADES

A logical demonstration? You mean to tell me
you can *prove* a shocking thing like that?

PHEIDIPPIDES

Elementary, really.
What's more, you can choose the logic. Take your pick.
Either one.

STREPSIADES

Either *which?*

PHEIDIPPIDES

Either *which?* Why,
Sokratic logic or pre-Sokratic logic. Either logic.
Take your pick.

STREPSIADES

Take my pick, damn you? Look,
who do you think paid for your shyster education anyway?
And now you propose to convince *me* that there's nothing wrong
in whipping your own father?

PHEIDIPPIDES

I not only propose it;
I propose to *prove* it. Irrefutably, in fact. Rebuttal
is utterly inconceivable.

STREPSIADES

By god, *this* I want to hear!

CHORUS

Old friend, WATCH OUT.
Upon this bout
    may hang your own survival.

What's more, unless
I miss my guess,
    the odds are on your rival.

That curling lip,
that sneer's a tip,
    and you'd be wise to heed it.

The tip? A trap.
But, *verbum sap*.
    I wish you luck. *You*'ll need it.

KORYPHAIOS

To Strepsiades.

And now, Sir, I suggest you brief the Chorus. Begin at the beginning
and describe your little fracas exactly as it happened.

STREPSIADES

Yes'm.
The whole damn dirty squabble from start to finish.

As you know,
we both went in to celebrate. Well, Ladies, a custom's a custom,*
after all, and there's nothing like a little music, I always say,
to get a party off to a good start. So naturally I asked him
to get down his lyre and sing a song. For instance, Simonides'
*Shearin' o' the Ram.**

Well, you know what the little stinker answered?
That singing at table was—Obsolete,
                    Old Hat,
                        Lowbrow,
                            Bullshit!

Strictly for grandmothers.

PHEIDIPPIDES

You damn well got what you deserved.
Asking me to sing on an empty stomach! What is this anyway?
A banquet or a cricket-concert?

STREPSIADES

You hear that?
A cricket-concert!
His exact words.

And then he started sneering at Simonides!
Called him—get this—Puny Pipsqueak Hack!
Was I *sore?*
Brother!
Well, somehow I counted to ten, and then I asked him
to sing me some Aischylos.
Please.

And you know what he replied?
That he considered Aischylos "a poet of colossal stature:"—
Yup,
"the most colossal, pretentious, pompous, spouting, bombastic bore
in poetic history."*

I was so damn mad I just about went through the roof.
But I gritted my teeth together, mustered up a sick smile
and somehow managed to say, "All right, son, if that's how you feel,
then sing me a passage from one of those highbrow modern plays
you're so crazy about."
So he recited—you can guess—Euripides!
One of those slimy tragedies* where, so help me, there's a brother
who screws his own sister!
Well, Ladies, *that* did it!

I jumped up,
blind with rage, started cursing at him and calling him names,
and he started screaming and cursing back and before I knew it,
he hauled off and—*wham!*—he biffed me and bashed me and clipped
    me
and poked me and choked me and—

PHEIDIPPIDES

And, by god, you had it coming!
Knocking a genius like Euripides!

STREPSIADES

Euripides!

A GENIUS??

That . . .

That . . . that . . !

Pheidippides raises his stick threateningly.

HALP! He's hitting me!

PHEIDIPPIDES

You've got it coming, Dad!

STREPSIADES

Got it coming, do I?

Why, you ungrateful brat, I *raised* you!

When you were a baby I pampered you! I waited on you hand and
foot!

I understood your babytalk. You babbled GOO and I obeyed. Why,
when you whimpered WAWA DADA, who brought your water?
DADA did.

When you burbled BABA, who brought your Baby Biscuits?
DADA did.

And when you cried GOTTA GO KAKA DADA, who saved his
shitty darling?

Who rushed you to the door? Who held you while you did it? Damn
you,
DADA did!

And in return you choked me,
and when I shat in terror,
would you give your Dad a hand,
would you help me to the door?
No, you left me there alone
to do it on the floor!

Yes, to do it on the floor!

CHORUS

YOUR ATTENTION, PLEASE!
Pheidippides
now makes his demonstration—

a proof which will,
I'm certain, thrill
the younger generation.

For if this lad
defeats his Dad,
    there's not an older man

or father in
this town, whose skin
    is worth a Tinker's Damn!

KORYPHAIOS

And now that Doughty Champion of Change, that Golden-Tongued
    Attorney
for Tomorrow, that Harbinger of Progress
                           —PHEIDIPPIDES!

To Pheidippides.

                                  Remember, Sir,
we want the truth
            —or a reasonable facsimile.

PHEIDIPPIDES

                        Gentlemen, Eloquence
is sweet, sweeter than I ever dreamed! This utter bliss of speech!
This rapture of articulation! But oh, the sheer Attic honey
of subverting the Established Moral Order!
                   And yet when I look back
on those benighted days of pre-Sokratic folly, upon the boy
I used to be, whose only hobby was horses, who could not speak
three words of Greek without a blunder, why . . .
                      words fail me.
But *now,* now that Sokrates has made a fresh Pheidippides of me,
now that my daily diet is Philosophy, Profundity, Subtlety,
and Science, I propose to prove beyond the shadow of a doubt
the philosophical propriety of beating my Father.

STREPSIADES

                     For the love of Zeus,
go back to your damn horses! I'd rather be stuck with a stable
than be battered by a stick.

PHEIDIPPIDES

              I ignore these childish interruptions
and proceed with my demonstration.
              Now then, answer my question:
did you lick me when I was a little boy?

STREPSIADES

                              Of course I licked you.
For your own damn good. Because I loved you.

PHEIDIPPIDES

                              Then *ipso facto*,
since you yourself admit that loving and lickings are synonymous,
it's only fair that I—for your own damn good, you understand?—
whip you in return.
                    In any case, by what right do you whip me
but claim exemption for yourself?
                              What do you think I am? A slave?
Wasn't I born as free a man as you?*
                              Well?

STREPSIADES

                              But . . .

PHEIDIPPIDES

                              But what?
Spare the Rod and Spoil the Child?
                    Is that your argument?
                                        If so,
then I can be sententious too. *Old Men are Boys Writ Big,*
as the saying goes.
                    A fortiori then, old men logically deserve
to be beaten more, since at their age they have clearly less excuse
for the mischief that they do.

STREPSIADES

                    But it's unnatural! It's . . . *illegal!*
Honor your father and mother.
                    That's the law.
                                        Everywhere.

PHEIDIPPIDES

                                        The *law?*
And who made the law?
                    An ordinary man. A man like you or me.
A man who lobbied for his bill until he persuaded the people
to make it law.
                    By the same token then, what prevents me now
from proposing new legislation granting sons the power to inflict
corporal punishment upon wayward fathers?

Nothing vindictive,
of course.
        In fact, I would personally insist on adding a rider,
a Retroactive Amnesty for Fathers, waiving our right to compensation
for any whippings we received prior to the passage of the new law.
However, if you're still unconvinced, look to Nature for a sanction.
Observe the roosters, for instance, and what do you see?
                                                A society
whose pecking-order envisages a permanent state of open warfare
between fathers and sons. And how do roosters differ from men,
except for the trifling fact that human society is based upon law
and rooster society isn't?

STREPSIADES

                        Look, if you want to imitate the roosters,
why don't you go eat shit and sleep on a perch at night?

PHEIDIPPIDES

                                        Why? Er . . .
because the analogy doesn't hold, that's why. If you don't believe me,
then go ask Sokrates.

STREPSIADES

                        Well, whatever your roosters happen to do,
you'd better not lick me. It's your neck if you do.

PHEIDIPPIDES

                                        My neck?

How so?

STREPSIADES

                Because look: I lick you. All right, someday you'll have a son
and you can even the score with me by licking the hell out of him.
But if you lick me, then your son will follow your precedent
by licking you. If you have a son.

PHEIDIPPIDES

                                And if I don't have a son?
You've licked me, but where am I? I'm left holding the bag,
and you'll go to your grave laughing at me.

There is a long tense silence as the full force of this
crushing argument takes its effect upon Strepsiades.

STREPSIADES

What?

But how . . .?

Hmm,

by god, you're right!

To the Audience.

—Speaking for the older generation, gentlemen,
I'm compelled to admit defeat. The kids have proved their point:
naughty fathers should be flogged.

PHEIDIPPIDES

Of course, I nearly forgot.

One final matter.

STREPSIADES

The funeral?

PHEIDIPPIDES

Far from it. In fact,

it may even soothe your feelings.

STREPSIADES

How to be licked and like it, eh?

Go on. I'm listening.

PHEIDIPPIDES

Well now, Misery Loves Company, they say.

So I'll give you some company:

I'll horsewhip Mother.

STREPSIADES

You'll *WHAT*???

HORSEWHIP YOUR OWN MOTHER?

But this is worse! Ten

thousand times worse!

PHEIDIPPIDES

Is that so? And suppose I prove by Sokratic logic the utter propriety
of horsewhipping Mother?

What would you say to that?

STREPSIADES

What would I

say?

By god, if you prove *that,*

then for all I care, you heel,

you can take your stinking Logics
and your Thinkery as well
with Sokrates inside it
and damn well go to hell!

To the Chorus.

—You Clouds got me into this! Why in god's name
did I ever believe you?

KORYPHAIOS

The guilt is yours, Strepsiades,
yours and yours alone. The dishonesty you did
was your own choice, not ours.

STREPSIADES

But why didn't you warn me
instead of luring a poor old ignoramus into trouble?
Why did you encourage me?

KORYPHAIOS

Because this is what we are,
the insubstantial Clouds men build their hopes upon,*
shining tempters formed of air, symbols of desire;
and so we act, beckoning, alluring foolish men
through their dishonest dreams of gain to overwhelming
ruin. There, schooled by suffering, they learn at last
to fear the gods.

STREPSIADES

Well, I can't say much for your methods,
though I had it coming. I was wrong to cheat my creditors,
and I admit it.

To Pheidippides.

—All right, boy, what do you say?
Let's go and take revenge on Sokrates and Chairephon
for swindling us. Are you game?

PHEIDIPPIDES

What? Raise a finger
against my old Philosophy professor? Count me out.

STREPSIADES
Show a little respect for Zeus.

PHEIDIPPIDES

Zeus?

You old fogey,
are you so stupid you still believe there's such a thing
as Zeus?

STREPSIADES

Of course there's a Zeus.

PHEIDIPPIDES

Not any more
there isn't. Convection-Principle's in power now.
Zeus has been deported.

STREPSIADES

That's a lie! A lot of cheap
Convection-Principle propaganda circulated by those windbags
in the Thinkery!

I was brainwashed! Why, they told me
that the whole universe was a kind of potbellied stove

Pointing to the model in front of the Thinkery.

like that model there, an enormous cosmical barbecue,
and the gods were nothing but a lot of hot air and gas
swirling around in the flue. And I swallowed it,
hook, line, and sinker!

PHEIDIPPIDES

Rave to yourself, Madman.

I'm leaving.

Exit Pheidippides.

STREPSIADES

O Horse's Ass, Blithering Imbecile,
Brainless Booby, Bonehead that I was to ditch the gods
for Sokrates!

*He picks up Pheidippides' stick and savagely
smashes the potbellied model of the Universe in front
of the Thinkery. He then rushes to his own house
and falls on his knees before the statue of Hermes.*

—Great Hermes, I implore you!

Be gracious,
lord! Forego your anger and give me your compassion.
Pity a poor old codger who was hypnotized with hogwash,

drunk on drivel.

O Hermes, give me your advice,
tell me what to do.

Should I sue?

He puts his ear close to the god's mouth as though listening to whispered advice.

What?

Ummm.

Good.

Got it.

DON'T SUE . . .

Go on.

Yes?

BURN DOWN THE THINKERY . . . SMOKE OUT THE
CHARLATANS . . .
INCINERATE THE FAKES!

Aye aye, Sir!

Shouting to his slave.

—Xanthias! come here!

Quick, get me your ladder!

Bring me an axe!

Xanthias runs up with a ladder and an axe.

Now
scramble up there on the Thinkery and rip up the tiles
until the roof caves in.

Shoo, boy!

Xanthias sets his ladder against the Thinkery, clambers up, and starts chopping at the tiles and prying them up with his axe.

—Quick,
bring me a torch!

Another slave runs up with a blazing torch.

By god, I'll fix those fakes
for what they did to me or my name's not Strepsiades!
Let's see if they can fast-talk their way out of this.

He bounds up the ladder to the roof, furiously firing the rafters and beams with his torch, while Xanthias pries at the tiles with the axe. The smoke billows up in clouds and the whole roof begins to glare luridly, while inside the Thinkery are heard the first signs of alarm and confusion.

FIRST STUDENT

From within.
FIRE! ! FIRE! !
HELP!

STREPSIADES
$$\text{Scorch 'em, Torch!}$$
Go get 'em!
When Xanthis stops to stare at the holocaust,
Strepsiades tosses him the torch, snatches up the axe,
and starts slashing furiously at the rafters.

FIRST STUDENT

Rushing out of the Thinkery and peering up
to the roof.
—Sirrah, what dost?

STREPSIADES
Dust? That's chips,
Buster. I'm chopping logic with the rafters of your roof.

SECOND STUDENT

From within.
Who roasteth our rookery?

STREPSIADES
A man without a coat.

SECOND STUDENT

Rushing outside.
But we're burning alive!

STREPSIADES
Hell, I'm freezing to death!

FIRST STUDENT
But this is Arson! Deliberate Arson! We'll die!

STREPSIADES
Splendid. Exactly what I had in mind—
He narrowly misses his leg with the axe and
then teeters dangerously on the roof.
oops!—
so long as I don't split my shins with this axe
or break my neck in the process.

110

*Wheezing, hacking, and gagging, Sokrates scuttles
out of the Thinkery, closely followed by an incredible
procession of emaciated, ghostlike Students, all
gibbering with terror. Finally, at the very rear,
squawking and clucking like two frightened roosters,
come Philosophy and Sophistry.*

SOKRATES

You there, sirrah!
What is thy purpose upon my roof?

STREPSIADES

Ah, sir,
I walk upon the air and look down upon the sun
from a superior standpoint.

SOKRATES

*Choking on the smoke and almost
incoherent with rage.*

Why, you—
agh!
I'm gagging . . .

argh
I . . .
grhuahg . . .
CAN'T . . .
TALK!!
Arrggghhh . . . .

*As Sokrates collapses into a spasm of choked
coughing, Strepsiades and Xanthias come scrambling
down the ladder from the roof. Then Chairephon,
totally covered with soot and cinders and his
cloak smouldering, streaks from the
holocaust of the Thinkery.*

CHAIREPHON

Yiyi!

HALP!
It's like an oven in the Thinkery! I'm burnt to a crisp.
I'm a cinder.

STREPSIADES

*Belaboring him with a stick as Xanthias
lashes Sokrates.*

Then why did you blaspheme the gods?
What made you spy upon the Moon in heaven?

KORYPHAIOS

Thrash them,

beat them, flog them for their crimes, but most of all
because they dared outrage the gods of heaven!

*Strepsiades and his slaves thrash Sokrates and
his followers, until the whole herd of thinkers,
followed by Philosophy and Sophistry, stampedes
madly toward the exit. Here they meet—and flatten—
Pasias and Amynias* returning to the Thinkery
armed with summonses and accompanied by
their witnesses. Exeunt omnes in a general rout.
Behind them the Thinkery with an enormous crash
collapses into blazing ruin.*

CHORUS

Now ladies, let us leave
and go our way.
Our dances here are done,
and so's our play.

Slowly and majestically, the Chorus files out.

page 11. *Strepsiades:* A name derived from στρέψις (turning, twisting, wriggling). That is, Strepsiades is etymologically The Debtdodger and his name is played upon throughout the play.

11. *desert to the Spartans:* The annual invasions of Attika by the Spartans and their allies during the first few years of the Peloponnesian War meant that maltreated or discontented Athenian slaves could easily desert to the enemy, and the fear of desertion was common in Athens.

12. *ponytails:* Pheidippides wore his hair long and curling in the style affected by the younger knights.

13. *bumbailiff:* B. B. Roger's solution, perhaps too English for American ears; but the pun is almost untranslatable. The Greek word here translated as bumbailiff is δήμαρχος, inserted as a surprise in place of the expected "bed-bug" or "flea."

13. *Blueblood Megakles:* Megakles was a common male name of the Alkmaionid family, one of the oldest and most aristocratic in Athens. It is largely because of the prominence of Alkmaionid names in the play that Pheidippides has frequently—and not improbably—been regarded as a caricature of Alkibiades, also an Alkmaionid and notorious for his dissolute youth.

Strepsiades' marriage to an Alkmaionid wife is, of course, a *mésalliance* between a prosperous farmer and a daughter of the dissolute and luxurious city nobility. Presumably, such alliances were not uncommon in the late fifth century, and Aristophanes clearly intends to show the progress of corruption in Strepsiades, ruined by his playboy son and his luxurious wife.

14. *hippos:* "Horse." A common component in aristocratic names, since in early Athens the ownership of a horse automatically meant membership in the military cavalry or the social chivalry.

14. *Pheidonides:* The name means Parsimonious.

14. *Pheidippides:* The compromise means Parsimonious Chevalier or The Scrimping Aristocrat.

15. *horse-god oaths:* As Poseidon Hippios, Poseidon was the patron god of horsemen. Cf. *Knights* 551 ff.

page 16. *Cosmical Oven:* The theory advanced in this passage is of uncertain provenance. In *Birds* 1001, Aristophanes attributes it to Meton, though the comedian Kratinos attributed it to Hippo in his *Panoptai,* and both Herakleitos and Parmenides held that the heavens were made of Fire. Here, however, it is probably best taken as a representative—and, for Aristophanes, representatively ridiculous—example of contemporary physical theory. Some of the Sophists may have held something like it; so far as we know, Sokrates did not.

But the metaphor of the Cosmical Oven is central to the play, and for this reason Aristophanes has placed a visible model of it in front of the Thinkery (cf. 11. 1473-74). Moreover, unless I am mistaken, the metaphor is a surprisingly consistent one, whose every detail and principle would have been instantly understood by an Athenian—but not an American—audience. For the principle here is that of an ordinary, humdrum, home-made charcoal-burner's "kiln," used incongruously as a diagram of highfalutin' Socratic physics, and it is in the appreciation of the details that the humor of the finale lies. It is, according to Aristophanes, a kiln designed for very slow heat and very little air (i.e., a πνιγεύς); in shape it is like an inverted bowl (i.e., a δῖνος—cf. 1. 1473), bellied at the bottom and tapered at the top; set inside it are charcoals (i.e., ἄνθρακες—1. 97) and *above* the charcoals are the swirling heated gases and flames (i.e., αἰθέριος δῖνος—1. 380) under whose steady heat wood becomes charcoal. Translated into the physics of the Aristophanic Sokrates, the humble charcoal-burner's oven becomes the Universal Crucible, in which the gods are the lightning and the slow, downward-burning heat of the heavens, the forces which slowly carbonize the world and the creatures below; in which living is a form of burning and the dead are only ashes. Against this background, with only minor modifications, Sokrates' student can demonstrate to Strepsiades the cosmical principles involved in the gnat's buzz and Sokrates can explain the thunder as elemental farting. And it is, of course, the same metaphor which informs the finale of the play where the Thinkery itself becomes an enormous blazing kiln. Sokrates chokes on the smoke (ἀποπνιγήσομαι—1. 1504), Chairephon is roasted alive (κατακανθήσομαι—1. 1505), while Strepsiades, like a blazing god, fires the roof *above* them.

Such, I believe, is Aristophanes' meaning. Because, however, charcoal kilns are unfamiliar nowadays, I have been compelled to make the Cosmical Oven an ordinary potbellied stove and to introduce a pseudo-scientific equivalent for Δῖνος, i.e., Convection-Principle.

16. *for a fee:* The perennial gibe. The Sophists expected to be paid for the instruction they gave, an attitude which seemed mercenary to the wealthy Plato and which Platonists since have never tired of condemning. Doubtless many of the Sophists were mercenary and several were rich men, but the mere fact of accepting a salary for professional services

rendered does not—except in artistocratic societies where cash payments are regarded as vulgarizing those who receive them—convict a man of intellectual dishonesty. But perhaps I am prejudiced. In any case, the sophistic movement made headway in Athens, not because the Sophists were greedy mountebanks in a gullible age, but because there was a rising class with a desperate need for new skills and techniques and for this class the existing education was worse then useless. If the New Education began by being *vocational*—offering precisely those legal and verbal skills which were so urgently required for the conduct of Athenian imperialism —it ended by being genuinely *revolutionary*, that is, by systematically questioning and overturning all the established beliefs of the old order. It could never have become this, however, had not the fact of payment *freed* the Sophists from the old order as much as it *bound* them to the new. Hence the hostility and open contempt of such conservatives as Aristophanes and Plato.

Sokrates, it is true, did *not* accept payment, and this is Sokrates' glory. But Sokrates' glory is not necessarily the Sophists' shame.

page 16. *The Technique of Winning Lawsuits:* Literally, "to overcome the truth by telling lies," i.e., the familiar accusation that the Sophists made "the worse cause appear the better." It was precisely this charge that was brought against Sokrates by his accusers later, and Aristophanes may be responsible for the suspicion. That some Sophists professionally claimed this ability is beyond dispute. Equally, however, the sophistic attack upon traditional beliefs must have seemed both perverse and illogical to staunch conservatives. Passionately held convictions tend, i.e., to defend themselves by their look of being self-evident: those who question them are *ipso facto* guilty of dishonesty or faulty reasoning. And this is especially true of an age when logic was in a state of comparative infancy. Plato, for instance, constantly attacks the Sophists for their devotion to specious logic (i.e., sophistry), and yet his own *Republic* contains dozens of logical fallacies and grotesque equivocations that even a schoolboy could detect. And presumably these are honest mistakes. But the Sophists normally receive no mercy.

17. *two kinds of Logic:* i.e., the so-called Just (or Major or Better) Logic and the Unjust (or Minor or Weaker) Logic, here rendered as Philosophy and Sophistry respectively.

The originator of the Doctrine of the Two Logics (or *Antilogoi*) was Protagoras of Abdera. If we are right in assuming that Protagoras' famous dictum ("Man is the measure of all things") means that the truth is subjective, then the same statement also implies that a proposition can be simultaneously both true and false. And it is a fact that Protagoras taught his students to argue *both* sides of a given statement with equal plausibility —presumably as an exercise in forensic virtuosity. The very willingness of Athenian courts to consider matter that would now be regarded as inadmissible supports the view that these exercises were practical in scope and not deliberate attempts to subvert justice. But for Aristophanes the *Antilogoi* are transparent sophistry, humbug on a huge scale, and he accordingly makes the debate between the two *Logoi* the climax of the comedy.

It is customary, of course, to translate Λόγος as "Logic" or "Argument," and this is the literal meaning of the word. But the issue here is larger, and to translate this way tends to obscure the fact that Aristophanes is talking, not about systems of formal logic, but about a whole system of Reason, discursive and nondiscursive alike. Λόγος also means Reason; but Reason includes several modes of discourse ranging from the work of the imagination to moral reason and strictly logical reason in the narrow sense. The so-called Just Argument, for instance, is not really an argument or a logical system at all; it is a personification of the kind of Reason spoken by a certain kind of society before logic, strict logic, existed: a Reason which expressed itself in education, in morals, in imagination, in the criteria of values and the justifications offered for those values. As opposed to the Unjust Argument, it represents the rational power of poetry—and the peculiar logic of poetic imagination—against the rational power of prose and formal logic (and for this very reason Aristophanes lets the Just Argument speak in splendid anapests while the Unjust Argument uses prosy iambics). In ethics, it represents the power of rational suasion—by means of models and parallels drawn from the great body of lyric and epic poetry—in contrast to a system of ethics, just as rational but rational in a different way, sanctioned by inferences drawn from Nature and animal existence (cf. Pheidippides' inferences from the life of the rooster, 11. 1427-29). In culture, it is the rational guidance of Custom (not Blind Custom), the corrective rightness of traditional experience as against the restless innovations and risky isolation from experience and history of the pure intellect. It is not what the modern world normally means by Reason, and certainly not what Protagoras meant, but it is, I think, what Aristophanes meant and what most Greeks would have understood him to mean. But for this very reason, because his *Logos* is not a logic but a prelogical discourse of the whole human reason, the Just Argument is helpless against his opponent. His case cannot be expressed logically, and yet it remains rational.

All this may seem like compounding old humbug with new, but it is the justification I make for translating Δίκαιος Λόγος as Philosophy and Ἄδικος Λόγος as Sophistry. Sophistry, of course, should be taken in the strict sense of the word, Philosophy in the loose and unprofessional sense (as in the catchphrase, "a philosophy of life").

page 18. *miscarriage:* Probably a conscious echo of Sokrates' claim to be a midwife of ideas.

page 21. *Spartan prisoners from Pylos:* Cf. Glossary, under *Pylos.* After their imprisonment, the Spartans must have been considerably emaciated.

21. *geological research:* Literally, "they are exploring the things under the earth." This was, in fact, one of the accusations brought against Sokrates by his accusers in 399 B.C. In substance the charge implies that scientific research is blasphemous, insofar as the very act of investigating Nature suggests that the inquirer has doubts about the received cosmology. In the *Apology,* Sokrates admits to having dabbled in scientific research in his earlier days; the later Sokrates, Plato implies, had quite outgrown such nonsense.

23. *And as patriotic as it is useful:* During the years preceding the Peloponnesian War, Athens sometimes confiscated the territory of rebellious subject cities. The land so confiscated was then divided by lot and portioned out among the poorer citizens of Athens. Such allotments, needless to say, were enormously popular—at least in Athens.

24. *a single lawcourt in session:* The Athenian love of litigation was notorious, and Aristophanes never misses a chance of hitting it. Cf. *Wasps.*

24. *Perikles squeezed it dry:* Cf. Glossary: EUBOIA.

26. *Bars of iron, like the Byzantines?:* Sokrates' statement that the gods are an expression coined by vulgar superstition causes Strepsiades to think of a less vulgar sort of coinage. And so he comes up with the Byzantines who, alone in the Greek world, used coins made of iron.

27. *the mystical couch:* Probably a very battered settee. The reader should perhaps be aware that the whole scene of Strepsiades' admission to the Thinkery and introduction to the Clouds is an elaborate "philosophical" initiation rite, probably paralleling initiation into one of the many Greek mysteries. Thus Sokrates' researches are *mysteries;* Sokrates powders Strepsiades as a *purification;* Strepsiades wears a *chaplet* and is forced to strip *naked* (like a candidate at the Eleusinian Mysteries) before entering the *cave* at the rear of the Thinkery (which reminds him of the cave of the oracular Trophonios, a Theban seer). After his entrance he must undergo an *ordeal* (whippings, bedbugs, etc.) before being vouchsafed rebirth as a *new man.*

27. *poor Athamas:* Cf. Glossary: ATHAMAS. Athamas attempted to kill his son Phrixos; when sentenced to be sacrificed for the attempt, he was saved by Herakles. The point here is that Strepsiades' mythology is inaccurate and his literary education has been neglected. But since no conceivable modern audience can be expected to know—or even to care—whether Athamas was killed or saved, I have deliberately intruded the two succeeding lines in the hope of making them seem Aristophanic and the situation a little clearer.

31. *That's why they write:* Presumably all the effusions which follow this are genuine examples of what happened when the Murky Muse inspired a dithyrambic soul.

119

41. *But I'm not a burglar:* According to the Scholiast, this line is explained by the customary Athenian procedure for searching a house in which stolen goods might have been hidden. The searcher was required to strip so that he could not, under pretense of carrying out his search, convey into the house of the accused the goods presumed to have been stolen. Sokrates' reply in the following line is an intruded gloss of my own manufacture, designed to give the situation a possible point for a contemporary audience.

43. *ARISTOPHANES:* In the Greek text the speech which I have here assigned to Aristophanes is given to the Chorus in accordance with the normal convention of the *parabasis*. But if the Chorus in a normal *parabasis* speaks *on behalf of* the poet, the parabasis of *Clouds* is unique in having the Chorus speak, in the first person, *as* the poet himself. Doubtless in the original version of this play, the *parabasis* was spoken by the Chorus on the poet's behalf; but in the revision Aristophanes has laid aside the mask and speaks directly for himself. In the circumstances it seemed unnatural to give the Chorus the poet's lines, and I have therefore brought Aristophanes on stage to speak for himself in person.

45. *a stranger / rescued the foundling:* Aristophanes had produced his comedy *The Banqueters* under the name of Kallistratos. His reason for so doing, he claims, was natural modesty and observation of Athens' neglect and mistreatment of her comic poets (cf. *Knights* 514-45); more likely, he was too young to enter the contest under his own name.

45. *Elektra in the play:* Cf. Glossary: ELEKTRA.

45. *dangling thong of leather:* The comic phallus. Despite the almost unanimous consensus of scholars that Aristophanic characters did *not* wear the phallus, and Aristophanes' explicit denial here, I am nonetheless convinced they did. My only argument is the text and the near impossibility of explaining the dramatic action of numerous scenes in the absence of the phallus. In *Clouds,* Strepsiades' little play on "finger-rhythm" (652 ff.) literally requires the phallus, as does his parting threat to Amynias 1299-1302). The masturbation-jingle in *Knights* (24 ff.) is unactable without it; the Wasps are stingless, etc., etc. Nor am I in the least deterred by Aristophanes' denial—the prize evidence of those who deny the phallus in Aristophanes—simply because it would be the height of ingenuousness, I think, to take Aristophanes' word for it, especially here. *The Clouds* may very well be a daintier, wittier play than the comedies of Aristophanes' rivals, but the disclaimers here are slyly contradicted by the play: several scenes are pure slapstick, Strepsiades beats his opponents with a stick, etc.

45. *a dirty dance:* That is, the *kordax.* Cf. Glossary: KORDAX.

46. *my celebrated simile* on the / *eels:* Cf. *Knights* 864-67.

47. *Paphlagon:* Cf. Glossary: PAPHLAGON.

page 47. *hard on the heels of the Levin rattled the steeds of Thunder:* A quotation from Sophokles' (lost) *Teukros.*

47. *How the moon, in dudgeon, snuffed her flame amongst the rack, and the sun in sullenness withdrew:* An eclipse of the moon took place in October 425, and a solar eclipse in March 424, just before the election of Kleon as general.

48. *your month is a consequent chaos:* An allusion to the confusion created in the Hellenic calendar by the Athenian astronomer Meton. Instituted in 432 B.C. and then gradually adopted throughout Greece, the Metonic calendar changes made for initial difficulties. Because the reform was not uniformly adopted throughout Greece, the same festivals in different places would fall on different dates, etc.

49. *stripped Hyperbolos of his seat:* Hyperbolos (cf. Glossary) had been appointed Athenian delegate to the Amphictyonic Council of Delphoi in 424 B.C. The Council was a religious and juridical federation of Greek city-states whose primary concerns at this time would have been the war and infractions of such "international law" as existed at the time. Presumably, this Council would have been responsible for smoothing the way to general Greek adoption of the Metonic calendar. Exactly what happened to Hyperbolos is not known; the Chorus says that it "stripped him of his crown" —which may mean, as Rogers suggests, that the wind blew off the sacred chaplet which he wore in his official capacity. From the animosity of the Clouds, it can be reasonably assumed that Hyperbolos had supported the Metonic reform.

51. *vulgarly called finger-rhythm:* δάκτυλος in Greek means both "finger" and "dactylic meter."

52. *Raising his phallus to the ready:* Cf. note on p. 120: *dangling thong of leather.*

53. *the female's a duchess:* An anachronistic pun of my own invention; the Greeks had ducks but no dukes. Literally, the Greek says "the male is a rooster (ἀλέκτωρ), the female a roosterette (ἀλεκτρύαινα)."

53. *You've made basket masculine, when it's feminine:* "Basket" is my own contribution. In the Greek, the word is κάρδοπος, "a kneading-trough," whose -ος termination is normally the sign of the masculine gender, though κάρδοπος is in fact feminine. This pun, of course, leads directly to discussion of Kleonymos, another instance of a masculine ending for an actual effeminate.

54. *Why, Amynia:* In the original, this whole passage is based upon a play on the Greek vocative (whereby the nominative *Amynias* becomes *Amynia*—which has the -α termination of the feminine nominative). Because English has no vocative, I have recast the play here as a confusion between singular and plural. For Amynias, cf. Glossary: AMYNIAS.

59. *witchwomen from Thessaly:* Throughout antiquity, Thessaly was famous

for its red-headed witches. Cf. Apuleius *Metamorphoses* I; Plato *Gorgias* 513 a.

page 60. *scorch out every word of the charges:* The charges would have been written down on a wax tablet.

65. *Expended as required. / No comment:* When asked to account for the expenditure of several talents (actually used to purchase the withdrawal of the Spartans), Perikles answered only: "I spent them as required."

66. *Even Hyperbolos:* Hyperbolos had evidently studied under the sophists for a fee of one talent—a large sum.

66. *Philosophy and Sophistry:* Cf. note on p. 117: *two kinds of Logic.*

67. *from the/neck up they are fighting-cocks:* According to a Scholiast, the Logics were garbed as fighting cocks and brought out in cages. This statement has rarely won the approval of scholars, who are quick to point out that it is contradicted by the references throughout the debate to hands, clothing, and other parts of the *human* anatomy. If I am right, the Logics wore rooster masks and a few feathers with perhaps a great vivid bustle of tail feathers; but from the neck down they were visibly human. After their adoption by the Birds, Pisthetairos and Euelpides appear garbed in this very way (cf. *Birds*). Such a solution allows Aristophanes to present the Logics as fighting cocks or as wrestlers as his dramatic needs required, and the text seems to me to support this.

69. *how Zeus escaped punishment after he imprisoned/his father:* Zeus dethroned his father Kronos and bound him in chains. The same argument is used by Euthyphro (cf. Plato *Euthyphro*) to justify his prosecution of his own father. But the argument here is interesting because it shows clearly the mythological rationale of the Old Education and the way in which the New Education refuted it. For the Old Education, mythology was a rational corpus of heroic behavior and morality was taught in mythological terms, quite despite the fact that the morality of mythology was incompatible in many instances with the operative moral values of the fifth century. The greatest artists of the older generation—Aiskhylos and Pindar—had in fact attempted to reconcile myth and moral behavior by rewriting the offensive myths and expelling their crudities or giving them new—and moral—interpretations. The exponents of the New Education quite naturally turned their characteristic invention—formal logic—against the Old Education by pointing out the inconsistencies of its morality and mythology. The same purpose informs many of Euripides' tragedies, and for this reason he incurred the suspicion and contempt of Athenian conservatives—quite despite the fact that his own artistic intentions were really very much like those of Aiskhylos, an attempt to harmonize mythology and morality. But because the morality was relatively new—or looked that way—and was supported by a logic which was destructive of the old morality, he was not understood by conservatives. Few artistic feuds seem, in fact, more futile than Aristophanes' with Euripides, since—

apart from dramatic differences—the two men basically believed the same things.

page 71. *Telephos:* Cf. Glossary: TELEPHOS.

71. *Pandaletos' loaf:* Cf. Glossary: PANDALETOS.

73. *the Old Education:* Readers interested in knowing more about the conflict between different views of education in fifth-century Athens and the rationale of the Old Education should consult the relevant chapters of Werner Jaeger's *Paideia.* Suffice it to say here that it was basically a curriculum comprising two major fields called respectively Music and Gymnastic. By Music was meant the education of the inward man; the schooling not merely of the mind, but of the emotions, the "soul," the feelings and the thoughts in their rational ensemble. The basic instrument of this inward education was poetry joined to music, a blend in which poetry taught by means of example and emulation and was sustained by music which was believed to inculcate the moral virtues. Gymnastic was, of course, vigorous and disciplined athletics. The intended product of this theory of education was a disciplined reason in a disciplined body, an outward grace which expressed the grace and harmony within, the whole person embodying the classical virtues: self-control, decorum, respect for others, piety toward the gods, moderation in all things, dignity and courage. It was, in short, far more what we would call moral education, education in "character," than intellectual training. It was also, for obvious reasons, the education of a restricted and exclusive class. It taught no skills, prepared for no career, and was obviously impractical for Athenian society of the late fifth century. For these reasons, it has always appealed to the exponents of "education of character," British public schools and their American imitators. Aristophanes put his whole heart into its exposition here, and I have done my best to overcome my own repugnance, though probably unsuccessfully.

It would, of course, have been a pleasure to modernize the debate and present it in topical terms as a struggle between the views of education represented—less than ideally, of course—by American universities and that preposterous pretence of education perpetrated by the professional "educationists" in the secondary schools of America. But this is a suggestion which might be adopted by a producer in search of a topical Aristophanes; for a translation, it is out of the question.

73. *A Voice from Afar* or *Hail, O Pallas, Destroyer!:* According to the Scholiast, the second of these hymns is ascribed to Lamprokles of Athens; the first to Kydeides of Hermione.

73. *their conduct was manly:* The point is precisely the manliness. The fashionable homosexuality of the Athenian upper classes was essentially borrowed from Sparta, where homosexuality was not only tolerated but even encouraged as a military virtue (because "lovers" would fight well for each other). Hence the contempt with which Philosophy regards the

effeminate homosexuals of the Athenian New Education. Only among the Athenian lower classes was homosexuality viewed with contempt. The modern image of an Athens populated exclusively by happy philosophical pederasts is largely due to the fact that the surviving literature is a leisure-class production; poor men were very rarely Platonists.

page 77. *Baths of Herakles:* Greeks normally named hot baths everywhere the Baths of Herakles. Another example of specious logic against which Philosophy is helpless.

77. *old Homer:* This argument must have hurt. Of all the poets, Homer was regarded by the Old Education as the greatest, the Bible of true belief. And now, like the devil, Sophistry quotes scripture.

78. *Peleus:* Cf. Glossary: PELEUS.

78. *Hyperbolos and swords just don't mix:* Because Hyperbolos presumably attempted to avoid military service.

79. *reamed/up the rectum with a radish:* The poetic punishment meted out to adulterers in Athens.

82. *Due date for debts:* Strepsiades does not actually say this. What he says is that the day he fears is "the-Old-and-The-New." By this he means the effective last day of the lunar month, the day on which both the last of the waning Old Moon and the first of the waxing New Moon could be seen. The-Old-and-The-New, in short, was the normal name given to the last day of the month, the day on which debts were payable. And this nomenclature continued to be used even when the calendar was no longer lunar. The term is, to modern ears, grotesquely unfamiliar, but it is also crucial to an understanding of the action, and for this reason I have had considerable misgivings about altering it. But upon reflection it seemed to me that "Due date" might just possibly do, and I have so rendered it. But see the note on this page: *Today's Dueday.*

82. *Call it an honorarium:* Aristophanes, that is, hints that Sokrates was not above receiving "tokens of esteem" from his disciples. This may be pure satirical malice, but then again it may not be. Sokrates' students were mostly rich aristocrats; he himself was poor. And in the circles which Plato frequented, a distinction was probably drawn between a payment and a "gratuity"—the common sophistry of "good society." But this is guesswork.

83. *with gladsome paeans plangent:* An echo, according to the Scholiast, from the *Satyrs* of Phrynichos—or Euripides' *Peleus.* Probably the latter.

83. *debouch from mine abode:* A very slight modification of Euripides' *Hekabe* 173 ff.

84. *Today's Dueday:* Cf. note above: *Due date for debts.* For a more literal rendering of Pheidippides' sophistic analysis of the-Old-New-Day in the following lines, readers should consult any prose translation of the play. I have preferred to use the "Dueday—two day" pun because it made the equivocation instantly visible as glib hocus pocus, though it also

meant a necessary change—a slight one—in the interpretation of Solon's legislation which Pheidippides offers. But I suppose most readers of the *Clouds* to be more interested in a comedy than in the details of Athenian debt legislation.

page 84. *to post their bond:* Before commencing a legal action against a defaulting debtor, a creditor had to post with the prytanies, as caution money to defray court expenses, the sum of 10 per cent of the amount of the debt.

85. *Precisely because they* are *magistrates:* A deliberate distortion of the literal meaning of the Greek. The text actually says: "They act like Foretasters; in order to devour the meal as quickly as possible, they have the deposits paid a day in advance." The Foretasters seem to have been officials responsible for sampling the dishes to be served at a public feast the following day.

87. *the National Honor:* The National Honor (and, one might add, the public interest) of Athens required that every citizen be as litigious as possible.

91. *tragedy / by Karkinos:* Karkinos was a frigid, fourth-rate tragedian with an apparent penchant for introducing querulous beggar-gods in his plays. Most of the fustian which follows is presumably the work of Karkinos or his son Xenokles. Talent did not run in the family.

100. *a custom's a custom:* The festive custom of *paroinia,* acording to Rogers, an old convivial tradition of singing at table.

100. *Shearin' o' the Ram:* Krios (which also means "Ram") was a wrestler, probably the victim of an overwhelming defeat in a wrestling match, and hence the "Shorn Ram." Simonides' poetry was very highly regarded by the older generation.

101. *bombastic bore / in poetic history:* The charge was common in antiquity. In an age of discursive prose and colloquial poetry, the gorgeousness of Aischylos and his extravagant metaphorical bravura made him look like a drunken lord of language. For Aristophanes, of course, Aischylos is the Model Poet who "makes men better citizens" as opposed to the Arch-Corrupter, Euripides. Cf. *Frogs.*

101. *One of those slimy tragedies:* A reference to Euripides' (lost) *Aiolos.*

104. *Wasn't I born as free a man as you?:* A parody of Euripides' *Alkestis* 691.

107. *the insubstantial Clouds men build their hopes upon:* This line and most of the two which follow it are Arrowsmith, not Aristophanes. I have intruded them in order to give just a little more resonance to the meaning of the Clouds. For although English has idioms in plenty which more or less parallel the Greek—to "have one's head in the Clouds," "to build on the clouds," "castles in the clouds," etc.—a little further rounding out seemed necessary. The Clouds are the patrons of visionaries and woolgatherers the world over; here they are cloudy deceivers, the shining hopes that deceive Strepsiades.

page 113. *Pasias and Amynias:* The Greek plays, of course, have come down to us without footnotes or stage directions other than what the Scholiasts tell us. And I admit that there is no textual justification for bringing back Pasias and Amynias here, nor is it suggested by any Scholiast. They are here because Pasias threatened to pay his bond and return with a summons, and because I think Aristophanes would have liked them to be foiled again, even at Strepsiades' moment of truth.

Glossary

AISCHYLOS, AESCHYLUS: The great Athenian tragedian (525-456 B.C.).

AKADEME, ACADEMY: Originally a precinct sacred to the hero Akademos and afterward used as a gymnasium and recreation area. The general Kimon planted it with groves of olives and plane trees. Only in the fourth century, after becoming the haunt of the philosopher Plato and his followers, did the once athletic Akademy become academic in the modern sense of the word.

AKROPOLIS, ACROPOLIS: The citadel of Athens.

ALKIBIADES: An Athenian politician (*ca.* 450-404) of great ability and brilliance. Of aristocratic Alkmaionid descent, he was related to Perikles and was, for some time, a devoted disciple of Sokrates. Distinguished by wealth, birth, and spectacular personal beauty, he spent his youth in lavish display and debauchery (Pheidippides in *The Clouds* has been thought to be a caricature of Alkibiades). After the death of Kleon in 422, Alkibiades became chief of the belligerent anti-Spartan party in Athens in opposition to the more conservative Nikias and was one of the primary advocates of the disastrous Sicilian expedition.

AMYNIAS: Son of Pronapes and one of Strepsiades' creditors in *The Clouds*. He was not, however, a professional moneylender but a notorious effeminate and wastrel, probably addicted to gambling.

ANTIMACHOS: A homosexual on a prodigious scale.

APOLLO: God of prophecy, music, healing, and light; his two chief shrines were at Delphoi (q.v.) and the island of Delos (q.v.).

ARTEMIS: Goddess of the hunt and the moon, sister of Apollo (q.v.).

ATHAMAS: King of Orchomenos and the legendary subject of a (lost) play by Sophokles. Having attempted to murder his son Phrixos (q.v.),

Athamas was sentenced to be sacrificed. He was crowned with a sacrificial wreath and dragged before the altar, but just before being dispatched, was saved by the sudden intervention of Herakles.

ATHENA, ATHENE: Goddess of wisdom and war and patroness of Athens. On her breast she wore the aegis, a goatskin plated with scales and a Gorgon's head in the center.

BACCHOS: See DIONYSOS.

BYZANTION: A city on the Bosporos and a subject-city of the Athenian Empire. Its siege by the Athenians under Kimon in 469 was celebrated.

CHAIREPHON: A pupil and disciple of Sokrates; his scrawniness and emaciated pallor are constantly ridiculed by Aristophanes.

DELOS: Small Aegean island sacred to Apollo.

DELPHOI, DELPHI: A town in Phokis, celebrated for its great temple and oracle of Apollo.

DEMETER: The Earth-Mother; goddess of grain, agriculture, and the harvest, worshipped in her shrine at Eleusis in Attika.

DIONYSOS: God of vineyards, wine, and dramatic poetry; also called Bacchos, Evios, Bromios, etc.

ELEKTRA: Daughter of Agamemnon and Klytaimnestra; with her brother Orestes she murdered her mother for having killed her father. In the *parabasis* of *The Clouds,* Aristophanes alludes to the famous scene in Aischylos' *Choephoroe,* when Elektra recognized that her brother Orestes had returned to Argos from the lock of hair left on Agamemnon's tomb.

EPHESOS: A city in Asia Minor (Ionia), site of a famous temple of Artemis.

EUBOIA: A large and fertile island northeast of Attica. In 457 Perikles planted an Athenian colony on the island and otherwise exploited it. As a result the island revolted in 445 and had to be resubjugated. This time, however, Perikles' treatment of the island was so severe that it was commonly said (at least by his enemies) that he had "stretched Euboia on the rack of torture."

EUPOLIS: An Athenian poet of the Old Comedy and a rival of Aristophanes. Eupolis claimed that Aristophanes had imitated him in *The Knights,* and Aristophanes countered by charging that Eupolis' *Marikas* was a plagiarism of his own *The Knights.*

EURIPIDES: Athenian tragedian (480-406 B.C.) whose character and plays were constantly ridiculed by Aristophanes. Euripides' mother may have been (though this is uncertain) a marketwoman who sold chervil, and Aristophanes never tires of twitting the tragedian about his mother's vegetables.

HERAKLES: Hero and demigod, son of Zeus and Alkmene; renowned for his great labors, his prodigious strength, and his gluttonous appetite.

HERMES: God of messengers and thieves; in Athens in every doorway stood a statue of Hermes (i.e., a herm, usually a pillar surmounted by a bust of the god), protector of the door and guardian against thieves—presumably because it takes a thief to keep another thief away.

HIERONYMOS: A dithyrambic poet and tragedian, notorious for his extraordinary shagginess, bestial appearance, and pederasty.

HIPPOKRATES: Athenian general and nephew of Perikles; his three sons, it seems, were all distinguished for their stupidity and were popularly nicknamed "The Pigs."

HYPERBOLOS: An Athenian demagogue, successor to Kleon on the latter's death in 422. Of servile origins, he seems to have been a peddler of lamps and then to have studied with the Sophists in order to advance himself politically. (At least these are the charges made against him by Aristophanes.) He was later ostracized and finally murdered by the oligarchical leaders in Samos.

KARKINOS: An Athenian tragic poet whose poetry and three sons are all ridiculed by Aristophanes. Karkinos' name means "Crab."

KEKROPS, CECROPS: Legendary first king of Attika and reputed founder of Athens. Hence "country of Kekrops" is equivalent to "Athens," and "son of Kekrops" to "Athenian." He is usually represented as twi-form, i.e., with the head and upper trunk of a man, but serpent-shaped below (symbolizing his earthborn origin).

KIKYNNA: An Athenian deme of the tribe of Akamantis.

KLEON: Son of Kleainetos; the most notorious and powerful of all Athenian demagogues. After the death of Perikles in 429 B.C., Kleon became, until his own death in 422, the leader of the radical democracy and the anti-Spartan extremists in Athens. An impressive speaker and a thoroughly unscrupulous and venal politician, he was bitterly loathed and attacked by Aristophanes. In 424 B.C., thanks to his coup in capturing the Spartan hoplites at Sphakteria, he reached the height of his power; so unchallengeable was his position that he was able to persuade the Athenians not to accept the handsome terms offered by Sparta in an attempt to recover her imprisoned hoplites. Filled with confidence in his military ability and tempted by the hope of further glory, Kleon took command of an Athenian army in Thrace, where, in 422, he was defeated and killed by the Spartan forces under Brasidas.

In Aristophanes' *The Knights,* Kleon is only slightly masked under the name of Paphlagon (q.v.).

KLEONYMOS: A corpulent glutton and part-time informer; Aristophanes' commonest butt for cowardice (i.e., throwing one's shield away).

KORDAX: A salacious dance commonly used in Athenian Old Comedy.

KRONOS: Father of Zeus, Hera, and Poseidon. Deprived of his rule by Zeus. Synonymous with "old fogy."

KYNTHOS: A mountain on the island of Delos, sacred to Apollo.

LEOGORAS: A wealthy Athenian gourmet, addicted to horse raising (or possibly to pheasant-breeding). Father of the orator Andokides.

LYDIA: A district of Asia Minor; under its greatest king, Kroisos (Croesus), it included almost all of Asia Minor from the river Halys to the Ionian coast. Its wealth and effeminacy were proverbial among Greeks.

MAENADS: The frenzied female worshippers (Bacchantes) of Dionysos (q.v.).

MAIOTIS: An inland sea (the modern Sea of Azov), northern arm of the Black Sea.

MARATHON: The famous battle (490 B.C.) in which the Athenian forces under Miltiades crushingly defeated the first Persian invasion of Hellas.

MEGAKLES: A name belonging to the Alkmaionid family, one of the proudest and most distinguished aristocratic families of Athens.

MEMNON: Famous hero, son of Tithonos and Eos (Dawn); killed in the Trojan War at the hands of Achilleus.

MIMAS: A mountain on the coast of Ionia.

NESTOR: King of Pylos and a hero of the Trojan War, famous for his wisdom and eloquence.

OLYMPOS: Mountain (app. 9700 feet, alt.) in Thessaly, covered at the summit with perpetual snow and reputed by the Greeks to be the abode of the gods.

PALLAS: The goddess Athena (Pallas Athene).

PANATHENAIA: The great Athenian festival in honor of Athena.

PANDALETOS: A professional informer.

PAPHLAGON: Aristophanes' (and presumably Athens') nickname for the demagogue Kleon (q.v.). The name is intended to suggest: (1) that Kleon came of slavish and foreign stock—i.e., was not an Athenian but a Paphlagonian—and (2) the sheer volume and violence of Kleon's rhetorical assaults (from Greek *paphlazein,* to froth, bluster, storm).

PARNASSOS: A high mountain to the north of Delphoi (q.v.); one of the chief haunts of Apollo and the Muses, but frequented also by Dionysos.

PARNES: A mountain in the northeast of Attika, forming part of the boundary between Attika and Boiotia. Near its foot was situated the deme of Acharnai.

PASIAS: One of Strepsiades' creditors; evidently a grotesquely fat man and probably a drunkard to boot.

PELEUS: Hero of mythology, husband of Thetis and father of Achilleus. According to legend, Astydamia, wife of Akastos, fell in love with Peleus but was rejected by him. Angered, she denounced him to her husband for having attempted to seduce her. Akastos thereupon invited Peleus to a hunting expedition on Mt. Pelion, stripped him of his weapons, and left him to be torn to pieces by the wild animals. When Peleus was almost on the point of death, however, the god Hermes brought him a sword.

PERIKLES: Greatest of Athenian statesmen of the fifth century, and from 461 B.C. until his death in 429, the almost unchallenged leader of the radical Athenian democracy. Of one of Athens' most aristocratic families (the Alkmaionids), he was nonetheless the politician most responsible for the creation of the extreme democracy of the late fifth century. To Aristophanes' critical and conservative eyes, it was Perikles who was responsible for the corruption of Athens, and Aristophanes never tires of contrasting the Athens of the Persian War period with the Athens of Perikles—corrupt, effete, cruelly imperialistic, avaricious, at the mercy of Sophists, clever orators, and impostors, cursed with a system (e.g., the law courts) which practically guaranteed further excesses and injustices. Worst of all in Aristophanes' eyes was Perikles' belligerent war policies (e.g., the famous Megarian Decree of 432) and the fact that, after 429, Athens was left to the mercies of men like Kleon and Hyperbolos who lacked Perikles' restraint and political genius. Like almost all the comic dramatists, Aristophanes was a conservative (*not* an oligarch), and although he distinguishes clearly between Perikles and his corrupt successors, he nonetheless holds Perikles responsible for creating the political system in which men like Kleon could thrive.

PHOIBOS: Apollo (q.v.).

PHRIXOS: Son of Athamas (q.v.); on the point of being sacrificed to Zeus, he was rescued by his mother Nephele.

PHRYNICHOS: The famous early Athenian tragedian.

PHRYNIS: Of Mytilene, a famous citharist and musician of the fifth century; his innovations shocked and angered contemporary conservatives.

POSEIDON: Brother of Zeus and god of the sea. As god of the sea, he girdles the earth and has it in his power, as Poseidon the Earthshaker, to cause earthquakes. In still another manifestation, he is Poseidon Hippios, patron god of horses and horsemen.

PRODIKOS: Of Keos, the famous sophist and friend of Sokrates.

PYLOS: Town of the southwestern coast of Messina whose siege and capture, along with the neighboring island of Sphakteria in 425-24, became a *cause célèbre* of the Peloponnesian War and the major source of Kleon's prestige and power in Athens. As a result of their defeat at Pylos and the capture of their hoplites, the Spartans were forced to sue for peace; every overture, however, was met by the determined refusal of Kleon, eager for the war to continue.

SARPEDON: Legendary hero, son of Zeus and Europa; killed by Patroklos during the Trojan War.

SIMON: A swindler, the details of whose peculations are unknown.

SIMONIDES: Of Keos, the great sixth-century lyric poet.

SOKRATES: (*Ca.* 469-399 B.C.) The great Athenian philosopher and teacher of Plato. In appearance he was almost grotesquely ugly; with his bulging eyes, fat lips, and a round paunch, he looked like nothing so much as a Satyr or Silenos. This, combined with his practice of strolling about the marketplace and accosting citizens with questions about truth, justice, beauty, etc., made him an apt target for ridicule, all the more since it is doubtful whether the majority of Athenians could, in fact, distinguish between Sokrates and the average Sophist. That this is the case can be inferred from *The Clouds* and Aristophanes' extremely sophistic presentation of Sokrates.

SOLON: Famous Athenian legislator (*ca.* 638-588 B.C.), whose achievement it was to have ended debt-slavery in Athens.

SOPHOKLES: The Athenian tragedian (495-404 B.C.).

TELEPHOS: Legendary king of Mysia and the subject of tragedies by Aischylos, Sophokles, and Euripides. Wounded by Achilleus while defending his country, Telephos was informed by an oracle that only the weapons which had given him his wound could cure him. Thereupon, disguised as a beggar, he made his way to Argos where, with the connivance of Klytaimnestra, he covertly took the young Orestes hostage. When the gathered Greeks were condemning Telephos for his hostility to their cause, the disguised hero made a speech in his own defense, but with such warmth and eloquence that the Greeks recognized him. When Achilleus demanded his death, Telephos threatened to kill the infant Orestes. Finally, Achilleus relented and agreed to give Telephos the weapon which had wounded him and which would cure him.

THALES: Of Miletos (*ca.* 636-546 B.C.), one of the Seven Sages of antiquity; renowned for his scientific genius and for having predicted an eclipse of the sun.

THEOROS: Flatterer, perjurer, sycophant of Kleon.

THESSALY: A large district in northern Greece, renowned throughout antiquity for its abundant supply of witches.

THETIS: The sea nymph, mother of Achilleus by Peleus (q.v.). Courted against her wishes by Peleus, she changed herself successively into a bird, a tree, and a tigress. But Peleus, acting on the instructions of the centaur Cheiron, countered by holding her fast until she assumed human form and consented to marry him.

TLEPOLEMOS: Hero and son of Herakles, the subject of a tragedy by the dramatist Xenokles, one of the sons of Karkinos (q.v.). In the play one of the characters describes how his brother was killed by Tlepolemos.

TROPHONIOS: King of Orchomenos, worshipped as a hero after his death. His oracle in a cave in Boiotia was celebrated throughout Hellas, and those who consulted him made it their practice to take honeycakes with which to appease the snakes who frequented the cavern.

TYPHO, TYPHON: A fire-breathing giant, frequently represented as a hurricane.

XANTHIAS: A common servile name.

XENOKLES: An Athenian tragedian, son of Karkinos (q.v.).

XENOPHANTES: Father of Hieronymos (q.v.).

ZEUS: Chief god of the Olympian pantheon; son of Kronos, brother of Poseidon and father of Athena. As the supreme ruler of the world, he is armed with thunder and lightning and creates storms and tempests.

SONIC
BOOM

SONIC
BOOM

GLOBALIZATION AT MACH SPEED

Gregg Easterbrook

RANDOM HOUSE / NEW YORK

Copyright © 2009 by Gregg Easterbrook

Published in the United States by Random House, an imprint of
The Random House Publishing Group, a division of Random House, Inc., New York.

RANDOM HOUSE and colophon are registered trademarks of Random House, Inc.

LIBRARY OF CONGRESS CATALOGING-IN-PUBLICATION DATA
Easterbrook, Gregg.
Sonic boom : globalization at mach speed / by Gregg Easterbrook.
ISBN 978-1-4000-6395-6
eBook ISBN 978-1-58836-903-1
1. Economic history—21st century.   2. Economic development—Social aspects.   I. Title.
HC59.3.E23 2009
330.9—dc22 2009022230
Printed in the United States of America on acid-free paper

www.atrandom.com

2 4 6 8 9 7 5 3

FIRST EDITION

Book design by Casey Hampton

For my older brother, Frank Hoover Easterbrook.
Whom I looked up to when a child, and do still today.

Contents

Introduction

A Trailer for the Docudrama of the Twenty-first Century

I n 2008, when the world realized the international economy had entered a sharp decline, I was sitting at a desk writing a book about why the international economy would boom. The decline that manifested itself in 2008 had the effect of focusing many people's minds. Those who lost jobs, or faced foreclosure, or saw their retirement savings damaged by swindlers masquerading as respectable bankers and Wall Street managers—their minds certainly were focused. My mind was focused on this question: Does it make sense to envision progress when the world seems to be sliding backward?

I came to the conclusion that this does make sense, and the result is the book you now hold. Before the downturn that became apparent in 2008, the larger global economic trend for three decades was rising prosperity for almost everyone, accelerating growth, higher living standards for average people, better education, increased ease of communication, low inflation, few shortages, and more personal freedom across most of the family of nations. History shows that when some crisis interrupts a larger trend, as soon as the crisis ends, the larger trend resumes. For example, global economic trends were mainly favorable before World War II; when the conflict ended, growth resumed, even in nations that were physically devastated by combat. All postwar recessions have ended in a resumption of previous trends. In places where natural disasters cause awful destruction, usually whatever larger trends were under way resume soon after the disaster stops; when the United States was hit by a manmade disaster in September 2001, the pattern of larger trends was not altered. Such precedents suggest that advancing global prosperity is likely to resume. If not this year, then soon, the global economy is likely to be fine. One purpose of a book is to step back from the drumbeat of headlines and consider larger trends. I write this preface knowing you may pick up *Sonic Boom* on a day when economic news is spooky. Notwithstanding, I believe a substantial rise in human prosperity is coming.

Here's the catch: just as favorable economic and social trends are likely to resume, many problems that have characterized recent decades are likely to get worse, too. Job instability, economic insecurity, a sense of turmoil, the unfocused fear that even when things seem good a hammer is about to fall—these also are part of the larger trend, and no rising tide will wash them away. For a writer sitting at a desk, the recession had a paradoxically useful impact, forcing me to spend just as much time contemplating the negative as the positive. The result is that the book you now hold, while envisioning the likelihood of a global boom, also warns that when it comes to anxiety, we ain't seen nothing yet.

What seemed scariest about the downturn that began in 2008 was not the dire unemployment rate, or specific data from bank lending departments or auto sales floors, but rather the fear that world economy was on the verge of unraveling. I don't think this will occur; I expect the reverse. But the fear may be here to stay. What happened in the economic downturn that began in 2008 was a trailer for the docudrama of the twenty-first century: a coming-attractions preview of the rest of your economic life. Don't worry about ordering tickets in advance, since you will be attending the show whether you wish to or not.

We're better off in a hectic, high-tech, interconnected world, for reasons *Sonic Boom* will spell out in detail. The coming global Sonic Boom may be the best economic news the world has ever received.

But being economically interconnected makes us feel vulnerable, because we can no longer control events—or at least, we can no longer believe events *can* be controlled. And that perception of loss of control is likely to accelerate. There will be tremendous pressure on government officials and policymakers to do something, anything, about the sense of accelerating change. Business leaders will be under tremendous pressure, too; soon, to the Fortune 500, Ralph Nader will seem like the good old days. New laws, policies and business plans might cushion the Sonic Boom, and this book will discuss them. But stop change? All the air, naval and ground forces in the world could not accomplish that. Get used to a ceaseless, low-grade sense of economic emergency, even if all goods and services are in ample supply, even if the local grocery store is fully stocked, busy and open twenty-four hours.

Why do I think a world boom is coming? Because though globalization may be driving you crazy, globalization is just getting started. The positive aspects—ease of communication, more freedom of speech, markets closely attuned to consumer demand, rising education levels in the developing world—are in their early stages. The world is going to become a *lot* more global. Though stress-inducing, this will be mainly good.

Because chip-based electronic devices are still relatively new and continue to rise in quality while declining in price, important technological improvements to the world economy are at hand. For example, fairly soon—meaning "really soon" at the current pace of change—most products will be manufactured using far less energy and producing less waste. That's the kind of advance for which we have all long hoped.

The conversion of the world to free economics remains in its early stages. You may not like free-market economics—let's hope someday there will be a saner, more compassionate system for organizing how we produce, work and spend—but it is inarguable that nearly all of the last century's improvements in standards of living for average people came from the free-market system. Just a few decades ago, most nations did not benefit from market economics. Most had controlled economies supervised by some form of dictatorship, or feudal economies—the feudal system, forgotten in the West, continues to be the primary tormentor of the world's poor—or economies that were free domestically but isolated behind import barriers. In the last generation, more and more of the world's economies have become reasonably free and begun to engage in reasonably open trade. Though the spreading of free economics is well-known, it's wrong to assume the impact has already occurred. Most of the impact lies in the future, because most of the world is just becoming accustomed to free markets, with their pluses and minuses. We should expect that in the near future, most of the world will attain the free-market advantages long enjoyed in the West, especially ample goods of rising quality and declining real-currency price.

Many of the benefits of the expansion of democracy remain in the future. A generation ago, according to United Nations figures, only one third of the world's nations held true multiparty elections; today 80 percent do, and the proportion continues to rise. Many nations have in recent years converted from despotism or autocracy to at least some halting form of democracy, while there is scant movement in the opposite direction. Dear Iran, North Korea and the Arab nations: become democracies. Do you really want to wake up some morning and find yourselves the world's sole holdouts against progress?

The concept of personal freedom, actively suppressed in much of the world through much of history, is only now spreading throughout most of the world. That people should make their own choices; that women should be as free as men; that individual decisions, not commands from palaces, should set the course of society—these are revolutionary concepts in many societies.

Until quite recently, only the Western nations benefited from technologically efficient agriculture and advanced manufacturing. Now most of the world is acquiring both, which means that soon billions of people will work with high productivity, rather than only those in affluent lands working productively.

One reason the United States and European Union have led the world in wealth and strength is that these are the first places where women achieved educational equality and personal freedom. Women could then contribute their ideas and effort to national success. As

women achieve educational equality and personal freedom in developing nations, the supply of ideas and effort available to the world will
roughly double!

And will an ever-more-interlinked globe reduce the odds of war?
Military spending is among the least desirable uses of social resources.
The best-case outcome for most defense spending is that it is totally
wasted—that is, military force is never used. Worst-case outcomes go
downhill from there. As most nations have begun spirited economic
competition, they have reduced their competition in arms buildups.
Stated in today's dollars, global military spending peaked in 1985 at
$1.5 trillion, and by 2008 had fallen to $1.3 trillion.[1] Owing to world
population growth through the period, military spending has declined
from $312 per capita in 1985 (in today's dollars) to $194 per capita in
2008. Depressing numbers receive extensive coverage in the media;
this splendidly positive number is unknown except to specialists.

Historically, the possession of military power has had a self-
fulfilling aspect: nations with strong armies tend to use them. If the
opposite is also true, then declining military spending ought to lead to
reduced conflict. So far, that is the case. Wars in Iraq and a few other
places are terrible exceptions to an overall trend of declining incidence
and intensity of combat. As discussed in more detail later in the book,
studies show that violent conflicts, both between and within states,
rose steadily from 1955 to 1989, hit their post–World War II maximum
in that year, declined steadily until 2003, the year of the U.S. invasion
of Iraq, and since have risen slightly but remain below the level of the
late 1970s. Owing mainly to this reduction in war, today a person's
chance of dying by violence is the lowest it has been in human history.
This is true broadly across the globe, except for a few places such as
Sudan.

Perhaps twenty years is too little time from which to draw conclusions. But interconnected economics have arisen at the same moment
that military spending has declined, and we should not be so cynical as
to refuse to entertain the possibility that this means something good is
happening. Hostile nationalism might reassert itself, but the globalized economy seems to make this less likely than in the past. In the
late 1930s, Germany's export sector was just six percent of the coun-

try's GDP; the value of trade was not pressuring that country to avoid war. Today people worry about a revival of hostile nationalism in Russia, but that nation's export sector is 22 percent of GDP. Belligerence would be bad business for Moscow; the loss of export income would almost certainly outweigh anything Russia might gain through threats of fighting. China has an extremely large export sector, and China so far is a historical rarity, a great state *not* attempting to establish a dominant military.

Except, perhaps, for the hushed agrarian sunrises of a prehistory about which we may only speculate, the centuries have been marred by endless attempts at conquest by force. Today, in the early stages of globalization, there have been two decades without superpower confrontation, while most nations have shown more interest in acquiring market share than acquiring territory. Economists have long maintained that if only people and groups stopped fighting each other and cooperated, prosperity would rise for all. What a sly joke if free-market economists turn out to be history's peacemakers!

But bear in mind the seemingly iron law of human events: new problems always arise to replace old. Suppose the economic downturn ends and what comes next is a flowering of productive efficiency, higher material well-being and decreased military tension. The same forces that are likely to bring about these desirable ends will also have many unhappy consequences. Sudden economic tumult will become more frequent. Job anxiety will be endless; even if unemployment goes down, millions will fear it could return again quickly. The treadmill of work-and-spend will run ever faster, demanding we keep pace. Many jobs will become more physically convenient but will blur with home life, meaning there is never a time when you are not "at work." The velocity of change could become dizzying. Winner-take-all accumulation of wealth at the top, already the worst fault of capitalism and among the least attractive aspects of American society, may worsen in the West while infecting newly free nations. Every little thing that goes wrong anywhere in the world will scare us. And we will *know* every little thing that goes wrong anywhere in the world.

Through most of the past, even the recent past, most people on Earth had little to do with most other people on Earth. Knowledge of the world beyond the horizon was slight: during the height of ancient Egyptian civilization, during the pinnacle of the Roman Empire or the apex of dynastic China, most people on Earth were not in any way affected by these societies—indeed, they did not even know they existed. Through most of the past, most men and women interacted only with those in immediately adjacent communities, while international trade was rare and hardly a factor in the typical person's life. As recently as a century ago, most men and women were not touched by what happened on other continents: someone living in the American Midwest in the nineteenth century, for instance, might read a book about the places now called Malaysia or Pakistan, but events in those lands would never affect that person. Now, if something explodes in Pakistan or a new product from Malaysia challenges a Midwestern product, we have live television images within minutes. Increasingly we live not in isolation from the rest of the nation or world but in constant interaction, which means constant anxiety. This development appears irreversible, so don't waste valuable time complaining.

To date, commentary has tended to declare the evolving interconnected global economy either utterly marvelous or dreadfully awful. When some new force comes into play in society, there is a natural initial tendency to view the force as either all good or all bad. Our mental processing systems prefer such clear-line categorizations; after all, we've already got too much to think about. Eventually, though, people begin to sort out the constructive and destructive impacts of the new force. This book will offer such a second-phase, mixed-bag understanding of global trends—the global economy basically will be fine, while most things become better for most people, but the pressure of change will become close to unbearable.

The prospect of a world more prosperous, more free and less militaristic, yet ever more nervous, is the topic of *Sonic Boom*.

Gregg Easterbrook
Colorado Springs, Colorado
May 2009

SONIC
BOOM

One

SHENZHEN

The city did not exist thirty years ago, yet today has nearly 9 million residents, about the same population as the five boroughs of New York. Many of its residents were born into rural poverty—and today live a lifestyle approximately equivalent to that lived in Brooklyn. In mere decades the people of the city have transformed a rock-bound fishing village of tarpaper shacks into a leading urban center, if one whose existence is unknown to most of the world. Engineers flattened hills to make room for two dozen skyscrapers of forty-five stories or more—the tally will be larger by the time you encounter this paragraph—plus the world's ninth-tallest structure, a 1,260-foot-high office tower. The city contains numerous hospitals and power stations, plus hundreds of schools, almost all built during the lifetimes of those who use them. Crisscrossing the city are thousands of miles of roads and transit lines connecting tens of thousands of shops and cafés with more than a million dwellings, all structures that did not exist thirty years ago. Paris and London took many centuries to build; Manhattan's core was constructed in roughly one century; the glittering new cities of the American postwar imagination, Atlanta, Dallas, Denver,

Los Angeles, Miami, Phoenix and Seattle, each required roughly half a century to reach their current status of impressive-when-viewed-from-orbit. This new city has outflanked them all, becoming the fastest-built great metropolis in human history.[1] You're forgiven if you have never heard of Shenzhen.

What is really impressive about Shenzhen is not its boulevards and apartment towers but its harbor. A dense tangle of docks, warehouses, quays, slips and monstrous cranes, the Port of Shenzhen has gone in a single generation from nonexistent to the world's fourth-busiest harbor. Cargoes borne by oceangoing container ships are measured in the prosaically named Twenty-foot Equivalent Units, corresponding to metal boxes the size of the trailer on a semi truck; a TEU typically holds about ten tons of finished products. In 2007, some 21 million TEUs departed from Shenzhen to the markets of the world—more cargo than moved through Los Angeles and Long Beach harbors combined, and Los Angeles and Long Beach are America's two busiest ports. Twenty-one million TEUs in a year equates to a trailerload of goods departing Shenzhen harbor *every other second.* Rotterdam and Hamburg required centuries to reach central positions in global commerce; Shenzhen did this in less time than one person's life span. Export totals for 2008 and 2009 are expected to be down, but the basic accomplishment won't change—Shenzhen fashioned itself into a city of global importance in a remarkably brief period. Lines of enormous cargo vessels leave Shenzhen low in the water owing to the weight of the electronics, clothing, industrial equipment, toys, furniture and other manufactured goods they are bearing to the United States, the European Union, Latin America, the Middle East and other destinations. Batteries are a common cargo because BYD, the world's second-leading manufacturer of batteries, is based in Shenzhen. By the time you read this, BYD may be the world's number-one battery maker—and a decade from now may become the world's leader in manufacturing electric cars. BYD did not even exist until 1996.

Though the people of Shenzhen, China, do not hear it, the sound their city makes is a sonic boom. There have been booms before in various parts of the world: some brief, some long-lasting, some that were followed by busts, some that simply petered out. What is occurring now is a Sonic Boom—noisy, superfast, covering huge amounts of territory. Nothing like Shenzhen has ever happened before: there has never been a great city built so fast, nor a productive economy established from so little, nor a society transformed in such a short time from isolationist and repressed to outward-focused and eager to be free. The international recession that began in 2008 has made the Sonic Boom quieter, to keep the metaphor, and is causing problems that may afflict many nations for many years. But Shenzhen represents the larger trend: growth, change and transformation at unprecedented velocity. Once the recession fades, the larger trend is likely to reassert itself.

Suppose you live in the United States. Where in America would you go to observe for yourself the restructuring of the world—to a Wal-Mart? To an office that runs a social-networking Web site? You should go to a harbor. The Port of Long Beach, south of Los Angeles, was as recently as the 1980s a relatively sleepy place where tramp freighters debarked to carry crushed steel from abandoned cars and rusting iron from torn-down bridges to developing-world blast furnaces that would recycle what America no longer wanted. Today the Port of Long Beach has its own sprawling highway system, one that looks from the air like a complex interstate freeway, to handle the ever-rising volume of trade. In 2007, more than 2,700 large vessels arrived at Long Beach Harbor, and unloaded about 7 million truckloads' worth of goods. Oceangoing container ships spend days or weeks at anchor waiting for a space to dock; trailer trucks queue up by the hundreds. Even as the international recession slows this activity, the Port of Long Beach is much more crowded and busy than a generation ago, though it has expanded significantly and continues to expand as fast as construction crews can pour fresh concrete.

In Brazil, in Flanders, in South Africa and Sydney and many other places, the restructuring of the world is best observed in the pace of operations at commercial seaports. The states of Pennsylvania and New Jersey are dredging the Delaware River to allow a new class of oceangoing container ships to reach Philadelphia; Shanghai is building a new port that will handle six times the volume of the already-bustling Long Beach Harbor. The harbor business is growing more rapidly than the fast-food business or the Internet advertising business, and may have more significance to the world's future. Quickly, what is Hutchinson Whampoa? The company is the world's largest operator of ports, employing more people than Honda Motors and the Intel computer-chip consortium combined.

As ports expand, so do ships. In 2006, the Odense Steelyard in Denmark launched the *Emma Maersk,* the world's longest container vessel. The *Emma Maersk* is longer than the nuclear supercarrier *Enterprise,* and was specifically built to take advantage of the long quays of Shenzhen. Numerous *Emma*-class trade vessels are under construction or scheduled to be laid down—many of them engineered to do nothing but transit between specific harbor pairs, such as Singapore and Rotterdam. Ship designers have for nearly a century spoken of the "Panamax," the largest vessel that can squeeze through the Panama Canal. Today they speak of the "post-Panamax," the even-larger vessels that will fit through the Panama Canal once its expansion, inspired by the sharp rise in global trade, is completed; and of the prospect of a "Kramax" ship if the Kra Canal, proposed for Thailand, is built. In 2008, the Mediterranean Shipping Company, based in land-locked Switzerland, launched the world's heaviest container ship, *MSC Daniela,* which weighs about a third more than the newest supercarrier, the *George H. W. Bush.* The vessels that really engage the attention of today's ship engineers are called "Malaccamax," meaning the maximum length and maximum draft of a ship able to traverse the Strait of Malacca. The Malaccamax vessels being designed at STX Shipbuilding in South Korea would be twice the length of the largest aircraft carrier.

The world's surge in port activity and commercial trading vessels, assuming this continues during the Sonic Boom this book foresees, is the epitome of the mixed blessing. Rising global commerce has created jobs in China and other developing nations, lifting hundreds of millions out of poverty; shipments of affordable and increasingly impressive-quality goods produced in the developing world keep standards of living high in the United States, Japan and the European Union. But at the Port of Long Beach, three ships arrive loaded for every one that departs loaded. The United States and European Union and Japan are buying like mad in the new globalized marketplace, but selling at a lesser pace. This has profound impact on jobs, community stability and the sense of anxious unease that characterizes much of Western life.

Before we move to those topics, ponder what the fantastic increase in ports and ships—and telephones and airplanes and broadband lines and other aspects of the Sonic Boom—represents to the world.

From the Industrial Revolution until the current generation, most nations threw much of their wealth and energy into building machineries for warfare. Nations eyed one another suspiciously, attempting to raise barriers to trade and intercourse, dealing with each other economically only when they believed it suited them at the expense of their partners. Now most nations put the majority of their efforts toward improving their standing in international commerce—that is, toward cooperative competition in which some members of the group may do better than others, but all members of the group become better off than if they had not participated.

Exactly as global trade has expanded, military spending has declined. Global military expenditure peaked in 1985 at $1.5 trillion in today's dollars and has fallen since, to $1.4 trillion in 2008.[2] Because the world's population rose during that period, total military spending might have been expected to rise. Instead it decreased, falling by almost 40 percent relative to population growth. In turn, the frequency and severity of worldwide combat has declined. According to the annual survey conducted by the Center for International Development and Conflict Management at the University of Maryland, the number of country-to-country conflicts in the world grew steadily from 1950 until peaking in 1989 and has dropped in most years since, to a 2008 level that is below the 1970s average: in the years after World War II, the number of global fatalities from combat peaked in 1989 and has tended to decline since.[3] Because television beams into our living rooms close-up images of belligerence wherever it occurs on any continent, it may seem that the world grows ever more deadly. The opposite is true, with a person's chance of being engulfed in war much lower than for most previous generations.

There are many theories on what caused World Wars I and II.

Cordell Hull, Franklin Delano Roosevelt's secretary of state, believed the root cause of both conflicts was the system of high tariffs and strict trade barriers in place at the time. These barriers gave nations little reason to cooperate, leaving them to channel their competitive urges into militarism. Hull pushed FDR to host the 1944 Bretton Woods Conference, at which the Allied nations agreed that when the fighting stopped, they would begin to engage in free trade, and would extend free trade to the defeated Axis powers, allowing them to recover. The Bretton Woods Agreement set in motion what we now call globalization. And since that moment, five hundred years of nearly continuous European conflict has ended, while more than fifty years have passed without great-power combat. Nuclear deterrence is obviously a major factor, and "low-intensity" warfare continues, but the interconnectedness caused by trade has been a leading reason the great powers have stopped shooting at one another. Global trade has increased twelvefold since World War II ended, partly because the average international tariff has fallen from 50 percent to 5 percent. Tariffs, once used to discourage international commerce, a deleterious purpose, are now merely used to raise money for governments. Big increases in trade cause most nations to stand to gain from a stable international system untainted by combat, and in the era of biggest-ever increases in trade, we observe a mainly stable international system untainted by great-state combat. As the transition toward knowledge-based economics makes ideas more valuable than physical resources, the incentive for war to seize resources declines. In the past, nations invaded other nations to seize the value of land or resources. Today it is more cost-effective to buy what you covet than to seize it, and so military spending and military adventurism are declining.[4]

Economists have long maintained that if only people stopped fighting one another and cooperated, prosperity for all would rise, while most nations would acquire incentives to get along rather than inflict harm. Because the new internationalized economic system has existed for only a few decades, we should be cautious about drawing conclusions: so far, however, the globalization of economics is guardedly positive for almost everyone. That countries are furiously devoting their energies to commercial production and trade, rather than missiles and submarines, can have unhappy effects, such as job insecurity and environmental harm, but its overwhelmingly positive side is inarguable. At this writing, China was breaking ground for the most expensive public-works project in world history—a $62 billion system of aqueducts to supply the populous part of the nation with fresh water for drinking and agriculture. Once completed, that system could be rendered worthless in mere minutes by precision-guided U.S. conventional weapons. That Beijing is investing such a huge amount in a structure vulnerable to rapid destruction from the air shows that the government of China believes it will never go to war with the United States. Capitalism causes all kinds of problems, but is so much better than militarism, there's just no comparison.

Clearly the last two years have been disagreeable ones for the world system. But many of the years before then were good, and what did the majority of Americans and Europeans do in those good years? Complain. The larger context of recent generations has been persistent focus on the negative, with little heed paid to the positive. Heeding the positive is not Pollyannaism—it is perspective. To achieve perspective, both positive and negative must be considered. There's an ample supply of negative. Yet most underlying global forces have mainly been good in recent decades; one shudders to think what the world might be like today if most underlying forces were not mainly good. Consider the underlying forces that point toward a Sonic Boom:

GLOBAL GROWTH ACCELERATES

Even taking into account the post-2008 slowdown, worldwide economic production has risen at a pace that is difficult to believe. In the last thirty years, China's gross domestic product rose from around $500 billion to $2.7 trillion—that is to say, five times as much new economic production in the last thirty years as all forms of economic production just a generation ago. China is not some spectacular exception to a rule; rather, it is the leading indicator of an extraordinary economic surge across most, although of course not all, of the globe.

Costa Rica, for example, increased its economic production from $8 billion in 1977 to $30 billion in 2008—more than three times as much new economic activity in the last three decades as total economic activity a generation ago. India increased its economic production from $400 billion in 1977 to $1.2 trillion in 2008, three times as much new economic activity created in the last thirty years as all forms a generation ago. (This chapter uses the period since 1977 as its benchmark not because Led Zeppelin broke up that year, but because modern Shenzhen is roughly three decades old.) Much of the new global economic activity does an end run around the wealthy West—for instance, the fast pace of construction in China has meant increased business for ArcelorMittal, the Indian firm that is now the world's leading steelmaker. Neither India nor China consult Washington or London about their steel trade—they're just taking care of it on their own.

If you're thinking, "Maybe all the growth helped only Asia," consider the U.S. figures. The U.S. economy produced $5.2 trillion in 1977 and $14 trillion in 2008—meaning twice as much new economic activity in the past three decades as all economic activity combined prior to then. Even considering the recession that began in 2008, if I'd told you in 1977 that the already mature, successful American economy nonetheless would grow another 170 percent in the next three decades, you may well have said, "Wow!" What is most important is the worldwide nature of recent decades of growth. In 2001, global average per-capita economic production was $5,000; by 2008, the average was $8,000, a 60 percent increase in less than a decade. Even if the recession in progress as this book was being written is unusually harsh, the first decade of the century still would be the best growth decade in human history, by a spectacular margin.

Nothing like the ongoing expansion of global economic activity has happened before: arguably, there has been more new economic activity in the last few decades than in all of previous history combined. Rising economic output is no panacea—there are environmental costs, and more important, much of the world's new output is distributed inequitably, the rich being too rich and the poor far too poor. Capitalism is, we can hope, a transitional form of economics that eventually will yield a "postscarcity" system able to eliminate want. You and I won't live to see that day, but postscarcity economics is not beyond imagination. Overall, it is hard to overstate how much better off the world is today because of the increase in global economic activity in the past few decades. Just consider India. In the 1960s, India was expected to collapse: mass starvation was widely predicted, along with urban breakdown for Calcutta and other cities. Instead, today India has multiple problems but is self-sufficient in food production, its malnutrition rate continues to fall, living standards are rising for most of its citizens, education rates are rising for almost all, and the country is holding together as a functioning, if fitful, democracy.

LESS POVERTY, WHILE A GLOBAL MIDDLE CLASS COMES INTO EXISTENCE

Thirty years ago, according to United Nations statistics, 1.3 billion people lived at the level of "high development," the standard of the United States or Europe; 2.5 billion lived at the level of "medium development," with reasonable material conditions and some access to education, health care, clean water and electric power; and 220 million lived at the level of "low development," meaning subsistence. By 2005, the figures were 1.7 billion at high development, 4.2 billion at medium development and 500 million at low development.[5] Those numbers convey that over roughly this period, the world has added 280 million people who live in miserable conditions, an awful sum. Yet in the same period, the world has added 400 million people who live in excellent conditions and a stunning 1.7 billion who live in decent conditions. Of the nearly 2.4 billion men and women who have joined the world's population in the last three decades—itself an amazing number—only one in nine has been born into terrible conditions, while conditions for the other eight fall somewhere on the spectrum of okay to really nice. During the current generation, more than 2 billion people have joined the human family at or above the level of "medium development"—and that is more than the *total* number of people who were alive a century ago. Imagine if that many new people had been born and the world had not been in a phase of economic expansion.

Rather than 500 million human beings mired at the level of "low development," the number might be 1 billion or even 2 billion.

Most of the rise in living standards has been in poor or southern nations, not the elite G8 powers. For centuries until roughly the present generation, North America and Europe enjoyed higher economic growth than other parts of the world, resulting in the United States and most European nations being affluent and powerful. Since 1990, the historical pattern has reversed; annualized economic growth in the United States and the European Union has been about 3 percent, while annual growth in developing nations has been about 6 percent.[6] Global average income per person has nearly tripled in inflation-adjusted terms since 1950,[7] with most of the income growth coming in the developing world. As recently as the mid-1990s, developing nations were producing 39 percent of the world's wealth, despite a far higher share of global population than the West. By 2008, developing nations were producing 46 percent of the wealth, reflecting a gradual shift of money and economic success toward the less-well-off. This growth shift helps explain why the developing world is mostly improving—a story missing from the Western media, which tend to report only violence in developing nations, ignoring progress—rather than descending into the predicted Malthusian calamities.

The biggest payoff has been in poverty reduction. Because one American in eight still lives in poverty or near-poverty—a shameful reality for an affluent nation—and because antipoverty programs in developing nations have a low reputation, Americans tend to think of poverty as a chronic problem that admits only of incremental reform. But progress against poverty is going much better than commonly understood. Merely in the five years from 1999 to 2004, 135 million people in the developing world graduated out of extreme poverty, as defined by the United Nations. Thirty years ago, China had 260 million people living in that state. Today the impoverished share of the Chinese population is down to 40 million,[8] still a distressing number, but one that reflects a dramatic rate of improvement. Since beginning to liberalize, China has pulled up out of deep poverty a number almost equivalent to the entire population of Brazil. As the New York University scholar William Easterly has written, globally, recent decades have seen "the greatest mass exit from poverty in world history." This has happened at a time when demographic pressure and resource demand were supposed to cause the developing world to descend into anarchy![9]

DEMOCRACY HAS THE UPPER HAND

Just a few generations ago, as the Nazi, Communist, and Imperial Japanese darkness spread across the face of the planet, the human experiment was down to a handful of nations that still advanced the cause of personal liberty—the United States, the United Kingdom, Canada, Australia, and not many others. We can thank our stars it turned out that free nations are stronger than dictatorships; in the twentieth century, in every case that the armies of liberty confronted the armies of despotism, liberty prevailed. Since the collapse of communism, dozens of nations have moved from some form of dictatorship toward at least partial liberty. Some nations are embracing liberty for reasons of self-interest: observing that the free countries are wealthy and strong, they move toward liberty in order to become wealthy and strong. Today the Arab nations are the primary holdouts against democracy and the open society; this is why they, despite in many cases possessing the fantastic advantage of oil reserves, remain weak.

China is the obvious example of a nation struggling to come to terms with liberty, but hardly the only one: Indonesia (recently a military dictatorship), India (recently a socialist controlled economy), and most of Latin America and many of the former Soviet states (recently dictatorships or controlled economies or both) have moved toward freedom, while no nation has backslid toward tyranny. At this writing, Bhutan was the latest to join the ranks of representative governments chosen by free ballot. Many of the world's young democracies are troubled. The essential point is that for a generation, totalitarian governments and feudal cultures have been in the process of being replaced by social orders based on at least some component of the consent of the governed.[10]

FREE ECONOMICS PREVAILS

A few generations ago only a small fraction of the world's societies practiced free economics. Most nations were Communist, or feudal, or controlled by aristocracies that resisted expansion of the middle class, or isolated from trade by tariff barriers or politics. Roughly around the time construction of Shenzhen began, the world's largest nation, China, switched sides on economics and began to adopt free markets. Today a majority of the world's nations have embraced some form of economic freedom. Is it a cliché to praise economic freedom? Yes, in the West, where economic freedom is now taken for granted. You would not be reading this book—or, most likely, any book—were it not for the forces of free economics. The spread of free economics is hardly without problems, in some cases serious problems, especially inequality; but the transition means that most of the world is shifting from inefficient to efficient means of production. As efficient economies become the global norm, living circumstances for average people should improve further.

PERSONAL FREEDOM PREVAILS

Most of the world is embracing, by varying degrees, personal freedom as an ideal. Just a generation ago, personal freedom was unknown, even actively suppressed, in China; today many of the 1.3 billion who live there are acquiring some form of personal freedom, and freedom is likely to expand in China over time. Russia, Germany, Japan and other nations that recently suppressed personal freedom today either promote the concept or at least, in Russia's case, admit its power. Across much of the developing world, especially in South America, repression has given way to at least partial recognition of individual human rights. In only a few nations, such as North Korea, does the concept of personal freedom remain taboo. In parallel to this trend, women's freedom is expanding in most nations. One century ago, owing to the repression of women, nearly half the world's population was denied personal rights. Now the official legal systems of most nations recognize the notion of women's freedom, while women's freedom increasingly is part of the day-to-day cultures in many, though not all, regions of the world.

DISTANCE SHRINKS

For millennia, distance meant that most men and women never traveled anywhere they could not reach on foot or riding an animal. For the majority of our ancestors, the concept of "travel," as we use the word today, held no meaning; they either lived their lives near their place of birth or migrated, taking a one-way trip that would never be retraced. To be a "traveler" was, to most of our ancestors, a rare, exotic existence. Even once sailing ships could tack into the wind, few people traveled, meaning most lived out their lives rarely meeting others unlike themselves. Trade for most of history has been very expensive and limited to specialty items such as spices, dyes and scientific knowledge. As well as being a physical obstacle to movement, distance was a physical obstacle to communication. As recently as the age of the Framers of the U.S. Constitution, a letter took weeks to cross the Atlantic, and the reply additional weeks to arrive—if either arrived at all. Real-time communication beyond one's own immediate sphere of acquaintances was impossible.

Since steam and then piston power, distance has become steadily less a factor in human affairs. Trains, diesel- or turbine-driven ships, and aircraft have made long-distance travel possible, while the comfortable modern car makes medium-distance travel convenient. Innovations have cut the price of personal travel so much that today huge numbers of Americans and Europeans have been to at least one other continent. Many of the roughly 1.7 billion well-off people in the world today believe that in order to vacation, they should travel a long distance from their place of residence. Distance costs have declined so much in commerce that heavy manufactured items, such as industrial equipment or cars, move routinely between continents; bulk commodities such as grain and coal are shipped around the world in vast quantities. Occasionally I teach seminars at my alma mater, Colorado College, whose campus sits within view of the freight railroad trunk line that runs along the Front Range of the Rocky Mountains. It is not unusual there to observe a lengthy trainload of coal, locomotives groaning, headed northward, passing a lengthy trainload of coal, locomotives groaning, headed southward. At first glance, trainloads of coal passing each other traveling in opposite directions can seem like absurd inefficiency. Actually what is happening is heightened efficiency, made possible by the declining obstacle of distance. Different grades of coal from different types of geologic seams are being shipped to different classes of facilities—power plants, coke-making factories, metal foundries. The result will be higher-quality products or more reliable electricity. Now even inexpensive items such as Happy Meals supplies and beach buckets move in global commerce. A barometer of social progress is that today far more resources are devoted to shipping toys around the world than once were devoted to shipping silks and perfumes for the wealthy.

Distance in communication has, over recent decades, all but vanished. Telephone contact from anywhere to anywhere is now practical and usually affordable; Internet communication costs so little that the marginal price is nearly zero; television and radio communication enable most of the world's population to get news from anywhere, and to experience entertainment that originates in far-off nations. With each passing year, distance means less, and the pace of decline in the significance of distance keeps accelerating. As distance declines in significance, there will be both good and bad. The good: friends separated by miles will stay in touch, societies will learn more about one another, emergencies will elicit faster responses, business will grow more efficient as companies get faster readouts on what the market wants. The bad: fear regarding distant problems will increase— there is no longer any place on Earth too far away to matter—and economics will become even more tumultuous and uncertain.

AS DISTANCE MATTERS LESS, DIFFERENCE SHRINKS

In centuries past, even contiguous societies were dramatically different—think of the social variation you would have encountered had you taken a horseback trip from Paris to Istanbul in the 1700s. A few decades ago, the United Kingdom was very different from nearby Portugal, China very different from nearby Japan, and so on. Now, as long-distance communication becomes cheap, as news and entertainment media spread nearly everywhere, and as almost all nations begin to compete economically in a global marketplace, differences between societies will decline. Groups will always have different customs, but most likely China of 2050 won't be that different from Japan of 2050. Pick another two societies, and the likelihood is that with each passing year of the coming century, there will be less difference. Countries and societies becoming more like each other will annoy many people on many levels, but will be good for economic efficiency, making the world more prosperous.

SOCIAL PROGRESS GATHERS SPEED

On the day I was born, in 1953, American schools were segregated; segregated housing and public transit were legal in many states; blacks were effectively forbidden to vote in several states; homosexuality was a source of shame and ostracism throughout the country, and a crime in much of the world (gays could still be jailed in the United Kingdom); for a woman to work outside the home as a professional was rare, and strongly frowned upon; workplace discrimination against women was legal; though the quota systems against Jews at Ivy League colleges were officially a thing of the past, prejudice against Jews remained widespread; Protestant preachers still commonly denounced Catholics, while Catholic priests still commonly said Protestants would go to hell; women who became pregnant out of wedlock were subject to vicious narrow-mindedness, while the purchase of birth-control supplies was banned in many states. In general, tolerance was low for differing religions, race, ethnicity, sexuality or even just unconventionality.

Today in American society, it is almost universally viewed as shameful to hold racial, religious or gender bias. A single woman with a baby is viewed as a hardworking person to be helped, not an abomination to be shunned. Openness toward others has blossomed across American life. Tolerance and openness have made significant advances in recent decades in most nations, while in only a few nations has prejudice risen. Not only is there substantial social progress, the rate of social progress seems to be accelerating. Maybe it's just a coincidence that societies have become more open and tolerant during the same period that communication and international contact have increased. Maybe; I doubt it.

ACCESS TO TECHNICAL PROGRESS GATHERS SPEED

What's haunting about current technical progress is not the addition of new gizmos but the accelerating rate of general access. Raymond Kurzweil, who in the 1970s invented the first practical device for optical character recognition and has since become a futurist,[11] notes there is steadily less time between an invention and its use by the average person. Kurzweil defines average-person use as something in the hands of at least 25 percent of the U.S. population. Looking back to the nineteenth century, forty-six years passed between the development of systems for wide-scale electricity distribution and the electrification of a quarter of America's homes; thirty-five years passed between invention of the telephone and common telephone access; thirty-one years separated the invention of radio and common radio ownership; twenty-six years passed between invention of television and common access to television; sixteen years between the development of the personal computer and a quarter of Americans possessing a PC; thirteen years between development of the cellular-relayed wireless call and a cell phone in every fourth pocket; seven years between development of the Web and mass access to the Web. So it's not just that lots of techno-stuff is being developed: the stuff is becoming practical and reliable faster, and falling in price faster. That means average people benefit faster—but also that accustomed ways of doing things, and of running the economy, are disordered faster.

INFLATION HELD IN CHECK

It is human nature to obsess over whatever is happening, while failing to appreciate what is not happening. One thing that has not happened in most Western nations in several decades is sustained inflation. In 2008, oil prices briefly hit $140 a barrel; the international price of coal doubled in the four years from 2004 to 2008 owing to strong demand in China and India; most prices of metals and ores have risen sharply in recent years. Yet chronic inflation has not occurred in the Western nations. Something that cost $100 in 1999 in the United States cost $126 in 2009, a historically mild inflation rate, while developing-world hyperinflation, which plagued wide regions such as Latin America as recently as the 1980s, has stopped except in a few places, such as Zimbabwe, where the degree of rampant government corruption would overwhelm any system of economics. The price-restraining impact of Sonic Boom economics does not benefit only Kansas or Spain; it benefits Malaysia and Ecuador, too. One reason so many have been able to escape poverty is that international competition is holding down the price of most essentials. Inflation might resume, of course, but so far, liberal international economics has been its foe.

When consumer prices rise 5 to 10 percent per year, as they did in the United States and parts of Europe in the 1970s, this is a calamity for average people. The inflation that paralyzed the United States and the European Union during the 1970s did not magically go away; no sparkling little fairies came in the night to repair the inflationary economy. Inflation has been driven into retreat by the advent of international interconnectedness, which increases efficiency faster than prices can rise, and which is accelerating the rate of technical improvement both in what we buy and how what we buy is manufactured. Americans complain that rates of growth of household income have been low during the last generation, which is true, without pausing to reflect that the same economic forces causing slow growth in household income are preventing prices from rising, or even placing prices into long-term decline. When judging living standards, falling prices are the same thing as rising income. The economists W. Michael Cox and Richard Alm of the Federal Reserve Bank calculate, for instance, that the typical new car purchased in the United States today costs 6 percent less in real terms than a new car cost a decade ago[12]—though today's new cars are packed with comfort and safety features previous cars lacked. Fifty years ago, Americans spent almost half of their after-tax income on food, clothing and shelter; by 2008, that number had declined to 33 percent, even taking into account the housing problems of that year.[13] Real-dollar declines in food costs, clothing costs and the prices of materials used in new-home construction—trends driven by a combination of technology improvements and freer international trade—explain why Americans spend ever-less of their disposable income on food, clothing and shelter, and such trends leave most Americans better off. During the past half-century, the primary area where real-dollar spending has risen for the typical person is health care, with 5 percent of after-tax income spent on health care in 1958, versus 16 percent spent in 2008. Though health-care costs are way up, outcomes hav e improved spectacularly (less disease, longer life) and quality has improved somewhat (a generation ago someone with chronic knee pain simply suffered; today arthroscopic surgery ends the pain).[14] Whether technology will eventually lower health-care costs is an open question—it might. Regardless, there is no doubt the average person is better off with the health-care services of the present than of previous generations, those infuriating HMO 800 numbers notwithstanding.

BROKERS BECOME GOATS, ENTREPRENEURS BECOME HEROES

For some time, theorists have been predicting that knowledge would become more important than physical resources. For instance, the MIT economist Lester Thurow said in 2002, "The world is moving from an industrial era based upon natural resources into a knowledge era based upon skills, education, and research and development." In 2007, the National Academy of Sciences estimated that 85 percent of economic growth is caused by new ideas[15]—nearly six times as much economic growth as caused by the combined impact of labor productivity increases, capital accumulation and natural resource discoveries. That ideas could be worth more than steel or silver may sound too optimistic—yet today this seems to be happening. Which would you rather possess, all the knowledge at a company such as AstraZeneca or Microsoft, or all the bauxite in a mine?

The importance of ideas in economic growth is intertwined with the rising importance of entrepreneurs and business innovators. There have always been entrepreneurs who open stores or restaurants, but most traditional entrepreneurial efforts have been small-scale and local. In the evolving global economy, entrepreneurs and venture capitalists have great incentives to devise ideas that can be duplicated throughout the world, bringing benefits to huge numbers of people. Surely you know the story of how two young guys founded Google in a Palo Alto, California, rental loft above a bakery, and less than a decade later had an enterprise worth more than several major oil companies. The rapid rise in significance of Google happened because its core ideas could be reproduced and marketed (or in this case, given away) very quickly and cheaply first to millions of Americans and Europeans, soon thereafter to the estimated 2 billion people worldwide who now have Internet access.

Increasingly, the world economy depends on innovative ideas that arise with entrepreneurs, are backed by venture capitalists, and can be rapidly, cheaply spread to much of the globe. Bankers and Wall Street brokers don't create anything, and as we learned in 2009, pilfer from what others have created. Those who do create are increasingly important to our shared economic futures. The rapidly spread idea is not confined to the software business, though software is the first example of a sector where it's hard to have a good idea but easy to spread a good idea once you've got one. In recent decades, many entrepreneurs have had important ideas concerning the industrial part of the economy— they're figured out ways to manufacture products at higher quality and lower cost, then rapidly spread those ideas. For instance, automotive fatalities in the United States and the European Union are down partly because antilock brakes, once found only on expensive sports cars, are now manufactured affordably and installed on almost all new cars. Since the 1980s, nearly 10 percent of the new jobs created in the United States can be traced to entrepreneurs and venture capitalists: entrepreneurs have a better track record at creating jobs than do government or large corporations. And we'd better hope entrepreneurs continue to succeed, because rising resource consumption in the developing world—developing-world resource consumption must continue to rise, to bring reasonable equality to the ways men and women live—would, if unassisted by innovation, quickly overcome the global economy. For the next half-century or so, until the human population stabilizes, running out of ideas will be a greater danger than running out of petroleum.

WOMEN DOUBLE THE WORLD'S SUPPLY OF IDEAS

Global literacy has risen from 74 percent a generation ago to 90 percent today, and essentially all the gains have been among girls and women. In the Western nations, women's equality is close; in many developing nations, personal freedom and equal protection under the law are still a long way off. Overlooked in thinking about women's rights and education is the role of rising women's freedom in economic growth. Half a century back, few women were productive in the paid workforce; those who were usually resided near the bottom rings, sewing garments or tending crops. As more women enter the paid workforce—not just in Western nations, but globally—the amount of global economic production should be expected to shoot up. Maybe it's just a coincidence that this is happening as women become more free. Maybe; I doubt it. In addition to contributing productivity, increasingly women are able to contribute ideas to the global economy. Women have been successful entrepreneurs even in the past—in the 1950s, a mathematician named Grace Hopper played an essential role in developing Univac 1, the first commercially marketed computer. But the total number of women involved in entrepreneurship and business development has been small compared to the number of men: most of the world's supply of technical ideas and business innovations came from men. As more women both in the United States and globally become engaged in economics, engineering and technology, the world's supply of useful ideas will increase. Suppose that by the middle of the twenty-first century, in most nations women have the same degree of freedom and social mobility as men—this is not an unrealistic goal. That would cause the world's supply of valuable ideas to double, further accelerating the rate of global economic growth and roughly doubling the number of minds that can be brought to bear on vexing future problems such as how to increase energy production while reducing greenhouse gas emissions.

CITIES ARE LOUD, CROWDED, AND GOOD

As Stewart Brand has pointed out, a core reason Europe and the United States became the first well-off, strong and free parts of the world is that they were the first to have significant shares of their populations living in large cities. As recently as the turn of the twentieth century, just 14 percent of people lived in cities, with nearly all large cities located in the West. In 2008, this balance fundamentally shifted. That year was the first in human history in which more people lived within cities than outside urban areas; and owing to population dynamics, there are now more city-dwellers in the developing world than in the West.

There are many things to dislike about cities—congestion, noise, smog (especially in developing nations), crime, the quiet hopelessness experienced by those who are rendered desperate for rent money—but cities are nothing if not incubators of human progress. As the writer Mathew Quirk has noted, "No country has ever become affluent until a majority of its population lived in cities."[16] The move from countryside to cities was an essential factor in Europe's transition from the Dark Ages to the Renaissance. When people live in cities, they interact constantly with others, sharing ideas and making breakthroughs. City living tends to be conducive to personal rights, social advancement and improved education. Urban living is also associated with declining poverty, and not just because people leave the farm seeking higher wages. Thirty years ago, China knew extreme poverty and had an 80 percent rural population; today China has fewer than 50 percent living in the countryside, with less poverty and much more economic growth.

Today nearly all city growth is occurring in the developing world. Heard of Kolkata, Yangon, Lahore, Chittagong, Abidjan, Tianjin? All these cities are larger than Chicago. São Paulo is a third larger than New York City. Global urbanization will trigger problem after problem, including more slums, but it is also an accelerator of progress—the likelihood is that every society that becomes urban-based will be better off and more free.

SMALLER FAMILIES MEAN BETTER EDUCATION AND MORE FREEDOM

The world's population has skyrocketed—almost doubling from about 3 billion in the late 1960s to more than 6 billion at this writing. Population growth is not the result of more births, rather of declining death rates: except in a few parts of the world, fertility and births-per-woman have diminished during the period of the population explosion. In the late 1960s, average global fertility was 4.8 live births per woman: today the average is 2.6 and continuing downward. In much of the European Union, average fertility is already below he replacement rate of 2.1; in Italy and Scandinavia, just 1.4. Euro malaise may have something to do with birth rates there, but fertility has dipped even in the perennially sanguine United States. American-born women now average two live births, just below replacement rate; the U.S. population would be declining were it not for immigration. Global population continues to soar despite reduced fertility because health-care advances such as vaccination, and nutrition improvements from high-yield agriculture, keep reducing death rates and lengthening the human life span.

Declining fertility rates in the developing world are the second half of the story of urbanization. Subsistence farming as still practiced in parts of the developing world, and by the overwhelming majority of current humanity's ancestors, entails backbreaking manual labor but requires little knowledge. In subsistence-farming environments, women have as many children as they can bear, because each new child is another set of hands. Education is deemphasized because book smarts are not needed to plow soil; indeed, book smarts may make you dissatisfied about a life of plowing soil. As the sociologist Dalton Conley has shown, the first two children in a family usually fare better in life than subsequent children, for many reasons; in large families, the final children born tend to fare poorly.[17] Once people move to cities and work in manufacturing or service industries, expectations about family size change. In city economies, education is vital to advancement; parents want fewer children, but invest more in each child, in order that the child can do well in life. In feudal rural environments, girls and women may be expected to do little more than fieldwork, babymaking and domestic chores; in cities, girls need education to prosper and help the family.

Because there is substantial "demographic momentum"—the huge number of young men and women who have not yet borne their own children—the global population will continue to rise for at least a few more decades, even as fertility declines. When you hear commentators decry a "birth dearth," bear in mind that this meaningfully applies only to Italy, Scandinavia and Japan: the populations of most countries will continue to swell for some time. But urban living, smaller families and better education and treatment for developing-world girls all point toward further increases in human progress.

"NETWORK EFFECTS" ARE JUST GETTING STARTED

Initially only small numbers of people or businesses had telephones, and unless you were reporting a fire, the phone wasn't good for much. Once many people and businesses had them, phones became valuable; once nearly everyone had a telephone, they became invaluable. Initially few people or businesses had Internet access, rendering the Web an expensive curiosity. Today Internet access is somewhat common, and the Web has become somewhat valuable. Once everyone has Internet access—and this is a realistic goal, except perhaps for the poorest nations of central Africa—the Web will be invaluable. Thus, although you may already be sick of the Internet, most of its benefits lie in the future.

The same holds true for many types of devices and services: the more people who get on a network, the more beneficial the network becomes, while, usually, the lower the network's price goes: the more people who sign up for cell phones, the less each call costs. Networks can increase in value exponentially even while declining in price. An Internet that links 100 million people is not worth ten times as much as an Internet that links 10 million people; the value increases by more than tenfold. It's easy to forget how young the Internet is—e-mail arrived in the late 1980s, Web sites were oddities until the late 1990s. The network value of Web communication and Web-based business is still new, while the network value of Web-based educational and artistic expression is barely starting. If the network doubles in the coming decade, Web benefits easily could treble or quadruple. Most of the global benefits of networked electronics lie in the future, and most future benefits will especially help the developing world.[18]

PLUG-IN FREEDOM

Why did China, for decades a pitiless dictatorship, begin taking steps toward a free form of life? Surely one reason was that trends in electronics were making the closed society impossible. During the 1960s and 1970s, Soviet and Chinese citizens knew almost nothing of the outside world, and many believed their governments' propaganda that most Americans lived in abject misery. But by the late 1980s, the expansion of electronic media and the arrival of computer-based communications made such fictions impossible to maintain. Had Tiananmen Square happened twenty years before 1989, no one outside Beijing would have known; in 1989, everyone in China knew. Today reports of official corruption, China's most sensitive topic, rocket around the country in days or even hours. Public antidictatorship demonstrations in Iran in 2009 were greatly aided by electronic communication. Historians may eventually argue that based on the numbers of people involved, the end of the Chinese Communist dictatorship is the greatest revolution the world has known. And while China is far from free and still held back by human rights abuses, its revolution against communism occurred without the violence that characterized other great revolutions, including America's. In his magnificent book *1984,* published in 1949, George Orwell worried that advanced electronics would become tools of dictatorial mind control, allowing a Thought Police. So far at least, electronics have been the reverse—their political impact has been to increase free thought while causing dictatorships to start turning into democracies.

DECLINING INDUSTRIAL EMPLOYMENT WAS ALWAYS CERTAIN TO OCCUR IN THE UNITED STATES

No measure of national economic success is more important than jobs; unemployment was the leading worry in the international reces-

sion of 2009. But it's a misconception that the new era of global competition has caused some kind of jobs wipeout in the United States.
For the last two decades, the U.S. economy has created more jobs than
it lost in every year except the recession years of 1991, 2002, 2008,
and 2009. As this book went to press, U.S. adult nonfarm employment
had fallen from its peak of 138 million, in December 2007, to 134 million; yet that very troubling number was still higher than anything in
American history before mid-2005. Unemployment was a danger in
2009 because job creation was not keeping pace with population
growth; by historical standards, job totals remained high.

Beyond that, there is no doubt that tens of thousands of good jobs
in the auto, steel, and appliance-manufacturing industries have disap-
peared in the United States, and will not return. But this would have
happened regardless of globalization, or silicon chips, or offshoring, for
that matter, regardless of whether Toyota had ever come into existence. Studies by Robert Lawrence of Harvard University and Martin
Bailey of the consulting firm McKinsey & Company show that about
90 percent of manufacturing job losses in the United States in recent
decades were caused by forces unrelated to international economics[19]—manufacturing job losses link to changing consumer demand,
ever-more-productive mechanized assembly lines, and the advent of
more reliable products that do not need to be replaced as often. Productivity increases in manufacturing have been steep. Fifteen years
ago, Boeing's main aircraft factory in Washington State required
twenty-two days to build a 737 airliner; today that factory builds a 737
that is technologically improved over earlier models, and completes
each plane in twelve days, thanks to such process innovations as cabin
insulation that is preformed rather than hand-fitted. This inevitably
means fewer heavy-manufacturing jobs at Boeing, but is the kind of
advance that would have happened whether there was globalization or
not. Brian Wesbury, chief economist at First Trust Portfolios, an economic analysis firm, calculates that U.S. manufacturing productivity
roughly doubled from 1950 to 1980, and in that time the share of
Americans who worked in manufacturing declined from roughly 30
percent to roughly 20 percent.[20] From 1980 to the present, U.S. manufacturing productivity roughly doubled again, and in that time the

manufacturing workforce fell from about 20 percent to about 10 percent of all jobs. Presumably, if manufacturing productivity doubles a third time, factory employment will decline to 5 percent of U.S. jobs.

Trends like this are really bad for the factory workers whose jobs are lost—but good for everyone else. Prices decline, goods rise in quality, and money is freed up for the many sectors of society where productivity increases are neither practical nor necessarily desirable. Here's a pop quiz: Did the United States manufacture more steel in 1970 or in 2007? The answer is 2007—106 million tons of steel made in America that year, versus 91 million tons of steel in 1970.[21] The 91 million tons of 1970 were forged by 531,000 workers, whereas the 106 million tons of 2007 were forged by 159,000 workers. Steelmaking has not fled the United States, as pundits and politicians claim, but rather become far more productive. This means fewer workers per ton produced—and also less resource waste and less air pollution. We hear about the jobs lost but not the rising output or declining pollution. Improved productivity holds down the cost of steel, and that makes cars, buildings, and other necessities less expensive. Had improving the manufacturing of steel somehow been outlawed in 1970, today far more Americans would have jobs at foundries—but metal prices would be much higher, meaning the total number of jobs in the United States would be lower. Many of today's more-productive U.S. steelworkers toil at mills owned by ArcelorMittal. In the late 1980s, when American business leaders thought the steel industry was yesterday's news, the Indian entrepreneur Lakshmi Mittal began to buy, at distress prices, old mills in America and other countries. Mittal was gambling that a global construction increase was in the cards, and also that he could improve the productivity of old steel mills. American business leaders who looked at the steel industry were proven wrong, while Lakshmi Mittal was proven right. Don't blame an Indian entrepreneur for being right!

Though better technology tends to reduce the number of jobs in manufacturing, everyone benefits from better products. Would you seriously propose that we prohibit improvements in technology? Today's cars, for instance, are much safer, more comfortable, more reliable— the car that refuses to start, a regular occurrence for prior generations, is now rare—and last many years longer than cars once did.[22] If improved technology had somehow been outlawed in the 1950s, there would be more autoworkers reporting for their shifts in Michigan, but we'd all be driving 10 m.p.g. finned Cadillacs with AM radios, drum brakes, underbody rust and no seat belts.

Consumer demand, for its part, will change regardless of tariff policies or congressional hearings. Thirty years ago, General Motors, Ford and Chrysler held 87 percent of the U.S. auto market; by 2008, their share was down to 51 percent, and likely will have dropped below half by the time you read this. Inevitably, closed auto plants result. Essential to this decline is that with each passing year, a smaller fraction of Americans want the kind of vehicles in which Detroit specializes. No one put guns to the heads of Big Three executives and ordered them to focus their product lines on ponderous low-mileage SUVs and pickup trucks, nor did masked gunmen order those U.S. auto executives to ignore the successful sales tactics used by their growing competitors, such as simplified product lines and emphasis on manufacturing quality.[23] American automakers made these choices of their own accord, and with each passing year, more consumers have, of their own accord, rejected the choices the Big Three made. In mid-2008, Toyota outsold General Motors in the United States, the first time since Herbert Hoover was president that any firm other than G.M. led American auto sales. Nearly all the vehicles Toyota sold as it passed G.M. were manufactured inside the United States by American workers earning about fifty dollars an hour in pay and benefits;[24] many were designed in the United States by American engineers and American auto stylists. Detroit carmakers had decades of warning about declining public enthusiasm for their products, yet Big Three executives focused on denying that there were problems, while zooming around in private jets and maximizing short-term bonuses to themselves. From 2005 through the middle of 2008, General Motors declared a staggering $68 billion in losses, while shareholders lost about $50 billion in value as the company's stock price plummeted below its levels of the 1950s. These losses happened *before* the financial-sector crunch that sent the company spiraling toward government-ward status. Yet during the period in question, G.M.'s

CEO and chairman of the board, Rick Wagoner, who made the inane decision to bet the company on very large low-mileage vehicles such as Hummers, placing this likely-to-lose wager even as gasoline prices were rising, paid himself about $30 million.[25] Globalization did not make General Motors executives greedy and stupid! They accomplished this entirely on their own.

During the same period of significant layoffs for Detroit automakers, Honda, Toyota, BMW and other firms created about 65,000 new auto manufacturing jobs inside the United States. These are the jobs that might have been kept by the Big Three, had its management not insulated themselves from reality. Some 335,000 Americans now work in production, sales, parts and service for foreign-based automakers, nearly the number that worked for General Motors at its peak. Georgetown, Kentucky, is today every bit as much an automaker's company town as Detroit once was: it's just that the automaker is Toyota. In 2009, every automaker was having a bad year—Toyota jobs may be gone someday, too—but the same forces that were closing auto plants in Pennsylvania and Illinois were opening them in Texas and Kentucky, and you can't have one without the other. Now consider: each year the United States has fewer heavy manufacturing jobs, but more white-collar jobs. Wouldn't our forebears think it was great news that their descendants are leaving the dehumanizing circumstances of the assembly line for white-collar employment? Getting millions of people out of factories and seated at desks is a tremendous social achievement.

DECLINING INDUSTRIAL EMPLOYMENT WAS ALWAYS CERTAIN TO HAPPEN EVERYWHERE

Some 6 million manufacturing jobs have been lost in the United States in the last thirty years, a serious blow to working-class families. In the same period, some 28 million manufacturing jobs have been lost in China—and when it comes to global economic forces, China cannot be both executioner and victim. Rather, the same factors at play in the United States and Europe, especially rising productivity and factory efficiency, are causing manufacturing jobs to be lost in China as well. India has lost manufacturing jobs in the last two decades, too. *Every* nation involved in manufacturing has lost factory jobs—and do we propose to outlaw improving the efficiency of factories?

IF RECENT ECONOMIC HISTORY HAD NOT OCCURRED AS IT DID, WOULD WE LIKE THAT BETTER?

Perhaps the internationalization of the economy and the fad for high tech eventually will backfire on the United States—this is a keen fear—but so far, most Americans are better off. Even considering that 2008 was a bad year, from 1990 to 2007, the inflation-adjusted GDP of the United States rose by 49 percent, excellent growth during a period in which the country was attacked both by man (on 9/11) and by nature (Hurricane Katrina). A core reason the U.S. economy continues to grow at a strong pace is that the world's largest nation, China, has become such a good customer: firms such as Caterpillar and John Deere have enjoyed record years at their Midwest factories, producing construction equipment for export to China, India and Indonesia.[26] A generation ago, China was closed to the outside world: not only did the West not benefit from production there, the West sold no products there. So would we be better off if the previous reality had continued, with China and many other nations still having closed economies? Had world trade not liberalized, U.S. economic growth almost certainly would have been slower than it has been. The same is almost certainly true of the European Union—growth would have been slower, and living standards lower, had international trade not liberalized. And there can be no doubt the dropping of trade barriers has been a benefit to the developing world, starting large numbers on the path out of poverty. The North American Free Trade Agreement, completed in 1994, may from some perspectives have been a raw deal for Indiana and Wisconsin, but was a fantastic gift to Mexico, helping the country become better off than it otherwise would have been.

And had globalization not happened, the West would be diverting considerable resources to military confrontation with China. This is easy to forget today, but the Anti-Ballistic Missile system that the

United States furiously built in North Dakota in the early 1970s was intended to stop a nuclear attack launched by China.[27] Indications that China was opening up to the world made the antimissile missiles seem less important, and the North Dakota system was decommissioned in 1976. Would we have preferred that this *didn't* happen? Think for a moment of the other military ramifications, had the United States and China not begun to cooperate: we'd be building supercarrier battle groups by the dozens to patrol Asian seas and confront China, wasting our national treasure on arms even if fighting did not break out. Which brings us to:

COOPERATIVE SUPERPOWER RELATIONS

What great-power relationship has ever resembled that now evolving between the United States and China? Think of great-power pairings of the past: the United States and the Soviet Union, Germany and the United Kingdom, England and France, England and Spain, the Ottoman Empire and the Holy Roman Empire, China and Japan, Rome and Carthage, Athens and Cairo—the list is almost entirely of pairs of belligerents. For millennia, great-power nations have related to each other through combat, imperialism, arms races and sponsorship of wars by proxy states. We should not be unrealistic about U.S.-Chinese relations: something could go terribly wrong. For the moment at least, the United States and China enjoy the most constructive relationship two great powers have ever achieved. That this has happened in the era of pumped-up international trade is not just some weird coincidence.

China exports vast amounts of products to the United States, causing America to seem in some ways dependent on China. But isn't China just as dependent on America? If the U.S. economy stopped functioning or American borders were closed to Chinese goods, China would instantly go haywire—and the Chinese people would blame their government. China holds some $1.5 trillion in U.S. Treasury notes, which would seem to make Washington dependent on Beijing. But isn't Beijing just as dependent on Washington? If China took some action that caused the dollar to tumble, China's own national wealth would plummet. Without its access to the American market, China might be staggering under the weight of internal poverty. Without its access to the Chinese market, the United States might stop running economically.

Nothing like this has ever happened before. The world's two most important nations are not angling to destroy each other; rather, they are for the most part engaged in cooperative competition that for the most part benefits both. We can hope this is the bow wave of the future for all the world—cooperative competition rather than conflict. Competition based on economics can be shallow, or enrich odious CEOs, or cause environmental harm, or have countless other defects. But when assessing world events we should always ask ourselves, "Compared to what?" China and the United States might have become enemies, eyeing each other across the control panels of nuclear missiles. Instead the world's two great nations are mostly getting along, and assisting each other's prosperity. Of course it would be ideal to take the positives of the emerging Sonic Boom international order—affordable goods, plentiful supply, focus on consumer demand—without the negatives. But that's like saying it would be nice to have flowers without rain.

Many people would like government to impose some kind of mandate to slow chaotic international economic change, if not to prevent such change entirely. Such actions inevitably would have the effect of favoring the politically powerful at the expense of everyone else: regulations to protect the market share and job numbers of one company or category of business would raise prices and reduce job creation for all who are not in that business. Western governments, for example, spent the 1960s and 1970s lavishing special protections on long-distance phone carriers; the result was high prices coupled with terrible service. And even special government protection does not assure permanence for any company or workplace. In 2009, in an all-out effort to prevent free-market economic forces from doing in two poorly managed firms, the United States government granted a bounty of favors and subsidies to General Motors and Chrysler, penalizing average taxpayers in the process. Even so, there is no guarantee General Motors and Chrysler will remain in business.

Most likely, government-administered attempts to prevent economic change simply would not succeed, unless stopping economic growth is the definition of success. Government rules should be used to reduce environmental harm or mistreatment of workers, or accomplish other modifications of the global economy, but not to dictate economic outcomes. *All* attempts to dictate economic outcomes have failed, regardless of what theory of control has been used. Think how poorly American policymakers, both conservative Republican and liberal Democrat, performed when they tried to dictate economic outcomes in 2008 and 2009, and both groups were willing (perhaps to our woe) to spend unlimited sums. Trying to dictate the outcomes of economic change is like trying to dictate the outcomes of biological evolution—tampering with one influence will change all others in so many unpredictable ways that the effort will just never work. And economic change happens by orders of magnitude faster than biological evolution.

We will never know for sure, but a good guess is that all possible government-imposed alternatives to the current superchaotic liberal international trade system would leave almost everyone worse off. So until such time as there may be postscarcity economics, economic change will bring an endless tumult of improved living standards wrapped with ribbons of stress, anxiety and dissatisfaction. Even in the boom years—and a lot of boom years are coming—we're going to feel unhappy about the economy. We'll feel unhappy because nothing will seem permanent. And nothing will be.

Some of the coming change-based anxiety may be little more than a reflection of human nature, since no one likes uncertainty. But let's not kid ourselves—some people and places are going to be shafted by the next phase of global transition. At the same time, the potential for social progress is fantastic. Right now, every principal theory of the Enlightenment is being tested in China. Because China is the largest nation in human history, the magnitude of the test far exceeds that of the one conducted in Europe in the seventeenth and eighteenth centuries. Western ideals—free economics, freedom of speech, personal dignity, rationality, consent of the governed—are spreading across the continents at the most rapid rate they ever have spread. The world seems to face two possible outcomes. Either the Western philosophy of life will fail when applied to the world as a whole, or it will succeed. If the former, the immediate global future may turn bleak. If the latter, there will be a Sonic Boom.

Two

WALTHAM

Waltham, Massachusetts, a city nearly three centuries old, had benefited from and suffered under global economic forces long before anyone heard the word *globalization*. Incorporated in 1738, Waltham sits along the Charles River, about ten miles west of Boston; at the time of the city's founding, this location was a rural area where children must have gone down to the water at night to marvel at the glow of Boston's gas lamps in the distance. In 1779, entrepreneurs built a small dam on the Charles by the foot of Waltham's main street. Power from the dam was employed to start a paper mill, which sold some of the paper upon which New England patriots and clergy debated the organization of the new republic being formed by former colonists of the British crown. Demand for paper was brisk in the new nation. A decade after the first mill, a larger dam and larger papermaking facility were completed. In 1813, the larger mill was converted into Boston Manufacturing Company, the first modern factory in North America. So far, so good.

Boston Manufacturing Company made textiles using ideas of the Industrial Revolution, which at that time was the Next New Thing. All processes were integrated into a single facility; raw materials came in the front door and finished products ready for sale departed by the back. Boston Manufacturing must have been a hellish place to work—hot, noisy, foul air, with low wages and a high rate of injuries. In 1820 its seamstresses went on strike, the first industrial labor walkout in the United States. The year 1854 saw another historic factory completed along the Charles, that of the Waltham Watch company, which would go on to manufacture 40 million watches of renowned reliability—on the moon in 1971, the cost-no-object superfancy chronometer given to Apollo astronaut David Scott failed, so he consulted his old Waltham wristwatch, which worked perfectly. Waltham Watch also built industrial instruments similar to watches. The factory's greater contribution was to pioneer what came to be called the American system of manufacturing: use of interchangeable precision parts, so that when a device malfunctioned, a replacement part could simply be swapped in. Thus Waltham helped bring about one of the major ideas of the nineteenth century, an idea that enabled the mass production that followed.

By the late nineteenth century, Waltham flourished, becoming a magnet for inventors drawn by the city's reputation for business innovation. Among other things, the chalk crayon and power steering would be invented in Waltham. The town had steam-driven fire engines before most large cities, one of the first electric trolley lines, and one of the country's first municipal water-purification facilities. But gradually Waltham's fortunes changed. In 1922 the Metz Car Company, which had been building a thousand automobiles per month, shuttered, throwing thousands out of work. Metz had gambled that brass would be an essential component of cars, but Henry Ford's durable steel automobiles were running away with the market. Waltham Watch workers went on strike in 1924, triggering a sequence of nine corporate takeovers and bankruptcies at what locals insisted on calling Waltham Watch regardless of who owned the facility. In 1930, Boston Manufacturing Company failed owing to the Depression; that same year, the Charles River pleasure cruise industry, centered in Waltham, ended because industrial pollution had made the river filthy. In 1951 the Waltham Bleachery and Dye Works, once the nation's biggest dye-making facility, closed. In 1957, disaster struck—Waltham Watch went out of business, done in by Japanese-made watches that sold for half the price because workers were paid a tenth the Waltham Watch wage.[1] By the 1960s, Waltham unemployment soared while housing prices plummeted. The town name became synonymous with a rusting, fading, unwanted way of life.

Today Waltham booms as never before. Simple square, shingled war-era housing still lines many streets, but corporate offices and fashionable restaurants occupy acreage that a generation ago was abandoned warehouses or closed taverns with doors nailed shut. Moody Street is bustling, and the view from Prospect Hill is agreeable. Rather than smart kids leaving Waltham, now they flock to the city, which has become a focal point of the Route 128 Corridor, the high-tech zone that is New England's answer to Silicon Valley. Atlas Ventures, Polaris and other leading-edge venture-capital firms have located in Waltham. The venture firms are investing in enterprises that may be the Google of tomorrow—Polaris, for example, backs Zink, a company attempting to develop inkless printing. (Laughing? They laughed at the Wright Brothers.) The defense contractor Raytheon is now based in Waltham, and employs thousands in the area. The retail chain Sports Authority has its flagship facility in Waltham, adjoining the gleaming basketball complex at which the Boston Celtics train. Most cities would be happy to host one corporate conference center: Waltham has two, though the town itself is sufficiently small as to require only a single public high school. Unemployment is low, housing values are strong despite the slow economy, and the city and surrounding county's 2007 average wage was $61,308, almost 50 percent better than the national figure. Japan no longer threatens Waltham, as Japan has become a high-wage country: as, likely, China someday will be. Venture capital and high-tech research are relatively rare in the developing world, so the low-wage nations don't undercut the businesses Waltham now features. The sprawling Waltham Watch plant that sat vacant along the scenic river for decades, wind whipping through its broken windowpanes—the factory is an icon of steam-era industrialization; most likely you'd recognize a picture—was at this writing being converted into upscale shops and condos.

The new Waltham is best represented by a company called Global Insight. From a glistening, futuristic office block along a small lake, Global Insight sells about $1 billion per year worth of economic analysis, mostly to companies trying to adjust to the new international marketplace. Global Insight's core contention is that globalization cannot be stopped: no laws or rules, not even military power, can prevent the eventual integration of international markets and production, so one must adjust or be cast aside in a Darwinian contest. The company doesn't call that good or bad, just reality. Since 2007, Global Insight has been the primary marketing adviser to Wal-Mart, the world's largest corporation: and never mind that Wal-Mart itself is a cause of contemporary mixed feelings about the economy and society, to say nothing of an accelerator of economic turmoil. Wal-Mart did not even exist until 1962, and by 2002 had more revenue than any other company. The firm cleaved to a buy-American-only policy through the 1980s, but by the early twenty-first century, its shelves were stocked almost entirely with products made overseas; countless small locally owned stores have been blasted off the landscape by Wal-Mart.[2] That advice on how the world's largest company should market itself would originate in Waltham, Massachusetts, would have seemed inconceivable to those writing the city's obituary half a century ago.

What caused Waltham's comeback? When the tech and biotech booms began, roughly in the 1970s, start-up companies wanted to be near major universities as sources of ideas and young hires. Silicon Valley's proximity to Stanford and Caltech is a reason Silicon Valley happened. Tech and biotech start-ups sought locations near Harvard and MIT, but could not afford Boston and Cambridge rents, so their scouts drove west along the Massachusetts Turnpike and found Waltham at the junction of the Turnpike and Route 128. The location is convenient to Boston's prestigious schools and also to the University of Massachusetts, which has one of the world's foremost human genetics programs. Rail and subway lines run directly from Waltham to Cambridge and Boston, and Waltham's land and housing prices were then low—not to mention its surfeit of abandoned industrial parks crying out to be turned into corporate office parks, or into "fabs" for small-batch, high-technology manufacturing. (Venture capitalists don't like to fund "factories," which sound too last-century; they fund "fabrication facilities," which sound nimble and flexible.) Waltham was further aided by the success of Brandeis University, founded in 1948 and by the 1970s an outstanding institution, and by the 1968 decision of Bentley College, a top business school, to relocate from expensive land in Boston to affordable land in Waltham. College is perennially mocked as a four-year vacation before real life begins, yet increasingly the American experience shows that colleges and universities are intimately linked to economic and civic success.

Around the same time the biotech start-ups and colleges arrived in Waltham, Raytheon made its commitment to the area. Though simple forms of manufacturing—"low-value-added," in economists' jargon—may be leaving the United States, complex manufacturing such as for aerospace, electronics and industrial equipment remains strong, with the result that America's share of total world income from manufacturing has been steady for the last two decades. Raytheon makes military missiles and radars; you may not care for missiles or radars, but the best come from the United States, assembled by the descendants of the engineers who, in a watch factory along a river, figured out the concept of interchangeable parts. The juxtaposition of aerospace production, tech start-ups, excellent universities and venture capitalism made Waltham desirable. By the 1990s, even river cruises resumed, the Charles having been elaborately cleaned by a multi-billion-dollar state project. Getting the Celtics to practice in the town was the cherry on the sundae.

Waltham's transition suggests why it is misleading to worry too much about the decline of traditional heavy manufacturing jobs, while not appreciating the rise of other forms of commerce. "One hundred years ago, pundits would have predicted total calamity for America if we surrendered our national economic base in agriculture, yet agriculture is now down to 2 percent of the economy and everyone including farmers is better off," notes Lenny Mendonca, a director of the consulting firm McKinsey & Co. "If the share of the economy that is heavy manufacturing declines but everyone is better off, this is no reason for panic. Old-style factories get so much attention because Ohio, Pennsylvania and Michigan are swing states that have decided recent presidential elections. But what's happening in Ohio, Pennsylvania and Michigan is only one of many things going on in the economy."

Massachusetts, its economy for two centuries based on old-style manufacturing from watches to textiles, today has little heavy manufacturing, and booms as never before. But this does not mean that there is any guarantee Waltham's newly comfortable position will last. Most tech and biotech start-ups in the area will fail, because the majority of new businesses fail—by the time you read this, Zink may be a gold mine or be out of business. Housing markets are notoriously fickle, as the country forgets and relearns on a cyclical basis; a generation from now, it may once again be impossible to unload a home in Waltham. International business competition is relentless and can knock out any seemingly secure corporation; a generation from now, India may be a significant player in the production of precision-guided weapons. Sports Authority has a dominant position in its market today, but K-Mart and Sears once seemed invincible. Should the highly paid types in the venture-capital and tech industries decamp from Waltham, then the entry-level jobs, at restaurants or maintaining buildings, also would decline. And while the Celtics may always play in Boston, they did not hesitate to leave the Boston Garden for practice sessions. If the price is right, they won't hesitate to leave Waltham.

Even in the places that are doing well there is no assurance about the future, including the near future. North Carolina's economy seemed doomed when the textile and furniture-making industries moved to Asia. Then Research Triangle Park and Bank of America's Charlotte expansion brought a high-tech and financial renaissance to the state, but who knows how long these will last? In 2005, every mayor and governor wanted to attract the financial industry; by 2009, none did. Pittsburgh's economy seemed fated for failure as employment in steelmaking dropped sharply from the 1970s to the 1990s. Then the city enjoyed a surge in employment in engineering and computer-systems design, triggered by the troika of the tech boom, global growth increasing the need for engineering companies, and the renowned engineering programs at Carnegie Mellon University. By the early twenty-first century, Pittsburgh was converting from a blue-collar beer-and-shots town to a white-collar city with relatively low unemployment and high wages.[3] But who knows how long this will last? Or consider Manitowoc, Wisconsin, where the town's principal factory, which made cookware, closed in 2003 as its owner outsourced production to Mexico. Today the factory hums anew, renovated and converted to more profitable "vertical" manufacturing (all work done in the same place, from raw materials to finished product) while, as Timothy Aeppel has written, a local aluminum mill has been reopened and a closed dockyard reopened to fashion wind-energy turbines.[4] In the 1990s, cheap labor overseas appeared to doom U.S. manufacturing; twenty years later, a weak dollar made manufacturing inside the United States increasingly attractive. The year 2008 was economically bad overall yet simultaneously the best ever for exports of made-in-the-USA goods, with $1.1 trillion in manufactured exports, surpassing the previous best year, 1998, when exports hit $915 billion, stated in 2008 dollars. So the pendulum swung back Manitowoc's way. But insecurity rules: in 2009, exports started to decline. Prosperity today could become pink slips tomorrow, and without warning.

———

The same global forces that have been keeping the Western standard of living high also have the potential to undo the Western standard of living. And that's the view from the prosperous places, such as Seattle or Austin, Texas! In the parts of the country struggling to adjust to the ever-changing new markets, things look scarier still. Even the places that replace old jobs with new ones will have little security about future employment. There is no escape from the clamor, uncertainty and constant upheaval of the Sonic Boom—and as the Boom gets louder, the headaches caused are going to make our collective temples throb. Let's consider some of the worst aspects of the Sonic Boom:

JOB INSECURITY

It's not in your mind—even before the recession, employers were downsizing or going out of business as never before. What are Cendant, CommerceOne and Excite@Home? Companies that grew from nothing to prosperous employers of thousands of well-paid people, to having market capitalizations exceeding that of Alcoa or Delta Airlines—then vanished, all going out of existence in the last decade alone. (Enron and WorldCom could be added to that list, but you already know about them.) When Ling-Temco-Vought, then one of America's largest conglomerates, crumbled during the 1970s, people were shocked that a highly capitalized giant firm could fail. Nobody's shocked when this happens anymore.

The most basic reason job insecurity keeps rising is "churn"—the modern economy creates plenty of jobs but also destroys many, leaving everyone constantly uncertain. In 2005, for example, a strong economic year, the United States gained 31 million new jobs, which sounds fantastic, but also lost 29 million existing jobs. The gain of 2 million jobs netted out as a plus, but an astonishing *60 million* Americans had some kind of job-status change in that year. An economy in which jobs flash in and out of existence like atomic particles in a physics experiment makes even those who have good jobs feel insecure. A generation ago, 15 percent of Americans told pollsters they were worried about being laid off;[5] now practically everyone worries about layoffs. That worry is likely to continue when international growth resumes. And the worry is spreading to every social class. During the recession in progress as this book was written, the category "professional and business services" had in the last year shed more jobs than the category "manufacturing."[6] Some employment totals, mainly in health care, kept increasing even during the recession. But think heart surgeons are safe from true market economics? Consultancies have sprung up that help Americans arrange surgery in Europe or Asia at a fraction of the cost of the same operation in the United States. It is only a matter of time until employer-paid health-care plans tell people needing elective surgery that they must fly to Bangalore for their care, and the insurers will be happy to pay the plane fare.

The acceleration of change in globalized commerce will make most Americans ever more unsure about their employment futures. Construction, school teaching, bus driving—there are some lines of work that will never be offshored, because they must be done within the nation where the services are rendered. Everybody else's job is up for grabs. The competition is no longer the nearest factory or the store next door. The competition is now the entire world.

Relentless media negativism on this point will make job anxiety steadily worse. In 2009, mainstream news outlets gave large-print (or its electronic equivalent) emphasis to any news of layoffs, spinning every story in the most negative way possible.[7] Layoffs are important news that must be reported, but giving them high emphasis created the impression that everyone was being laid off, when nine out of ten people weren't. Generating a negative sense about the economy can be a self-fulfilling prophecy, since many economic decisions, from capital investments to consumer purchases, are influenced by whether we think conditions will improve or decay. What's doubly troubling for the future is that the mainstream media were relentlessly negative about job news even when the economy was in great shape. In 2006, when Visteon closed an auto-parts factory in Indiana, throwing nine hundred out of work, this was national news. In 2007, when Honda decided to build a state-of-the-art factory in Indiana, to employ about two thousand, this made no national newscast. If on jobs the media report only bad news, ignoring the good, the sense of employment insecurity will be with us indefinitely.

The mainstream media have been spinning employment news with maximum gloom in part because they themselves are going through a period of contraction. Even when the global economy was going gangbusters in the 1990s and the early twenty-first century, many mainstream media outlets were losing customers, revenue and jobs, owing to technological change, primarily caused by the Internet. Baby Boom reporters and newscasters may subconsciously identify with factory workers: both types of job classifications are becoming less numerous owing to trends in technology. Like autoworkers, many in the media think, *If only change would stop, then we'd be fine.* Change is not likely to stop, and probably cannot be stopped. But the travails of news organizations color their understanding of the economy, causing them to perceive the world as worse than it is.

Yet even if we lived in an ideal media environment where bad and good news were granted balanced perspective, job insecurity would still be seen as worsening. Rob Valletta, an analyst at the Federal Reserve Bank of San Francisco, has found that roughly a generation ago, in 1984, the typical American laid off because of downsizing or other industrial change found a new job that paid 14 percent less than the previous position; by 2004, the typical new job of the laid-off worker paid 17 percent less.[8] That's not a huge change, but is a clear negative for many who lose jobs owing to the accelerating pace of change in economics. Further, Valletta found that adjusting for aging trends in the population, median job tenure for middle-aged men dropped from about thirteen years a generation ago to about eight years in 2006 (while median job tenure rose slightly for middle-aged women). For the median job tenure to be eight years means an awful lot of middle-aged men have short job tenures—and that's not good, considering middle age is when the typical person's income requirements peak.

Job insecurity is nerve-wracking, and the advent of the two-earner family doesn't necessarily solve the problem; rather, it may result in households where two adults have job insecurity instead of one. As Peter Gosselin showed in his excellent 2008 book *High Wire,* the chance that someone in an American family will suffer a loss of income—pay cut, corporate downsizing, temporary or long-term unemployment—in any given year has risen from 17 percent in 1980 to 26 percent today.[9] A one-in-four annual chance of bad news about work is stress city.

Job insecurity also threatens to overturn a basic premise of American life, namely, the one-way nature of the middle class. For generations, Americans have accepted that breaking into the middle class requires hard work; the unwritten reward is that once you're in, you're always in. The assumption is that people who attain white-collar jobs, or secure homes in nice neighborhoods, will never backslide out of the middle class, losing the privilege of a single-family home or dropping backward from a salaried position to hourly labor. A 2008 survey by the Pew Research Center found that 78 percent of Americans think it is becoming harder to maintain a middle-class standard of living; that 28 percent had gone backward economically in the previous five years; that although 65 percent of Americans say they live better than their parents did, only 49 percent believe their children will, in turn, have better lives.[10] The same poll also found that the number of Americans who agree with the statement "I can afford the things I want" has risen steadily, and in 2008 stood at an all-time high of 52 percent. Thus in 2008, large numbers of people were anxious even if they possessed the means to afford what they wanted. A majority of Americans and Europeans have a middle-class lifestyle now, but fear they will not be able to keep that lifestyle in the future.[11] Quiet desperation, which Henry David Thoreau called the biggest trepidation of daily life, is being replaced by noisy nervousness.

SOMEONE WILL BECOME RICH TODAY—AND IT WON'T BE YOU

Since 2005, according to Internal Revenue Service statistics, there have been at least 300,000 households in the United States earning at least $1 million annually. Three hundred thousand is the population of Saint Paul, Minnesota—America has produced the equivalent of an entire city of millionaires. Since 2006, all members of the Forbes 400 have been billionaires; even in 2008, a down year for opulence, a net worth of at least $1.3 billion was required to qualify for this club. You know about the obscene bonuses showered upon Wall Street and bank executives in 2008 even when they performed terribly—for instance, in 2008 Merrill Lynch lost $27 billion, yet handed out $3.8 billion in executive bonuses. Cases of grand rewards for dubious performance are not flukes. In 2008, the twenty-five highest-paid hedge-fund managers in the United States earned an average of $464 million,[12] even as their funds were losing an average of 18 percent. Not only is such extreme pay for losing money ridiculous, in the case of hedge funds it's far from clear that their managers do anything socially useful.[13]

The people who run public corporations do perform socially valuable roles, but often are paid too much. Studies by the Economic Policy Institute show that in 1965, the typical CEO made 24 times the annual salary of the typical hourly worker; by 1999, the typical CEO was making 300 times as much as the typical worker, though today the average has dipped to a mere 262 times as much.[14] Executives who are showered with millions of dollars for showing up at an office and sitting in a chair speak in lofty terms of their "compensation," not "pay," as if they were noble philanthropists. Corporate boards—whose members are usually CEOs themselves and thus have a self-interest in sustaining high pay for CEOs—claim executives must receive millions of dollars annually to give them an incentive to perform. Because what, otherwise they would clock in and sit at their desks reenacting Civil War battles with miniature soldiers, refusing to answer the phone? For almost anyone who works for a company or government agency, keeping your job and your salary is your incentive to fulfill your tasks. Any non-executive-suite employee who said, "I refuse to perform any duties because my salary doesn't incentivize me" would promptly be fired.[15] When CEOs demand huge bonuses merely to carry out their duties, they not only pick society's pocket, they insult our intelligence.

Considerations such as these make wealth concentration a bitter topic. Adjusting for inflation, in the last three decades income for the poorest fifth of Americans has risen by just 2 percent, while income for the richest fifth has risen by 63 percent.[16] The poorest fifth are still better off, because the inflation-adjusted size of the economy has grown, meaning they are receiving a slightly larger piece of a somewhat larger pie. As Brad Schiller, an economist at American University, has noted, adjusting to today's dollars, the bottom fifth in the United States earned $181 billion in 1970 and $447 billion in 2007.[17] But the top fifth have seen a far higher rise in adjusted terms, and the top 1 percent has been overwhelmed with increased riches.

The issue may not be as simple as it seems, however, since the same forces that are creating excessive wealth at the top are also benefiting the average person. While income for the top 1 percent has soared since 1980, income for the middle class has, adjusting for inflation, grown by just 15 to 23 percent, depending on how one performs the calculation.[18] Still, average people's income has risen—even in the current weak economy, middle-class income is the highest it has ever been in the United States. Falling after-inflation prices of most goods and services means the typical person's somewhat higher income today buys a higher standard of living than that of thirty years ago. Home electronics, jet travel, full-featured cars (air-conditioning once was found solely in luxury cars; now no new model sold in the United States lacks it), eating in restaurants and other living-standards measures once rare for the middle class are now common. Suppose a generation ago we had shifted the social compact away from free economics. Then there would be no infuriating news stories about avaricious hedge-fund managers paying themselves $464 million, and I certainly would like to live out the rest of my life without having to read another one of those stories. But there might also be no rising standards of living for typical people, stagnation might mean terrible levels of unemployment, and low-cost developments fostered by chaotic free competition, such as the affordable cell phone, might never have happened.

"Compared to what?" Never forget this critical question. In recent decades, the rich have gotten a lot richer while the middle class has grown only somewhat better off and poverty has declined, but not by anywhere near as much as should have been achieved. (The U.S. poverty rate, 22 percent in 1960, fell steadily to its all-time low of 11.3 percent in 2000, and by 2007 has risen to 12.5 percent.[19]) Isn't this preferable compared to, say, decades in which the average did not gain, or was clobbered by inflation? Inflation harms average people far more than it harms the well-off. The same free-economics forces that are allowing very large numbers of people, in the United States, Europe and elsewhere, to improve their standards of living are also allowing small numbers of people to become objectionably rich. A dynamic of moderate gains for large numbers coupled to large gains for small numbers is preferable to many other possible outcomes. In an ideal world, income gains would be concentrated in the middle. In the less-than-ideal world we have, obscene wealth might be moderated—see a suggestion below—but shifting the social compact away from free economics easily could backfire by harming the middle.

INEQUALITY WILL GET WORSE

Brace yourself, because the same forces that in recent decades have made some haughty, overbearing people very wealthy are likely to accelerate. Ideas—business innovations, inventions, movies—are rising in value compared to labor and resources, while ideas are becoming easier to produce for sale than was once the case, since it costs a lot less to manufacture an idea expressed as better software than an idea expressed as a better refrigerator. As ideas become worth more than resources or labor, pay premiums will rise for people who have marketable ideas. That is all but certain to mean more excessive wealth at the top. Already the growth is vivid in physical evidence, such as yachts clogging marinas. According to studies by Ron Haskins of the Brookings Institution, today the bottom half of American households holds just 3 percent of the country's wealth and assets, while the top 1 percent holds a third of the wealth and assets.[20] The top 1 percent has ten times as much as half the country! Inequality of this sort is nearly certain to grow worse in the United States and other nations.

The conundrum is that the same forces likely to cause inequality to grow worse are also likely to create benefits for almost everyone. Suppose there were some form of legislation that made ideas less valuable or that forbade the inexpensive reproduction of inventions, biotechnology, management concepts and so on. Wealth surplus at the top would screech to a halt. But average people would be penalized—there would be no free-content Web sites, no generic drugs, no fifteen-dollar overnight delivery, no cheap MP3 players loaded with ninety-nine-cent songs and so on. Attempts to stop repugnant wealth might also impede economic growth. For instance, as this book went to press, Congress was considering legislation that would tie CEO bonuses very closely to company performance. Since many CEOs are overpaid, this is the kind of legislation that's easy to root for. But if corporate bonuses were tied very closely to how much money a firm makes in a given year, the unintended consequence might be to discourage research and development—which cuts into profits in the current year and probably won't produce any benefits till after the current CEO has left his post. Thus, regulating bonuses by tying them tightly to corporate numbers sounds tempting, but could have an unpleasant, unintended result, discouraging investments that spawn innovation. My personal proposal for reigning in executive pay: limit a CEO's income to one hundred times the annual income of the lowest-paid worker in the firm. Only an appalling egotist could claim to deserve, for shuffling papers and initialing memos, more than one hundred times the income of a cafeteria worker. Formally stating CEO pay as a multiple of an underprivileged person's means might shame top executives into being content with millions rather than dozens of millions: taking into account the current federal income wage, one hundred times the lowest worker's pay would be $1.5 million. If a $1.5 million annual income isn't enough to motivate a business executive, then the problem lies with that person, not with society. More important, in the times-the-lowest concept, the CEO could make more only if those in most need got raises, creating a positive incentive rather than a perverse incentive.

HOUSING STRESS MAY BECOME PERMANENT

The tight mortgage market and soft housing prices that began in late 2007 in the United States represented serious issues for many people—but mortgage terms and real estate values are cyclical, and all past snafus in both resolved themselves. Stamped above the front door of every home and townhouse should be the legend WARNING: HOME PRICES SUBJECT TO BOOM-AND-BUST CYCLES. The decline of housing prices, coupled to foreclosure threats impacting those ranging from totally honest men and women who experienced unexpected setbacks to those who signed gimmick loans or "liar loans," was viewed as an economic disaster: a "crisis," according to presidents George W. Bush and Barack Obama and countless others.[21] This depends on your point of view—to many, it was good that housing prices declined. Housing prices had entered a bubble phase, and it is healthy when bubbles end. No bubble has ever lasted forever; the more a financial bubble expands, the worse when it bursts. Toward the end of the housing bubble, first-time home buyers had been priced out of the market: after prices fell, a first-time home purchase became possible again for many, especially young people. Falling housing prices were bad news *for people who already had houses,* mainly the middle-aged. Falling housing prices were good news for people hoping to make their first purchase. The needs of the young are almost entirely unrepresented in the mainstream media, which is dominated by Baby Boomers, so this part of the situation went unreported. Arguably, the media's promotion of the idea that declining housing prices represented some unprecedented emergency that justified unlimited federal spending—though home prices have gone boom-and-bust many times before, there was a real estate price bust cycle from about 1994 to 1997 that cured itself without any government intervention—actively harmed the young. How? By pushing Washington to adopt policies that subsidize those in houses at the expense of those living in apartments. This happened in part because the needs of the young are almost entirely unrepresented in politics, too. The Baby Boomers running Congress borrowed wildly, without accountability, for programs to help people who already had houses, sending the bill for the borrowing to young people who don't yet own anything. For that matter, the Baby Boomers running Congress borrowed wildly, without accountability, for people who already had great jobs at banks and on Wall Street, subsidizing them and sending the bill to young people who just got out of college and couldn't find a job.

The sense of general panic caused by declining home prices is another leading indicator of stress-based economics. According to the Case-Shiller Index, U.S. housing prices slowly rose by 47 percent from 1994 to 2004; then rose very fast, gaining another 29 percent, to their peak in 2006; then fell just as fast, by the end of 2008 back almost exactly to the level of 2004. But that's still a 54 percent gain from 1994! Stated in today's dollars, these figures mean a house worth $400,000 in 1994 would have zoomed to a peak value of $975,000 in 2006 and then by the end of 2008, been worth $615,000. If you were told in 1994 that your house would be worth 54 percent more by 2008, wouldn't that have sounded good? Suppose you haven't owned a home since 1994: you bought one more recently. Even after the drop, the typical American home was worth roughly a third more in 2008 than in 2000—roughly a 5 percent annual rate of return, compounded. This means Americans who followed the standard financial strategy regarding homeownership—put 20 percent down, buy only what you can afford, don't strip your equity by reckless refinancing, never engage in real estate speculation—were doing fine, in fact coming out ahead, during a period national leaders called a "crisis."

Extensive federal intervention in the housing market, via the bailouts of Fannie Mae and Freddie Mac, affecting individual home-

owners, and by Federal Reserve actions to lower mortgage costs artificially, are likely to have long-term negative consequences for anyone
who doesn't already own a house, by making it easier for present owners to stay put and harder for young people to acquire homes. This will
add economic stress during a period when stress levels would rise even
if the housing market were in some kind of perfect equilibrium.[22]

The larger financial worry regarding housing is not short-term vari-
ations in price, but rather a long-term sense that costly houses are essential to a successful life. In her prescient 2003 book *The Two-Income
Trap,* Harvard professor Elizabeth Warren warned—long before anyone outside the banking profession had ever heard the term *subprime
mortgage*—that housing expenses could be the undoing of the American middle class. Warren analyzed the budgets of middle-class families and found that most had relatively little trouble affording clothing,
food, appliances and similar needs. But spending on homes was skyrocketing, she found, because of the desire to locate in neighborhoods
that are safe, confer status and offer high-quality public schools.
School-district nervousness, Warren wrote, was causing middle-class
Americans to overinvest on housing—real estate agents are now the
gatekeepers of the good public school systems, which on paper are
open to anyone, but in actuality only to those whose parents can afford
the right house. Overspending on housing to get into good school districts, or for reasons of snobbery, seems ironic when many of the over-
spenders themselves, as children, simply lived wherever they lived,
attended whatever school was down the block and turned out just fine.
Warren's book cautioned of a reckoning based on people signing mortgages they could not afford. When the housing-price and mortgage
crunches first manifested in 2007, the president, the Federal Reserve,
Fannie Mae, Freddie Mac and Wall Street all claimed they had no way
of knowing there was a problem brewing. As Warren's work shows,
there were plenty of warning signs that the system ignored. And the
underlying problem—the confluence of the desire to live in an impressive house, coupled to worries over the quality of public schools—
will be with us long after the credit-market foul-ups of the moment
have been solved.

IT'S FUN TO ORDER CHAMPAGNE, BUT EVENTUALLY THE WAITER BRINGS THE BILL

For the last decade America's national savings rate has hovered between zero and minus 4 percent, meaning we borrow more than we earn—and if you're borrowing more than you earn, when interest is factored in, you are falling behind. Occasional borrowing may be smart; constant borrowing creates the sense of endlessly falling behind. Much of the housing bubble that ended in 2006 was inflated by America's collective inability to think ahead to the day the bill comes due. Zero down! No payments until next year! Zero-down deals are great in the year you sign them, then become monsters later.

Mortgage and housing difficulties have been made worse because Americans began to misuse the best backstop form of borrowing, home equity. Federal Reserve figures show that adjusted to current dollars, home-equity borrowing rose from $245 billion in 2000 to $1.1 trillion in 2007—a stunning rise not only in absolute terms, but also considering it happened during a period when the economy was strong, so people should have been paying down debt, not borrowing more. As Vikas Bajaj has written,[23] "Too many Americans came to regard a home as an A.T.M. with three bedrooms and 1.5 baths." Americans by the millions took out home-equity loans to finance vacations, renovations, big SUVs. As a result, according to the Federal Reserve, in 2007, for the first time ever, the typical equity value in an American home was less than 50 percent. When you borrow against the value of your home, you both increase your debt load and assign to someone else part of the value that previously belonged to you. Significant home-equity borrowing will boomerang unless two conditions obtain: housing prices rise and interest rates don't. Any sensible person knows prices cannot rise ad infinitum while interest rates stay low ad infinitum. But Americans have not acted sensibly when it comes to debt, and this contributed to the sense of economic instability that washed over most of the world in 2009.

Perhaps Americans don't think sensibly about debt because they are following the examples set by the White House and by Congress!

Leadership starts at the top, and American government—Republican and Democratic officeholders alike—puts dishonest mortgage brokers to shame when it comes to gimmick borrowing. National debt was $5.7 trillion when George W. Bush took office, and was $10.8 trillion when he left office in 2008. Adjusted to today's money, the $800 billion increase in the national debt ceiling approved by Congress in 2008 exceeds the *entire* national debt of the year 1975.[24] That's just for one year's undisciplined borrowing, and the borrowing binge got worse under Barack Obama in 2009, as the national debt ceiling was increased again, to nearly $13 trillion. In turn, the official debt ceiling covers only borrowing for current costs—not included are long-term obligations for Medicare and Medicaid, Social Security, federal employee pensions, care and benefits for injured Iraq and Afghan war veterans, the ongoing Fannie Mae–Freddie Mac megabailout or the bailout of irresponsible home buyers who lied on their mortgage applications. It took the United States 209 years, from 1789 to 1998, to compile the first $5 trillion in debt; it has taken just ten years to compile the second $5 trillion. The third $5 trillion will come even faster, with more being added to the national debt for the banking sector and automaker bailouts, plus huge amounts of debt-backed spending under the rubric of economic stimulus, plus Federal Reserve decisions to buy up mortgage-backed securities no one wants.

If you borrowed, borrowed, borrowed, you could live high for a while—but then you'd need to sell off your possessions, which is exactly what is happening to the United States as its leaders continue their borrowing binge. America's federal public debt was 29 percent of its GDP when George W. Bush took office in 2001; had already leaped to 36 percent in January 2008, before the financial meltdown began; stood at 43 percent as President Barack Obama completed his initial round of bailout and budget actions in winter 2009; and is on course to hit 60 percent by the end of 2011. The amount of the U.S. economy that's been promised to someone else via borrowing is on track to double in just eleven years! If any young person borrowed in such a rash way, he or she would be sternly admonished by grown-ups as irresponsible. But it's the grown-ups in Washington, of both parties, who have taken to borrowing like mad to avoid ever having to face a tough decision. In 1781, George Washington insisted that taxes rapidly pay down the Revolutionary War debt, lest his contemporaries "ungenerously throw upon posterity the burden which we ourselves ought to bear." If only Washington's spirit still could be found in Washington! Every penny of the $1 trillion to $2 trillion expended on the Iraq War has been borrowed, the grown-ups running the country today—perhaps that should read "grown-ups"—being unwilling to tax themselves or their constituent groups, handing the bill instead to those who cannot yet vote. The gigantic and ever-compounding national debt that will be inherited by those now young, as they enter their workplace and child-bearing years, will worsen their sense of economic anxiety. Even if the overall international economy goes well during a Sonic Boom, today's young will be dragged down by being expected to pay off what their elders so recklessly and selfishly borrowed.

THE SAME FORCES THAT MAKE FOR A NIMBLE, FLEXIBLE ECONOMY MAKE FOR CUMBERSOME, EXORBITANT HEALTH CARE

As the Sonic Boom grows louder, many Americans will need to adjust to a reality of frequent job changes—the moving-van industry will be happy!—and hybrid careers. Traditionally, a person either worked all his or her life for a big corporation, or for a small local business, or for government, or was self-employed. To switch among any of these categories was considered a major move, and usually final—a person might decide to leave big business for self-employment, say, but the break would be permanent. Future workplace paths are likely to be a lot less well lighted. Men and women may end up switching back and forth among categories of employment several times in a working lifetime.

We should not romanticize the Gray Flannel Suit lifestyle of spending one's whole career at a single employer: many who did so found it stifling and draining, all building up to an empty feeling at retirement. Frequent job-switching and even work-category switching may have nerve-wracking aspects but otherwise keeps people fresh and helps the rate of idea exchange, which serves to cross-pollinate the world.

Historically, men and women have sought to spend an entire work life with the same employer for four reasons: seniority, lethargy, pen-

sion checks and health care. As ever less of the labor population be-
longs to a trade union, seniority becomes less of a factor in determin-
ing pay, while in the white-collar world, the trend is away from
seniority as the first factor in promotion. As for lethargy, many people
never think of changing jobs simply because staying put is easier. As
for pensions, the problem of having your hands tied by a corporate-run
pension is lessened, though hardly solved, by the portable 401(k)
owned by you rather than held by an employer.[25] The sooner all pension instruments are owned by employees, the better.

Then there's health insurance. According to the Kaiser Family
Foundation, in 2007, privately purchased, basic family health insurance cost on average $5,799 per year, versus an average cost of $3,281
for workplace group plans. Federal law allows someone who leaves a
company with group insurance to buy the policy for an additional year
at the group rate, but that's purely a patch on a tire losing air. Individuals have considerable trouble obtaining private health insurance, for
reasons that make perfect sense to insurance companies and no sense
to society as a whole. If you've got a preexisting condition, either no
one will insure you or the charge will be a knockout punch. Even if a
job-hopping person does succeed in obtaining new policy after new
policy, this means constant turmoil: figuring out new plan details, finding new doctors who take the plan. The postwar American model of
health insurance—premised on secure corporations providing coverage to long-term employees who will never leave—does not function
in a globalized world. America must make a fundamental choice: either national health-care coverage (of the high-quality kind, as delivered by the French system) or nationally mandated, standard-feature
private coverage that anyone can buy at the same price regardless of
health condition or type of employment. It's ridiculous that our cell
phones work wherever we go but our health-care coverage does not.

JUST IN CASE THIS IS NOT ENOUGH INSECURITY FOR YOU . . .

There are many other reasons to dislike, or at least worry about, the approaching Sonic Boom reality. Record levels of immigration causing
constant social change; ubiquitous media fixation on whatever's not

perfect; "data smog" in which an outpouring of mutually contradictory information creates paralysis about what to take seriously; the accelerating pace of life; the ongoing decline of institutions, which leaves us feeling at sea with no one to trust.

And that's before climate change! Artificially triggered climate change is almost certainly in progress, and may bring levels of upheaval that would be distressing even if everything else about our lives held constant. Global political, cultural and economic systems will undergo extraordinary rates of change *at the same time the climate changes*. Much of humanity's footprint is where it is—farm regions, coastal cities, industry along waterways—owing to prevailing climate. And the prevailing climate is about to stop prevailing. The situation is as though a bus were spinning uncontrollably on a patch of ice when a mechanic popped his head in the door and said, "Excuse me, I'm here to disconnect the brakes."

Three

YAKUTSK

Yakutsk, Russia, is home to a marvelous newly built performing-arts center, to the world's leading museum of wooly mammoth fossils, and to Yakutsk State University, where ten thousand students take classes in engineering, geology and medicine. Flowing past Yakutsk is the starkly beautiful Lena River, whose vast watershed offers some of the largest serene natural vistas remaining on our planet. But despite the nature preserves and the university, Yakutsk is not a destination travel guides recommend, for it is the coldest major city in the world. Located in Siberia just below the Arctic Circle, Yakutsk has an average January temperature of minus 22 Fahrenheit.

Hey, wait—global warming is coming! Someday, Yakutsk may boast of mild weather and become a prime ecotourist destination. The scientific consensus is that temperatures will rise in the twenty-first century—in the most important scientific statement so far, in 2005, seven Western science academies, led by the U.S. National Academy of Sciences, declared, "There is now strong evidence that significant global warming is occurring."[1] The short version of the evidence: global mean temperatures have risen at least one degree Fahrenheit in the last century, ocean temperatures are rising (because most of our planet's surface mass is water, not land, this may matter more than other measures), sea ice is declining somewhat, spring is arriving progressively sooner in many parts of the world, and, most important, the level of greenhouse gases in the atmosphere continues to rise. The signals are sufficiently strong that in 2006 President George W. Bush's Climate Change Science Program declared "clear evidence of human influences on the climate system."[2] Exactly how the climate will change is unknown—perhaps the warming will turn out to be just a blip in nature's scheme of things. But even artificial climate change that is minor to nature's scheme could be enormously disruptive to the world's economy. Supposing a Sonic Boom begins, the best case is that simultaneous climate change will make the boom even more chaotic than it otherwise would have been. Worst case? Let's skip the worst cases.

Most global-warming commentary tends to focus on environmental effects. Think instead what climate change could do to the world's flows of money, economic activity and power. Climate change will produce its own set of winners and losers. Some areas now impoverished will prosper, while other areas now desirable will falter. Political alliances will shift; trade patterns will change; fortunes will be made and lost. Entrepreneurs and business people will rush from region to region asking: "Global warming, what's in it for me?" Global warming may cause economic convulsions unparalleled by any event other than World War II. And this will happen at the very time millions of men and women across the world are facing rapid economic change caused by Sonic Boom forces. If you think the globalized landscape is in upheaval now, just wait a few years.

Consider Siberia. For centuries, Russian poets have lamented that their homeland is cursed by this foreboding, frigid expanse. What if Siberia were to become a temperate, inviting expanse? Many minerals are known to reside beneath the Siberian permafrost; some geologists think as much oil as lies beneath the Saudi peninsula may be present. If Siberia warms, its minerals and oil may become accessible, leading to a huge improvement in Russia's national wealth, plus an increase in global commodity supplies, moderating prices for everyone. (Yes, in this event, greenhouse gases from fossil fuel combustion would cause permafrost melting that frees up more oil supply leading to more greenhouse gases. Surely you accept by now that God has a sense of humor.) Siberia's soil has never been depleted by controlled agriculture. If that soil is tillable—currently a subject of debate among specialists—a new breadbasket region would be added to our pale blue dot, just in time to meet the food needs of a rising population. More generally, climate change could open Siberia to urban development: construction of cities and factories might be just the beginning. If Siberia warms, this could represent the largest addition to the world's supply of land available for development since the sailing ships of Old Europe first beheld North America. And the wealth generated by a usable Siberia might catapult Moscow back to great-power status.

Climate change could be a boon to other parts of the world. Alaska, Canada, Greenland and Scandinavia, most of whose territories are now too cold, might experience a rip-roaring gold rush. Examine a globe: by accident of geography, except for Antarctica almost all the world's high-latitude land is in the Northern Hemisphere. Only a relatively small portion of South America, which narrows as one travels south, is at high latitudes, and none of Africa or Australia is, with Cape Town being roughly the same distance from the Equator as Cape Hatteras, and Melbourne about the same distance from the Equator as Manhattan. High-latitude land that is currently cold is the land likely to grow more valuable in a warming world, and that land is held entirely by well-off nations: the United States, Canada, Russia and the Scandinavian countries. No poor nation will benefit from high-latitude warming, because no poor nation—other than Nunavut, the sparsely populated Inuit territory in the north of Canada—possesses any significant amount of high-latitude territory.

Climate change could have amusing real estate consequences. The Gulf of Bothnia might become the favorite resort area of trendsetters, while the Laurentian Mountains of Quebec become the new Poconos. The chilly, parched Gobi Desert lies adjacent to the fastest-growing, most crowded region of the world—if climate change brings rain and fair winds to the Gobi, China's land crunch might be solved. Today hardly anyone wants acreage in the Dakotas: global warming could change that equation. And in a warming world my hometown of Buffalo, New York, might become the vacation paradise of the stars. Hollywood celebrities and hedge-fund managers may build mansions on the Lake Erie shoreline outside Buffalo. They'll sit sipping Heitz Martha's Vineyard cabernet, watching the sun set behind the slag towers of the abandoned steel mills, and remarking on the ideal weather.

For every climate-change winner, there will be a loser, and losing in the game of climate change could be highly disagreeable. Real estate markets of the American southwest, for instance, may stall if climate change causes temperatures in Arizona, Nevada and Southern California to become stifling. If Houston becomes even more humid, who would wish to live there? Sea-level rise could turn much of Florida—where the water table is already high—back into swampland. Those swank waterfront homes at Nantucket and Sag Harbor, in the Outer Banks, along the Mexican Gold Coast? Fish reefs if the seas rise.

Sea-level rise could imperil many of the world's waterfront cities, such as Singapore and San Francisco, while rendering uninhabitable much of Bangladesh and Egypt. Developing countries whose low-lying riparian areas are already overpopulated could find those areas gone. The National Academy of Sciences estimates sea levels will rise from a few inches to three feet during the twenty-first century: the bottom of that range would be manageable, the top a disaster.[3] Although global warming is expected to be felt more at high latitudes than in the tropics, equatorial nations tend with a few exceptions to be poor or less developed, leaving them more vulnerable than the mainly prosperous northern lands. Heat will hurt the equatorial countries, and they will be least able to afford a response. I once lived in Pakistan, where summertime temperatures often exceed 100 Fahrenheit, where the average person has only an electric fan for cooling, and where the electricity fails every other day. Imagine if highs in Pakistan hit 110 Fahrenheit—tens of millions of poor people would suffer, while the nation overall would falter as heat made productive labor close to impossible.

Global warming and climate change sound like the same thing, but climate change is the greater danger. Suppose Earth's climate changes in such a way that the rain now falling on agricultural areas falls instead on deserts or at sea. If what are today breadbasket regions become too dry to till owing to climate change, over the course of decades the world would adjust—but food shortages might plague societies, causing great suffering in developing nations. The reason predicted Malthusian famines have not occurred is that, since World War II, farm yield has always increased slightly faster than population growth. We take for granted that even with an expanding global population, a plentiful harvest will always come in. The phrase "crop failure" has not been spoken in world politics since the Soviet wheat failure of the late 1970s. Should the climate change rapidly, farm-yield increases may stop. If food shortages begin, other issues we now carp about will instantly seem inconsequential.

If rain declines in what are now agricultural belts, it may increase in areas that now wish they received less rain. Already the Indian subcontinent is lashed by annual monsoon deluges that cost lives and bring destruction. In 2006, nearly *three feet* of rain fell on Mumbai (Bombay) in just twenty-four hours, killing hundreds, shutting down the city and causing a cholera outbreak. Imagine if climate change makes the monsoon season worse. Or merely if seasonal storm patterns change: in the last twenty years the relatively mild monsoon that helps supply rainwater to China's agricultural region has been shifting toward the sea, and freshwater that falls into the sea is, from humanity's perspective, wasted. Partly to compensate, China is depleting its groundwater at a worrisome rate.

Even supposing artificially caused global warming does not have extreme consequences such as significant sea-level rise or dangerous heat in equatorial nations, many other forms of disruption will occur.[4] Today the Central Valley of Chile is wild and hauntingly picturesque, one of the few major regions left on Earth where man enters as a guest. The Central Valley also has tremendous potential for zero-emission hydropower and plantation forestry—trees growing rapidly under plantation conditions subtract carbon from the air faster than trees growing naturally. If climate change set loose by greenhouse gases threatens society, the magnificent Central Valley of Chile may be converted to hydro dams and tree farms, and large numbers of people will move to this now-secluded region to run the anticarbon economy that may take hold there, while current residents are displaced.

This kind of disruptive change may come to many other places now tranquil. The James Bay region north of Montreal is already the world's leading hydropower producer; its output of clean electricity could go way up if more dams and reservoirs are built. Solar power collectors—which are likely to be large—will be built in many rustic areas now remote from the pulsing of technology. Already there's a movement to prevent solar power collectors from being located in California's Mojave Desert, and the movement is led by . . . environmentalists, who don't want high-tech devices, even high-tech clean-power devices, marring desert panoramas. At current rates of polar sea ice melting, the entire Arctic Ocean may be navigable within a few decades.[5] Oceangoing container ships will be able to speed their transit times between North America and Asia, cutting costs for consumer goods, but a Wild West atmosphere may come to what is now one of the quietest parts of Earth. Some geologists believe there are stupendous amounts of petroleum and natural gas below the northern polar ice. If that ice melts, who owns the prospecting rights? Already the United States, Canada, Denmark, Norway and Russia each assert jurisdiction over the North Pole; in a warming world, Greenland might declare independence from Denmark and claim the North Pole, too. Today the idea of nations going into combat over the North Pole sounds like a comedy sketch—but wars have been fought over less than may be at stake.

Reforms to prevent climate change need not lead to privation or slower economic growth, if energy conservation policies are adopted and green energy development is successful. (Remember, by greenhouse-effect standards, nuclear energy is green.) In 2008, three Brookings Institution scholars studied the "carbon footprints" of America's hundred largest metropolitan areas.[6] Making their Top Ten list of cities with the smallest carbon footprints—that is, where greenhouse emissions are lowest per capita—were Los Angeles, New York City, Portland, San Diego, San Francisco, San Jose (the city of Silicon

Valley), and Seattle. These are among the most prosperous, economically vibrant cities in the world, yet are already ahead of the curve on
reducing greenhouse gases. The Bottom Ten, with the highest carbon
emissions per capita, all were cities lower on the prosperity scale—
Indianapolis, Lexington, Nashville and Toledo among them. This kind
of indicator suggests that reducing greenhouse gas emissions need not
mean restricting affluence. Rapid global growth during a Sonic Boom
might mesh with conversion of wide areas of the world to a low-carbon
lifestyle based on clean energy and energy efficiency; that would make
the world a better place to live. In turn, conversion to clean energy
might help drive Sonic Boom growth.

But unless the concept of artificially triggered global warming is totally wrong, which seems unlikely,[7] tremendous upheaval caused by
climate change is a possibility over the coming decades.[8] Even supposing a favorable sequence of events—society adapts while
greenhouse-gas buildup gradually comes under control and then is reversed by advances in clean-energy technology—turmoil will be widespread, during the period when the long-sought full economic
liberalization of the world will itself bring turmoil. Or, as economists
say with cool detachment, "creative destruction." Two categories of
turmoil will hit simultaneously, and both are just getting started. It is
common for men and women to think, "Life is too fast and chaotic, if
only things would settle down for a while." Life is on the verge of becoming faster and more chaotic, though maybe things will settle down
in the twenty-third century!

———

Even if the future holds mainly positive developments, and there's a
good chance this will happen, the conjunction of rapid economic
change and unpredictable climate change will introduce new categories of uncertainty into our lives. Many of them won't strictly speaking be caused by climate change, but could be amplified by it. The
more interconnected the world becomes, the less chance we'll be able
to determine which cause led to what effect. Economies might boom
and most people do well, yet events seem a whirling blur of disorder.
Here are some themes to watch for:

THE WORLD CAN NO LONGER BE UNDERSTOOD

Once, for most people, it was enough to understand one profession and one town. Today job and social requirements are in constant upheaval, while events anywhere on the planet can impact any town anywhere. Even if the impact is welcome—a beneficial new product is made available, another country becomes democratic—the sense of having no grasp of what's going on is maddening.

Does it seems as though no matter how much you know and learn, you'll never really be on top of things? Guess what—you won't. This is especially true of economics, as is shown by the utter failure of learned, highly paid economic specialists to anticipate what began in 2008.[9] If you did nothing all day long except try to understand what was happening in the world economy, by the time you figured it out, things would have changed so much that your knowledge would no longer be valid. There's a reason economists spend far more time studying the past than analyzing the present! A world of 6 billion souls, most of them now economically free and about half of them politically free, with very large numbers of them freely communicating, is a world that simply cannot be grasped. You may know many important aspects of that world, but you will never understand the totality. No one will ever understand it. This is not necessarily bad, just something to adjust to.

LIFE HAS BECOME FANTASY BASEBALL

Fantasy baseball leaguers are obsessed by statistics, whose microscopic ups and downs they follow to . . . let's just say excess. This is emblematic of a larger phenomenon—too many statistics changing so fast that it is impossible to make heads or tails of them. Americans now obsessively follow the day-by-day and even hour-by-hour vacillations of the Dow Jones Industrial Index and similar Wall Street measures, though stock trends are only tangentially related to overall economic health—stocks can rise when the economy falls and vice versa—and though many stock-price movements are driven by herd-psychology factors that tell us little or nothing. In one sequence in March 2008, the Dow Jones fell 3 percent one day, then rose 3.7 percent the next day, was down 1.6 percent two days later, then a few days later rose 3.7 percent followed by a 2.4 percent decline the next day followed by a 2.2 percent rise the subsequent day. By the fall of 2008, during the financial-institution meltdown, it was not unusual for the stock market to fall 5 percent one day, then rise 5 percent the next. There is no possibility that the underlying value of the economy was changing as quickly as stock prices changed. Where once only a small fraction of Americans and Europeans paid attention to Wall Street and bourse fluctuations or even knew where to find the numbers, now everyone can see the readout minute by minute on the Internet or in the "chyron," those screen-bottom crawls on news channels. Now many people fret about minute-by-minute stock movements, wondering why the changes are happening and what they portend. Most likely there is no specific "why," and unless you intend to buy or sell stock that particular week, most likely the changes won't have any impact on you. But we follow and fret.

Political polls now change almost daily, and millions follow such minute vacillations. When the Internet arrived, men and women starting checking for news updates once or twice a day; now many check twice an hour. Computer and cell-phone services can be configured to alert you of news events or celebrity tantrums on a minute-by-minute basis. At every moment, something happens somewhere; we check obsessively, looking for some larger trend of good or bad, but in most news there is no larger trend. Economic statistics—leading indicators, consumer confidence, factory output—once were gauged quarterly or yearly. Now indicators are revised weekly or even daily, and there are now so many, often mutually contradictory, that you could spend an hour each day merely reviewing them all and still have no idea what's going on. Indeed, many highly paid corporate economists and Wall Street analysts do spend an hour each day reviewing the leading indicators, and as was learned with the tech crash of 2000, the mortgage securities crash of 2007, and the Wall Street crash of 2008, they still have no idea what's going on. The writer David Shenk calls this problem "data smog."[10] With each passing year there is increased data, and the data are more easily obtained. But the data do not bring clarity. Rather, they function as smog—making it harder to see into the distance.

INFORMATION DRIVES OUT KNOWLEDGE

The ancient Greeks had considerable knowledge, though compared to us, little information. For instance, the Greeks believed matter was made from four elements: the latest count is 119. Today's typical American high school student has at his or her disposal more facts about science, biology, geography, physics and astronomy than was known to all the great Greek thinkers combined. Yet were they alive today, we would seek out the ancient Greeks for their wisdom. The ancient Greek philosophers achieved a sense of perspective about human affairs. When we think about our lives today, *perspective* isn't the first word that pops to mind.

Modern press reports are chock-full of facts, yet often after reading or watching such reports, we feel we know less than when we started. The Internet already offers more words and information than could be found in the Great Library of Alexandria, yet the Internet seems a source of befuddlement rather than enlightenment. Information can drive out knowledge, and there are ever-more-vast amounts of information coming quickly and cheaply. Two principal impacts of the Sonic Boom will be major improvements in the ease of communicating information, coupled to broader access to information at lower cost. It is impossible to oppose the improved exchange of information, and indeed, as technology and globalized economics set free the sort of information once controlled by elites, the next revolution in human equality will be achieved. A flowering of science and innovation could be the bonus. But when information changes from a stream (the Greeks) to a river (the present) to a Niagara Falls (the near future), how will we ever slow down enough to achieve knowledge?

THE ADVENT OF MULTIPLE MEDIA PERSONALITY DISORDER

We know that electronics, car engines, printers and other standbys of daily life have become more powerful and easier to use. So have the news media. Between the Web and five hundred channels of cable, it's amazing how much faster, more compelling and more accurate news has become. From a business-model standpoint, what are the goals of most news media? First to make us uneasy, so that we feel we need more news; second to make us discontent, so we feel we need the products offered by the advertisers who support news transmission. And though their profits may be shrinking, their business performance is improving: the media are getting ever better at making us feel uneasy and discontent!

A century ago, well-informed Americans had two basic sources of news: newspapers that appeared daily, but offered little international content, and analytical magazines published months after the events they described. If your sole news sources were a daily newspaper and two or three serious magazines, you could stay on top of your reading and obtain the sense of more-or-less grasping the world; plus, when there was a disaster, usually you wouldn't hear until after the recovery had begun. As recently as twenty-five years ago, television news was available for only a small portion of the day—during the dinner hour, then again for a half-hour before bed. That amount of news was possible to digest. Today in the United States there are three 24/7 national news channels; many cities have a 24/7 local news channel; dozens of other channels broadcast at least some news content; most major nations have at least one round-the-clock news channel. Now anyone can use the Web to check hundreds of newspaper worldwide—say, *The New York Times, Los Angeles Times, Chicago Tribune, The Miami Herald,* plus *Le Soir, Pravda* and the *Pakistan Times,* while also using the Web to check multiple newscasts. There is no way any human being can handle it all.

The media focus on the upsetting or the shocking to hold our interest, and the sheer availability of the "platforms" to supply whatever is upsetting or shocking keeps arcing upward. Anything burning or exploding anywhere on the globe immediately becomes the lead everywhere—making us feel the world is falling to pieces, even if most things for most people are fine. News channels increasingly have flashing red bars on the screen (red connotes danger) or urgency-suggesting crawls that say BREAKING NEWS! (even if the "breaking" news is no more than a press conference). Once a news broadcast would show one person speaking or perhaps a pair of people conversing; now it is common to have four or five faces on the screen, often shouting at one another, because studies find that televised emotion is compelling and holds the attention of viewers. And just as the media become ever better at quickly and accurately providing to our televisions and computers scary images or clips of people shouting at one another, advertising is getting ever better—through focus groups, Zip code analysis and other techniques—at making us feel whatever we own now just doesn't cut the mustard. Advertising is supposed to make you discontented with what you already possess, else why would you change products? And we are constantly exposed to more advertising, an average of sixty-one minutes daily, according to a recent study.[11]

Because the media are ever more efficient at scary-sounding coverage, flashing-red stories now crowd out other concerns, such as holding government accountable. Television news now often uses helicopter footage to create a theatrical sense that events are more dramatic than they are. When a small fire broke out in a subway station in Bethesda, Maryland, in 2007, no fewer than four television news helicopters came to circle the station closest to the problem—though you really can't see much of what goes on inside a subway from the air![12] The point of the helicopters was to create a sense of cinematic drama (though no one was harmed in the fire), keeping viewers' eyes glued, in the same way that local news now shows radar traces of bad weather hundreds or even thousands of miles from the station's viewing area, just to have something scary (and bright red) to talk about.

Because so much media time is spent on scary information or anger, little time is left for stories of reforms that worked or people who benefit society. A person who causes terrible harm is sure to get saturation media coverage; a person who makes the world a better place may be ignored by television and the Web. Suppose there were a publication called *Consensus Today*. A current copy could have page-one articles on how the air pollution in Los Angeles has declined to a tiny fraction of its 1960s level, thanks to cooperation among activists, industry and regulators; the reforms that allowed New York City to transform from a murder capital to one of the world's safest cities; how volunteer work is at an all-time high and charitable giving remains high despite the slow economy; how global malnutrition is at an all-time low. But if *Consensus Today* existed, no news channel or Web site would pick up the content.[13]

The result is Multiple Media Personality Disorder: a universal, low-grade nervous tension from which there may be no realistic escape, given that freedom of the press includes the freedom to sensationalize. Just wait until scary news reports are tight-beamed directly to your neocortex! Media and political scare tactics make the world seem ever more ominous when actually life is ever safer. Crime, accidents, disease, even gun violence are in long-term decline in all Western nations; longevity is rising almost everywhere. But from the commentary that surrounds us, and is ever more efficiently and cheaply delivered to us, the impression is given that everything's getting worse. There may be no solution to this: communication technology cannot be prevented from improving, while the First Amendment protects media inanity with the same power it protected publication of the Pentagon Papers.[14] We simply need to be aware that in the Sonic Boom, major segments of society will get steadily better at making people feel uneasy. It will be in their business interest to make people feel that way.

TECHNOLOGY DOESN'T RULE US YET—BUT THE NIGHT IS YOUNG

So far, technology-based economics and factory automation have made life better. Would you return to cars before seat belts and air bags? To searching for a pay phone rather than carrying a cell phone? To an urban summer without air-conditioning? To the medical care and hospital technology of any decade before the present? Most technology has become steadily safer and less wasteful; today's large suburban-style refrigerators, for example, consume about two thirds less energy than the small-box fridges of the recent past. But just because consumer technology and cheaper production have been good to us so far is no guarantee that this will always be the case. The Luddites could be right in the end. Automation could take over not only factory production but much white-collar work, completely skewing the jobs equation. If artificial intelligence becomes possible, there is no telling what might happen. That technology will backfire is a legitimate fear, and as technology continues to proliferate owing to the Sonic Boom—soon there will be computer chips in hundreds of everyday products—we may stop making fun of antitechnology sentiment. Yet how, on a practical basis, might technology be reined in? You can't pass laws against thinking.

MORE STRESS MILESTONES

The high school prom, college graduation, marriage and a death in the family were once the typical stress milestones of life. Now, with frequent job changes, a less-stable nuclear family and nonstop news of whatever is bad in the world, stress milestones may come far more frequently. We would all like a slower, more predictable life—and that's just not going to happen.

INTELLECTUALS AND BUSINESS LEADERS ABDICATE THE FATHER-FIGURE ROLE

For centuries, people have looked to the top figures of the business and intellectual worlds as father figures for society. Even if you had a good relationship with a good father, you still need other father figures, since your own father inevitably will cross the river. In recent decades, business leaders have abdicated the father-figure role—today most CEOs seem to care about little beyond cackling as they count the gold they have stolen from shareholders, workers and taxpayers—and the public has stopped believing that business leaders are people of character. For centuries, millions looked for life guidance to the examples of public-spirited intellectual figures, such as, in the twentieth century, Albert Schweitzer or Upton Sinclair. Today's intellectuals often seem arrogant, self-focused and contemptuous of the average person. One reason America has, in recent years, made icons of sports coaches is that they are among the few types of individuals in the limelight who still play the father-figure role—attempting to help others reach their goals, rather than just grabbing for themselves. Business leaders and intellectuals, who once took this role, today in many cases simply don't seem admirable, and this problem is likely to get worse.

DEINSTITUTIONALIZING INSTITUTIONS

Government, law, the military, politics, medicine, religion—all these, too, have declined in credibility in recent decades. What big institution do you really trust or believe in? Chances are the answer is "None." Up to a point, loss of belief in institutions is healthy. Just two generations ago, many men and women naively thought business leaders were always honest and government officials always had the public interest in mind. Today, free flow of information, rising levels of education and healthy doses of skepticism allow most Americans to see the countless faults and failings of big institutions. But the feeling that institutions cannot really be trusted—that they are more like necessary evils than human achievements—adds to the sense of being adrift in a world that cannot be understood. Once millions of people could say to themselves words to the effect of, "Whatever else happens, at least I belong to/work for/worship at a great institution that is widely respected and making the world a better place." Every year fewer people think this way—instead, they feel rootless and compelled to face the world alone. All this adds up to:

THE SUPER BOWL OF STRESS

The economic reinventing of much of the world will occur simultaneously with artificially triggered climate change and further decline in the public standing of politicians, intellectuals, the media, business leaders and institutions. It's going to be the Super Bowl of stress. Chances are it's going to go well. Chances are it won't be relaxing.

Four

ERIE

The city of Erie, Pennsylvania, was resisting Sonic Boom economics long before there were silicon chips—or telephones, for that matter. In the 1840s, when John Tyler was president and California not yet a state, three railroads of differing width converged at Erie, all serving the city's sheltered port inside the peninsula that is today Presque Isle State Park. A tremendous upheaval of economic change had occurred in the transportation industry in a single generation, as the stage carriage yielded to water canals, and the canals then yielded to railroads.[1] Great Lakes ships arrived at Erie to transfer grain and ore to the three competing railroads for transportation to destinations along the East Coast. Freight that needed to move from one rail line to another also came to Erie to be unloaded, then loaded again onto railcars that could ride tracks of different widths. All this unloading and reloading made for plentiful jobs. By the time the three incompatible railways met at Erie, families in this corner of Pennsylvania might have thought that if economic transformation would just come to a stop, there would always be secure work for their descendants.

Then, in the early 1850s, federal authorities began a push for

standard-gauge tracks, hard upon the success of standard-gauge legislation in Britain. If the railroads standardized, much of the unloading
and reloading would be eliminated. Fearing job losses, in 1853 the
Erie City Council passed a series of laws attempting to forbid railroad
standardization, and to authorize the town's police to sever rail lines
and destroy bridges on public property at the first sign of standard
tracks. In effect, Erie's citizens were trying to stop globalization, or at
least the nineteenth-century equivalent. Standard-gauge tracks would
bring lower shipping costs, along with faster shipping—having to
transfer cargo from one type of train to another is economically inefficient, while through-transit cuts costs. Once the Golden Spike was
driven in Utah in 1869, and transcontinental rail service established,
it became possible to travel, or send products or mail, from coast to
coast in a few days—an idea that would have seemed like sorcery a
century before.

Needless to say, standard gauge moved forward, while Erie did
not.[2] The city's attempt to prevent economic change failed, and in fact
backfired by causing railroads to circumvent the area. Buffalo, to the
north, became a new Great Lakes center for transshipment; Cumber-
land, Maryland, to the east, expanded as a rail center; and Erie entered
a period of self-imposed decline in the 1850s and 1860s. Then luck
turned back Erie's way. The Bessemer Converter, invented in 1855
and proliferating by around 1870, enabled mass manufacturing of
steel. Before these devices, steel had been a prohibitively expensive
specialty material, while iron was the common construction metal.
Once steel became affordable, builders and manufacturers wanted
steel, steel, steel and more steel for the bridges, ships, trolleys and tall
buildings of an expanding nation. Its lakeside location made Erie a
good choice for the steel boom, and for nearly a century the city enjoyed a strong economy as a steelmaking hub. Through the same period the fish dinner rose in popularity, and trawlers operated from Erie.
But by the early 1970s, Erie's nineteenth-century-style steel mills had
ceased operation, while commercial fishing was banned in the Great
Lakes, owing to water pollution caused mainly by . . . steelmaking.
The city's economy faltered again. Overall, the Pennsylvania steel industry declined more than steelmaking in other states, because Penn-

sylvania steelmakers fought for protectionist legislation from Congress; protected against competition, Pennsylvania steelmakers did not innovate, clung to outdated methods, and ultimately fell out of the business.[3] That's an important lesson to remember today, as some American and European industries demand protectionist legislation; historically, innovation has produced recoveries, while protectionism has only ensured an industry's doom. At any rate, a visitor to Erie in the 1970s might have declared the city destroyed by modernity.

Except . . . today a factory in Erie builds some of the largest, heaviest and most expensive products sold in the international marketplace. Erie's products are being snapped up by international customers as fast as they can be made, with the leading buyer being China. The product is the world's most technologically advanced, fuel-efficient railway locomotive.

In the mid-1990s, Wall Street viewed freight railroads as dinosaurs. General Motors sold off its locomotive division, and General Electric, which owned a century-old locomotive factory in Erie, considered shuttering that plant. Instead, G.E. decided to gamble on renovating the Erie engine factory while designing a new line of diesels that used less fuel, and emitted less air pollution, than existing models. The company believed that oil prices would rise, causing rail transportation to increase in importance—on a pounds-per-mile basis, trains need less fuel than trucks, so when oil prices rise, railroads become more profitable and trucks less so. General Electric also believed that strict antipollution regulations would be imposed on railroads, previously exempt from the smog-control rules such as those that govern cars.

Both projections turned out to be correct. Beginning around the turn of the twenty-first century, rising global oil prices triggered a choo-choo renaissance: shippers returned to rail, and savvy investors such as Warren Buffett began buying up rail stocks. Then, in 2004, the federal government issued strong antismog rules for locomotives. Suddenly, every rail line was signing deals for General Electric's Evolution diesel engine, a 207-ton, 4,400-horsepower behemoth that uses less fuel and emits 40 percent less pollution than previous locomotives. By 2005, the company was selling the Evolution as rapidly as the Erie factory could build the locomotives, though at about $2 million each, the new engines cost more than competitors'. But the Evolution's lower fuel consumption offered long-term savings, considering that a locomotive typically is in use for thirty years. Most U.S. and Canadian railroads placed big orders for Evolution locomotives, and the Chinese national railway ordered hundreds. Looking ahead, General Electric has begun to design an even more fuel-efficient hybrid locomotive that, like hybrid cars, would recapture some of the energy otherwise lost during braking. In the mid-1990s, Wall Street analysts believed the General Electric locomotive division would go out of business. Fifteen years later that division was setting sales records, with the three thousandth Evolution delivered in March 2009.[4]

That heavy industrial products made in the United States can still hit a home run in the international marketplace is half of the Erie story; the other half is General Electric. No company reinvents itself more often or more successfully than G.E., whose menu of home appliances, medical devices, jet engines, locomotives, movie and television entertainment, lighting systems, green-energy technology, financial services and other products reflects constant determination to sell the best possible goods while staying one step ahead of the global market. General Electric is among the world's largest corporations, posting $183 billion in revenue in 2008, and among the world's oldest large corporations. General Electric had a rough ride in the 2008–2009 recession, with its stock price falling, its dividend cut and its credit rating dropping from decades of triple-A to double-A. In March 2009, company officials held a peculiar five-hour marathon financial disclosure session in the same 30 Rockefeller Plaza theater used to stage *Saturday Night Live*—General Electric owns NBC— hoping to convince analysts and journalists that the company's capital-lending division was not a bank and did not share the kinds of problems afflicting the banking industry. This was a very G.E.-like move; rather than claiming proprietary secrecy, the company released unprecedented amounts of data about its internal details. Though General Electric's stock price remained weak, its core businesses did not: while many big corporations took losses in 2008, G.E. had a net income of $17 billion that year. General Electric has succeeded for a century though it operates in turbulent business spaces where change is ongoing. The reason is an internal culture in which new ideas are continuously dreamed up, tested, discarded or fielded. In this, General Electric may serve as an exemplar for what the Sonic Boom will require of everyone involved with private enterprise. But first, back to those choo-choos.

———

In the mid-1990s, Erie seemed headed for yet another dose of economic bad news. General Electric, the town's leading manufacturing employer, was a good company but hardly perfect: it had just built one of the all-time-clunker industrial products, the AC6000 locomotive. General Electric engineers had set a goal of producing the most powerful rail engine ever, one that cranked an incredible 6,000 horsepower. But the AC6000 proved unreliable, and reliability is crucial to the rail business. General Electric's basic idea for the AC6000 also was poorly thought through. For heavy loads, railroads often couple together three 4,000-horsepower locomotives; G.E. figured that two 6,000-horsepower units would cost less to buy and require fewer crew members. Had the company asked its customers, the railroads, before starting the project, General Electric would have learned that spreading "tractive effort" across many sets of powered wheels is essential to getting long lines of railcars up and down inclines. In many rail applications, three moderately powered engines are better than two musclebound units, making the AC6000 an answer to a question no one asked. When the megalocomotive tanked in the marketplace, Wall Street analysts urged General Electric to get out of the rail business, to concentrate instead on trendy sectors such as finance. After all, analysts claimed, not only were the engines being built in a century-old facility, everybody knew that heavy manufacturing was a dying business, while financial products were the wave of the future! By 2009, heavy manufacturing would remain a profit center for General Electric, while the company's financial division would be the source of nearly all the company's problems.

"Sometimes you need a crisis to change bad habits and old assumptions," said John Dineen, the Erie factory manager, as we walked through a 450-acre complex where no one looked twice at an entire train engine rolling through a building. "The fear that General Electric would go out of the locomotive business got everybody here at the plant to focus on competitiveness." For instance, factory hands as recently as the 1990s were still paid using the nineteenth-century "piecework" system, under which an individual benefited by maxing out his or her specific assignment, but did not care about the overall output of the factory. The plant's union agreed to switch to "standard work," the Japanese-style system in which all are equally responsible for overall factory performance. Under piecework, an employee who has a useful production idea doesn't share it, because keeping the idea to himself allows him to produce a higher piece rate than others, and thus earn more pay. Under standard work, an employee who has a useful idea immediately shares it.

Engineers converted the Erie facility from an old-style factory where everything was bolted to the floor, and process change was discouraged, to a contemporary flexible factory in which most machines are on wheels or a compressed-air base, allowing rapid rearrangement. Thousands of boxes, worktables and other detritus were removed from the factory floor to create an open feeling and, not coincidentally, to allow workers to see what their comrades were doing—or if they were goofing off. Small cranes and simple robots were positioned so that workers rapidly can swing bulky parts into position without having to wait for help from one of the ponderous overhead cranes. When an overhead crane moves in a factory, all work comes to a stop, for safety reasons; so the fewer overhead crane "picks," the less wasted time. Rather than rummage for tools and wander around the factory looking for parts, at the start of each shift a worker would receive a wheeled kit containing everything he or she needed that day.

These are "lean manufacturing" techniques pioneered by Toyota a generation ago, when the company resolved to make better cars than General Motors by revolutionizing what happened on the factory floor. Consumers care only about what a product is and what it costs, but how that product is manufactured is half of business success. One reason American industrial production lost ground relative to global competition was that stultified management and featherbedded unions resisted change on the factory floor. In 1999, when General

Electric decided to stay in the engine business and gamble on the Evolution model, it took the Erie factory ninety-two days to complete a locomotive. By 2008, the factory was building an engine in fifteen days. And though built much more rapidly than its predecessors, the Evolution has no reliability issues—just as Toyota got its foot into the door of the American market by making cars much more reliable than those on the loading docks in Detroit. Between the corporate commitment to advanced fuel-efficient technology, and a labor commitment to leaner and smarter work, in a single decade locomotive manufacturing flip-flopped from General Electric's problem child to its pride and joy. Some 40 percent of G.E.'s locomotives are shipped to China, which is rapidly building rail lines and is desperate to reduce fossil fuel use and air pollution, already owning three hundred Evolution engines and signing orders for many more. It's an urban legend that the United States only buys from China, never selling manufactured products in return.

General Electric's turnaround of its locomotive business syncs with a decision the company made in 2003—the kind of decision that may serve as an archetype for what commercial enterprises must do to stay strong in an ever-more-interconnected world. At the time, G.E. decided that rather than make incremental, tinkering changes in products, it would seek dramatic new ideas. The ideas would not be acquired from entrepreneurs or start-up firms; rather, they would be developed inside the company. And General Electric's overseas research divisions would have the same freedom to innovate as those at the company's central research complex, a huge, college-campus-like facility in Niskayuna, New York, outside Albany.

The decision to make General Electric more ideas-oriented came from Jeffrey Immelt, who attained the CEO post in 2001. Immelt has worked for G.E. his entire adult life. He said, "I started off in plastics sales, and immediately it was clear to me that we did much better selling a superior product. My next assignment was the appliances division, where things were the same—superior products sold well, the not-so-good products sold poorly regardless of price. This told me, first, that customers really know what they are buying. Second, it told me that if a company wants above-average profits, its products must be clearly better than the competition's. Not slightly better, clearly better. That made new ideas essential."

Immelt and an assistant, Beth Comstock, asked each General Electric division to propose ideas with enough sales potential that at least 8 percent of the company's annual sales growth could come from new concepts. "There was tremendous resistance at first, because inevitably some of the ideas would fail, and in a bureaucracy, managers do not want their names associated with failed projects," Comstock said. "We had to convince people that it's okay to have a failed idea, that this would not be held against them in a promotion review." Since most entrepreneurs and inventors do their initial work alone, they don't care how many failed ideas must be discarded until a good one is found, since only they know about the failures. In a big organization, by contrast, everyone knows everything and corridor gossip can be a career killer. This discourages corporate managers from swinging for the fence with a revolutionary idea, which exposes whoever backs the idea to criticism. Corporations also often base promotions on "measurables," or the completion of specific tasks by specific deadlines. Because many new ideas fail, and successful ones can't be pushed until they are ready, innovation tends not to produce measurables.

But swinging for the fences was just what Immelt and Comstock wanted. Eventually the two persuaded General Electric's internal corporate culture that incubating bold ideas would be rewarded, while making an expensive mistake would not end anyone's career. "It's okay to make a mistake and can even be a beneficial learning experience— what we don't tolerate is making the same mistake twice," Immelt says. The new-ideas initiative resulted in projects that either have already produced hot-selling products, or are likely to in the future. They include the hybrid-powered railway locomotive; a jet engine that uses less fuel and makes less noise than today's models; a magnetic-resonance image scanner that sets itself to the type of medical test being done (previous MRI machine required elaborate set-up work by radiologists); a simplified MRI scanner that costs less than previous models (intended for the developing world, the low-cost scanner may also allow many U.S. clinics to afford such devices); glowing plastic that serves as a light source; holographic storage devices that can hold hundreds of movies on a disc the size of a DVD; circuit breakers that revolutionize the half-century-old design typical to houses; advanced wind turbines for generating electricity; an extremely efficient power-generating turbine that uses less natural gas than previous models; and home curtains that absorb warmth from sunlight in winter but reflect warmth in summer. There have been dud ideas, too, of course. The appliance division backed a complicated double range that proved impossible to install in an existing kitchen without ripping out the wall, and G.E.'s own Universal Studios was aghast at a DVD engineered to crumble three days after being exposed to air. That goal was a rental movie that would not need to be driven back to the store. But the self-crumbling DVD did not test well in focus groups, and Netflix leapfrogged this particular market sector anyway.

Immelt not only encouraged free thinking and new ideas, he backed the plan with $100 million in annual research funding. A common knock against U.S. corporations is that they do not invest enough in research and development. Short-term incentive structures are the culprit. Spending for R&D can depress the current quarterly profits on which executive bonuses are based, while not yielding benefits until years down the road: many CEOs prefer to pump up a firm's current stock price, cash out their options, and leave the lack of innovation for someone else to deal with in the future. For example, during the 1980s, General Electric spent about $1.5 billion researching an unorthodox type of aviation engine called an "unducted fan," which, in the end, no aircraft maker bought.[5] That $1.5 billion might instead have been profit, added to the company's dividends and executive bonuses. Late in the 1990s, G.E. began another R&D project to develop an improved jet engine; the project had a $1 billion research budget. Wall Street analysts began saying the 1990s effort was a repeat of the unsuccessful initiative of the 1980s, and urged General Electric to cancel the project, thus boosting the company's short-term stock price. (Wall Street firms would rather see corporations seek short-term profits than long-term innovation because today's returns improve stock market numbers, justifying bonuses for Wall Street managers.) Instead G.E. stood by the 1990s research initiative, which produced an unusually fuel-efficient jet engine. In 2006, that engine was chosen to power Boeing's next generation of airliners—assuring twenty years of profits for G.E.'s aviation propulsion division. Had General Electric canceled its jet-engine research to save a little up front, the company would have lost a lot. This lesson may be increasingly important in a Sonic Boom world, where a dollar spent on research and innovation today may become a hundred dollars later, while a dollar cut from costs today will never be more than a dollar.

Roughly a century ago, General Electric made substantial research investments to develop indoor lighting and low-cost radio transmission and reception, correctly wagering that both would be future boom industries; today, G.E.'s biggest research investment is in improved energy production. "In health care, electronics and other fields there is tremendous ferment of innovation, yet in energy, everything we do is fifty years out of date," Immelt notes. General Electric's wind-energy division is already recording $4 billion in annual sales; the company is spending freely to develop over-the-horizon turbines that would be built at sea and unseen from land, solving the aesthetic objection to wind power. General Electric has developed a concept that may prove important to America's future—a system of burning coal for electric power that uses substantially less fossil fuel than current generating stations, and may reduce or even eliminate greenhouse gas emissions. There are many environmental objections to coal burning, especially that coal contains the most carbon of any fossil fuel, and thereby is a leading greenhouse-gas malefactor. In 2008, former vice president Al Gore called for the immediate worldwide elimination of coal use;[6] he might as well have called for the immediate worldwide elimination of foul language. There simply is no scenario in which the world does not mine and burn fantastic amounts of coal over the next few decades— at least if poverty is to continue declining. Rich nations such as the United States get about half their electricity from coal, and even if alternatives such as wind generation continue to grow in use, the United States will be burning very large amounts of coal indefinitely. Many developing nations, especially China, India and Indonesia, are even more coal-dependent than is the West, while having less capital to build alternative power sources such as nuclear or geothermal. Large-scale global combustion of coal is in the cards for the next few decades and cannot be wished away.

The trouble is that when it comes to producing power from coal, "everything we do is fifty years out of date." The majority of the world's coal-combustion facilities burn pulverized coal at the base of a boiler—a process that has not changed meaningfully since before World War II, and which is extremely inefficient, wasting more than half the energy value of the coal. The wasted energy means more coal must be consumed, thus increasing greenhouse emissions. Advanced combustion systems might not only reduce pollution associated with coal but also raise efficiency, so that less coal is consumed in the first place. About a decade ago, at a time when many energy-industry analysts believed coal was about to become passé, General Electric concluded that rising natural-gas prices, coupled to ever higher prices for nuclear power and the lack of a big breakthrough to make solar power affordable, meant that clean combustion of coal would be a major future business sector. So—how to do it? Oil companies have long known how to gasify coal, a process that is similar to refining petrochemicals; turning coal into a gas before combustion dramatically increases the energy efficiency of power plants. But oil companies are not in the electricity-generating business, and don't seem to want to enter it. So G.E. purchased a coal-gasification concept originally designed by Chevron, and perfected the idea until, in conjunction with the construction firm Bechtel, General Electric was ready to build advanced coal-electricity stations. Burning coal as a gas, rather than in pulverized pellets, cuts coal consumption by about 30 percent per unit of electricity generated—meaning 30 percent lower greenhouse emissions and a big cut in the pollutants that contribute to acid rain. Burning coal in gaseous form also makes it possible that all carbon dioxide can be pumped back into the ground—"sequestered," in the clunky term-of-art—eliminating greenhouse gases entirely.

You may remember the clunky term *sequestration* from the 2003 State of the Union Address, during which President George W. Bush rhapsodized about a planned government project to build a superadvanced prototype coal-fired power plant that would produce no greenhouse gases. Five years later in 2008, after $1.3 billion had been wasted and nothing built—it was, after all, a government project— Bush canceled the plan, called FutureGen.[7] One year after that, with President Barack Obama in the White House and Congress eager to spend in the name of economic stimulus, the FutureGen idea was revived with another $1 billion in appropriations. Perhaps sometime before Halley's Comet returns,[8] the FutureGen project actually will turn a spade of earth. What's maddening is that this is a case of the perfect driving out the good—while government officials of both parties bicker about how to experiment with a conjectured perfect future power plant, General Electric is ready today to build far more efficient, cleaner power plants with technology that is already available.

Coal-gasification power plants would cost about twice as much up front to build, compared to traditional pulverized-coal power plants, though would save money over the long term by using less coal: in the same way that if you paid extra to buy a high-mileage hybrid-powered car, after a couple years of buying less gasoline you'd come out ahead. Because coal-gasification plants cost more up front, most regulatory agencies (power production is regulated by states) refuse to issue permits for their construction, despite their long-term benefits. In 2008, the Virginia State Corporation Commission, which regulates electricity production, rejected an application from American Electric Power, a large utility, to build an advanced coal-gasification power plant that would cut greenhouse gas emissions by 90 percent. Virginia's government *refused* permission to build the power plant of the future! At this writing a medium-size coal-gasification generating station was under construction in Indiana by Duke Energy, a utility long considered the nation's best-run power company. General Electric was chomping at the bit to build lots of advanced coal-gasification power-generating stations; they would be good for the company, and would help restrain greenhouse emissions. If the United States imposes federal regulation on greenhouse gases, then state public-utility commissions almost certainly will allow numerous coal-gasification plants to be constructed, and G.E. once again will have a hot new piece of merchandise. This succession of events is likely to become more common in a Sonic Boom world—a company not only will need to develop a useful product, but also locate the product in the context of complex global issues, and navigate political and regulatory obstacles in order to win permission to sell.

Coal-derived electricity with much lower emissions, high-efficiency jet engines, wind turbines far out of sight at sea: all sound good. We tend to think of economic turbulence only in negative terms—of jobs lost, or the ends of familiar ways of doing things—but new economic ideas can also be positives, ushering in cleaner production, safer technology, more affordable products, new jobs in new fields. In mid-2009, General Electric decided to open two new factories in the United States, in Schenectady, New York, and Lexington, Kentucky, to build batteries for high-efficiency hybrid locomotives and to build an advanced hot-water heater that requires far less power than standard models, respectively. The company also decided to open another U.S. research center, near Detroit. The new facilities will employ more than two thousand people in high-paying jobs, and two of the three are being located in traditional union towns. Their common thread is advanced use of energy.

Energy is an economic sector where the sensible person might root for some nice turmoil, as traditional approaches cause greenhouse gases, waste resources and render much of the world reliant on Persian Gulf dictatorships. Significant aspects of the coming Sonic Boom will find their impetus in improved forms of energy production and use. Some existing jobs will be lost in the process, while many new jobs are created, and society benefits overall. Rather than obsessing about losses, as do politicians, we should look forward to the improvements. Trying to stop change did not work for Erie, Pennsylvania, in the 1840s, and will not work for any American or European city or industry today.

———

Situated in the woods along the Mohawk River, General Electric's flagship research center covers hundreds of acres in a dozen buildings. Before Immelt, engineers at the center performed their research, then sent memos up the chain to headquarters; executives rarely met the science staff. Immelt had a fancy visitors' lodge built along the riverbank. He asks executives of both G.E. and its big customers to come to the research center on a regular basis and brainstorm with the technical personnel. This, he thinks, leads to the kind of new ideas strong enough to outflank opponents in the evolving everybody-competes-with-everybody global marketplace. It has also led to a new way of thinking about thinking—the notion that industrial innovation should be spread broadly across the world, not confined to the West.

General Electric's ideas search is not confined to its U.S. divisions; the company has research centers in India, China, Germany, Qatar and, soon, Detroit. The China research center, in Shanghai, is devoting most of its budget and personnel to finding relatively inexpensive ways for Chinese power plants to burn coal with less waste and reduced emissions. The Indian research center is in Bangalore, the city that has become an embodiment of globalization owing to its customer-service call centers.[9] Some four thousand engineers and other technical staffers work in the Bangalore research center, and not just finalizing details but studying their own basic ideas. Chemical engineers in Bangalore devised Valox and Xenoy, two industrial resins that allow recycled plastic to be fashioned into material indistinguishable from virgin plastic. General Electric unveiled Valox and Xenoy in Japan, where laws mandate that cars contain recycled materials, but where buyers strongly prefer all-new products; these resins solve that problem, at least for automotive plastics. An American company uses its Indian division to devise a product first marketed in Japan—this really must be the twenty-first century. A year after Xenoy and Valox were perfected, G.E. sold its plastics division to Saudi Basic Industries, for about $12 billion. Plastics manufacturing requires petrochemicals, which Saudi Arabia obviously has; the recycling resins made G.E.'s plastics business valuable, as many countries are beginning to require recycling of industrial materials. So the full sequence was that an American company used its Indian division to devise a product first marketed in Japan, and now a Saudi company manufactures the product. Stories like this will be increasingly common.

Many Americans and Europeans might respond that globalized economics are fine so long as Americans and Europeans are the ones doing the thinking—the prestigious, high-value work—while other nations run the production lines. Yet allowing everybody in on the thinking is what will benefit the world, including Americans and Europeans. As recently as roughly twenty years ago, when China and India, the world's two largest countries, were either closed societies (China) or closed economies (India), huge amounts of available brainpower in those places went to waste. Now millions of people in China and India can get up-to-date technical, economic and political information; can communicate with anyone in the world; and have begun to traffic in ideas. Because those countries produce a higher percentage of engineers and scientists than other nations—30 percent of college degrees awarded in India and China are in the hard sciences—the world's rate of technical progress should accelerate. Immelt notes, "People think we hire Chinese and Indian engineers because they work for less. We hire Chinese and Indian engineers for who they are in their own right, because they have become the sources of good, original engineering ideas." Many Americans and Europeans, accustomed to sitting atop the economic hill, might feel that something has gone badly wrong if developing-nation engineers and managers have begun to do an important share of the world's economic thinking. Something has gone right—free economics, free speech and freedom of expression are expanding from the privileged nations to most of the globe. Everyone will be better off as a result, though there are sure to be some changes that the people living at the top of the hill won't like.

Five

LEIPZIG

Leipzig, Germany, near the eastern boundary of that nation, is a very old city that in many senses has seen it all. First documented in the year 1015 when the Holy Roman Empire reigned, during the twelfth century Leipzig began to stage an annual trade fair that is the world's oldest regular festival of commerce. Beginning around 1165, residents raised the glorious Saint Nicholas Church, which today has wings in the Romanesque, Gothic and neoclassical styles. In addition to his lifelong habit of leaving children gifts of candy, which started the legend of Santa Claus, Nicholas was the patron saint of merchants, wholesalers, pawnbrokers, prostitutes and the falsely accused, a good mix for a commercial crossroads city. Leipzig acquired a cityscape of magnificent medieval architecture, and prospered during the Reformation centuries. The University of Leipzig, one of the world's oldest, was founded in 1409. In the 1760s, Johann von Goethe, a University of Leipzig student, consumed copious amounts of wine in Auerbach's Cellar, a café still in business today, and a scene of his masterwork *Faust* involves rowdy drinking at Auerbach's. One of the continent's first rail hubs opened in Leipzig in 1839.

During World War II many of the storied medieval buildings were destroyed by firebombs, followed by Leipzig being made part of Soviet-controlled East Germany. On September 4, 1989, thousands of people gathered at Saint Nicholas Church to demand the end of the dictatorship under which they suffered. This began the anti-Communist mass movement that led two months later to the fall of the Berlin Wall, followed by the reunification of Germany. Today the city has returned to its Middle Ages status as an island of education and affluence. Porsche sports cars are manufactured in Leipzig, while Amazon and DHL have major operations there—watched over, surely, by Saint Nicholas.

Just outside Leipzig, at an abandoned military base, is Waldpolenz Solar Park, the world's largest thin-film photovoltaic power-generating facility. Basically, Waldpolenz is 275 acres of glistening solar cells lying on the ground, interrupted only by workers' access walkways and roads for tour buses. The installation makes 40 megawatts of electricity, enough to power about twenty thousand homes. That is not a huge amount in the grand scheme, about 5 percent as much electricity as made by the undamaged nuclear reactor that still functions at Three Mile Island in Pennsylvania. Needless to say, the facility only runs in daylight, while power is needed on a twenty-four-hour basis. But Waldpolenz is on the leading edge of many types of changes to the global economy, changes involving how energy is produced, priced and used. To a coal miner, Waldpolenz represents something ominous. To most people the facility represents something terrific: an eventual future in which much if not most of the world's power is produced without fossil fuel. It is fitting that such a facility should rise not far from the history-packed streets of a thousand-year-old city.

Germany would seem a poor candidate for solar power, given its perpetually overcast weather. Solar power can be generated in cloudy conditions, just not as well as in full sunlight. A solar cell in Germany will produce about two thirds as much electricity as would the same unit in Arizona, but since power costs more than twice as much in Germany as in the American southwest, solar alternatives may still be desirable beneath Deutschland's clouds. In fact, overcast Germany is the world's leader in production of electricity from solar conversion. In the same way that Japan became an economic power despite having no petroleum, Germany is a solar power despite having relatively few sunny days.

Resources are nice, but a lesson of the Sonic Boom is that being smart about what you have is more important than what you have. As Mariah Blake has written, "Already Germany, which is about as sunny as Juneau, Alaska, is home to almost half the world's solar generating capacity," with 15 percent of the nation's electrical grid supplied either by solar or wind power.[1] Germany made a national policy decision to reduce fossil-fuel use, and nuclear power is extremely unpopular there (though zero-emission nuclear generation has caused no problems in neighboring France, which draws nearly all its electricity from uranium). To maximize the appeal of solar power, Germany allows any entrepreneur, or any homeowner, who places solar converters on the roof or anywhere else to sell the electrons produced to the power grid at about 70 cents per kilowatt hour, quite a high price. This is a subsidy—fossil-generated power sells for 30 to 40 cents per kilowatt hour in Germany, and for much less in the United States—but the decentralized concept of allowing anyone whose home or business generates power to sell it to the grid at an attractive price has led thousands of Germans to become solar entrepreneurs. The solution is far from perfect—central power stations must still be standing by to generate the electricity that solar users require in darkness, while ratepayers are charged more than they would be if not for the expensive solar inputs. But Germany's approach has given the nation a head start toward a postfossil future. This is a disruptive change, though a beneficial disruptive change; and a lot more beneficial disruptive changes await us in the near economic future.

"The energy market is one of the largest in the world, yet the least innovative," says Robert Metcalfe, the inventor of the Ethernet, founder of 3Com and now a Massachusetts venture capitalist. "Many of the products are not what people want, many of the markets exhibit no genuine competition, and the oil industry especially is an oligopoly. In the 1960s, when AT&T had a cartel over telephone service, the phone market was poorly served, there was no competition, phones were attached to the wall and very expensive to use, and the big players claimed no other situation was possible. A bunch of inventors, entrepreneurs and venture capitalists attacked AT&T—and look what happened. Now phone service is far cheaper, better and even uses fewer resources, since it's all low-power devices based on miniature parts. Energy is ripe for the same sorts of fundamental change that results in better quality at lower price, even as we eliminate waste."

One new idea Metcalfe backs is to employ the carbon dioxide released by fossil-fuel burning to grow algae, which would be converted to biodiesel for trucks or biobased aviation fuel. Sound ridiculous? When dark, gooey stuff first was pumped from the ground in Titusville, Pennsylvania, in 1859, if you'd told anyone alive then that by 2009 the world would be burning 80 million barrels of petroleum daily, they would have responded, "That's ridiculous." And not just owing to the volume involved. Colonel Edwin Drake, who sunk the wells at Titusville, was searching for oil to sell as a patent medicine. That petroleum could be burned for energy hadn't occurred to anyone at the time. To a power plant, carbon dioxide is a pollutant; to algae, it is a nutrient. Metcalfe, one of the most accomplished inventors of our day, is trying to figure out a cost-effective way to grow algae rapidly, then use it as a feedstock for liquid fuel: algae molecules convert into hydrocarbons more efficiently than corn or soybean molecules convert into ethanol. Tests conducted by Pratt & Whitney, which builds engines for military and civilian jets, show algae-derived fuel would not only be greenhouse-neutral—the algae subtracts from the air the same amount of carbon it releases when burned for power—but also have higher energy content than some petroleum-based jet fuels.[2] If Metcalfe can make large-scale algae production affordable, he estimates it would be practical to add algae racks to about one thousand of the world's coal- and natural-gas-fired power plants, reducing their greenhouse footprints while producing fuel that replaces petroleum. Depending on how oil prices move and what kinds of carbon-emission regulations are enacted, a power plant that uses its carbon dioxide to make algae for biodiesel or aviation fuel might be more profitable than a conventional generating station. So—three cheers for scum!

Many new power plants need to be built around the world, and it's important they be as clean and as close to carbon-neutral as possible. If you're worried about global warming now, just wait until 2050, by which time global energy consumption is expected to double, even as-suming major strides in energy efficiency.[3] All projections point to a doubling of global energy need by mid-century,[4] mainly owing to developing-world growth: because developing-world growth is a must, to reduce poverty, we can't conserve our way out of this problem. Global power production must rise. This means there will be two tremendous challenges happening simultaneously: to increase energy supply, yet reduce greenhouse-gas emissions while doing so.

Making more of something while generating less pollution is cer-tainly possible. Over the last few decades, the U.S. petrochemical in-dustry has increased its output—not by shifting production overseas, but rather by making more petrochemicals in America—while halving toxic emissions. But the double-challenge nature of the energy future means a lot of upheaval is coming. Some power utilities, especially ones wedded to old-style production, may go out of business. Lots more surface mining of coal may occur in the Rocky Mountain states, bringing land-use problems to what are now unspoiled areas—Wyoming's coal contains fewer pollutants than West Virginia's, which will make it increasingly desirable. Mining of oil shale and tar sands, already happening in Alberta, Canada, may happen in the United States if oil prices rise again. True competition may come to electricity production, presenting consumers with options as confusing as cell phone plans. Things we currently take for granted, such as the local gas station always having fuel for sale, might not always be so. Con-gestion pricing of roads may cause cars to be left in driveways, creat-ing a new impetus to invest in more mass-transit systems. Suburban developments may be designed for energy efficiency and reduced auto use, causing new areas of the United States to look more like Europe and less like a set for *Desperate Housewives*. Because power costs least in the middle of the night, businesses may shift activities, even office work, into the wee hours.

Big changes in the energy economy will be disconcerting. Big, dis-concerting changes also represent a tremendous opportunity! Gener-ating more energy while consuming less oil and emitting less carbon dioxide is a *knowledge* challenge. The reason artificially triggered cli-mate change seems unstoppable today is that the knowledge that will be used to stop this problem does not yet exist. Based on what is known today, climate change might be headed off only by drastic steps such as gasoline and electricity rationing. As the researchers Stephen Pacala and Robert Solocow of Princeton University have shown, even using extremely optimistic assumptions based on current knowledge—fifty times more wind turbines than today, twice as many nuclear power plants, doubling the m.p.g. ratings of all the world's cars—greenhouse-gas buildup in the atmosphere will continue for decades.[5] It would be nice to think that existing green energy forms can solve climate-change problems, but then, it would be nice to think a chest of doubloons is buried in the backyard. Even best-case scenarios show that solar, wind, geothermal, nuclear and other existing technologies either can't be expanded fast enough to impact overall greenhouse-gas accumulation trends, or are so expensive as to be impractical. Globally, existing green energy forms produce only about 1 percent of the world's power. Even if existing forms are expanded very successfully, that amount is likely to increase only to 3 or 4 percent.

But that's where the opportunity comes in. Clean energy may be the number-one economic growth opportunity of the next few decades. As all nations grapple with transforming their energy economies, the American styles of brainpower, technical skill, entrepreneurial enthusiasm and can-do spirit will be especially essential. Greenhouse gases are likely to be regulated inside the United States, if not this year, then soon. Once American entrepreneurs and engineers invent the technology and devise the business strategies that make greenhouse controls practical, other countries will adopt these ideas and strategies voluntarily.

Today smog and acid rain are declining almost everywhere in the world, including much of China—you should have seen how bad the smog was in Beijing ten years *before* the 2008 Olympics—yet no international treaties govern or even mention smog and acid rain. In the early 1990s, the United States began a "cap-and-trade" system to reduce acid-rain emissions by allowing power-plant managers, rather than federal regulators, to decide among themselves which facilities should make cuts at what rates. Since then, acid-rain levels in the United States have declined by more than half, and the cost of the program has been far lower than projected. In 1991, petroleum chemists in California discovered a way to "reformulate" gasoline to remove, at the refinery level, pollutants that would otherwise end up in auto exhaust. Reformulated gasoline became mandatory in the state in 1992, throughout the United States in 1993, and in Mexico in 2002. Smog levels have been declining in these places since, with Los Angeles today averaging a hundred fewer ozone-alert days per year than it did in the 1970s. Because the technical aspects of reformulation can now be duplicated cheaply, China, India and other developing nations are in the process of modifying refineries to produce cleaner fuels. Diesel fuel was reformulated in the United States beginning in 2006: urban soot has begun declining as a result, and this may reduce asthma incidence. Reformulating gasoline not only worked to reduce smog, it is also not expensive.

Because customers don't see the chemical improvement in the fuel they buy, nor can they see that power plants now emit much less acid rain, low-cost programs to reduce smog and acid rain do not receive the credit they deserve. Polls show that most Americans think air pollution is getting worse; in fact air pollution has been declining for a quarter-century, even in Los Angeles and Houston. Other governments have noticed that smog and acid rain can be reduced at low cost, which is why many nations, including China, are putting anti-smog and anti-acid-rain rules into effect voluntarily, because they realize it is in their self-interest to do so. If Americans understood that smog and acid rain are declining, cheaply and without harm to the economy, they would be more likely to support the next step, greenhouse-gas controls. And if engineers and entrepreneurs devise ways to reduce greenhouse gases cheaply, the world may adopt these ideas voluntarily, too. There may never be a need for a 192-party ultra-complex Daughter of Kyoto treaty, because once the necessary knowledge exists, nations will control greenhouse gases of their own volition.

———

Customers worldwide spend about $7 trillion a year on energy, roughly the GDP of Japan and Germany combined. By way of comparison, the entire U.S. "information industry"—news media, Hollywood, Internet providers, television networks—had a little over $1 trillion in revenue in 2007. The sheer amount of money in energy makes it a tempting target for economic innovation, yet despite the vastness of the energy industry, energy innovation remains rare. The petroleum economy—drilling, refining, distribution through filling stations—has not changed meaningfully since the 1930s. All nuclear power reactors in use in the United States were completed before 1975, and employ technology that is antiquated compared to what's possible today. Utility companies keep building old-fashioned pulverized-coal power plants, rather than the far more efficient, and lower-polluting, coal-gas plants that are possible. The technology for transmitting electricity has barely changed since Thomas Edison and George Westinghouse duked it out over whether to use direct or alternating current—which is significant because nearly a third of electricity vanishes to transmission losses. Major modernization of global energy production would be needed even if climate change weren't on the horizon.

One reason the energy economy changes so little is capital requirements. Petroleum companies and electric utilities have invested heavily in the current gasoline-station and central-generating power infrastructure, and so are reluctant to switch systems. This isn't a sinister plot, just economics. A reason the Internet expanded so quickly is that relatively little capital investment was required for the hardware, and the software, once designed, could be copied for free. By contrast, the energy economy is entirely based on hardware, most of it big, complex and costly. Edison favored the transmission of electricity via direct current, but the materials of the late nineteenth century could carry direct current only about a mile; so alternating current was chosen, even though it is inefficient. Today materials exist that can carry direct current long distances, meaning that transmission losses could be eliminated, which would allow the disconnection of countless power plants: but building an all-new energy-transmission grid would be fantastically expensive. The International Energy Agency estimates that in order to reduce greenhouse gases at the same time world energy production doubles, $45 trillion will need to be invested in the global energy economy by 2050.[6] To reach $45 trillion by then, 2 to 3 percent of the world's economy would need to be devoted, annually, to capital-

izing energy projects. That is a ginormous amount of money. The nature of energy dollar figures should draw ever more smart people into
this field, improving the odds of technical advances. But the capital
obstacles mean that even if things go well, it will take decades to re-
build the industry around cleaner production. In 2007, American venture funds placed about $2 billion with entrepreneurs and start-up
firms pursuing green energy ideas. That's a lot of money to you and me,
but a token amount compared to the capital requirement for restructuring a major industry.

The improvements that are possible using existing technology are
the obvious first step. The National Academy of Sciences said in 2002
that cars and SUVs could be big, safe and comfortable and yet average
about thirty miles per gallon, rather than the current U.S. average of
about twenty miles per gallon, if existing fuel-conservation technology
were applied and horsepower reduced. Horsepower is the overlooked
aspect of the gas-guzzling problem, in the United States at least.
Twenty years ago, the average new passenger vehicle sold in the
United States had 120 horsepower. For 2008, the figure was 230
horsepower, almost a doubling. Not only is rising horsepower the root
cause of America's terrible m.p.g. numbers, it is the root cause of road
rage, as that horsepower is used for running stoplights and cutting
other drivers off. Today even family cars such as the Ford Taurus or
Toyota Camry have so much horsepower that they can achieve zero to
sixty in under seven seconds, which is the acceleration rate of a 1960s
Corvette. Sensible reductions in horsepower would reduce gasoline
consumption, lower the price of oil, reduce greenhouse gas emissions,
and make the roads a less hostile environment in which driving is less
stressful.

Existing conservation technologies such as the compact fluorescent lightbulb can make helpful reductions in energy waste, considering incandescent lightbulbs—a nineteenth-century design!—are just
5 percent efficient, wasting 95 percent of the power they draw. Australia has outlawed the sale of incandescent bulbs, requiring high-
efficiency lighting; America will ban the outdated bulbs in 2014.
Here's a factoid you may not believe, but which is true—replacing just
one Edison-era lightbulb in every American household with a compact

fluorescent would be the equivalent, in greenhouse terms, of taking 1 million cars off the road. Old-fashioned lightbulbs cost 75 cents each, compact fluorescents about $4 each. That makes the latter seem more expensive; but using a fraction of the power and lasting five to ten times as long, the compact fluorescent is cheaper overall. And if you don't like compact fluorescents because you think they produce inferior light—just as no one can tell Coke from Pepsi in a blind taste test, when focus groups are shown the light of incandescent bulbs and compact fluorescent lamps without being told which comes from which, they can't tell the difference.[7] At any rate, light-emitting diodes or metal-halide bulbs that use barely any power may fairly soon supplant the compact fluorescent design.

Today's U.S. coal-fired power plants are 37 to 40 percent efficient—meaning 40 percent of the energy value in the coal becomes electricity—while typical Chinese power plants are just 20 percent efficient. Advanced-design power plants that convert coal into a gas, the kind discussed in chapter four, can achieve about 60 percent efficiency. If all new coal-fired power plants were the 60 percent efficient type, an important step would be taken against greenhouse-gas accumulation. Those pre-1975 vintage nuclear reactors? New designs are simpler from an engineering standpoint, use less uranium per megawatt, and are "passively safe"—even if their cooling systems fail, they can't melt down. Passively safe nuclear reactors generate electricity without greenhouse-gas emissions and without any threat to public health. The United States has not commissioned a new power-generating reactor station during the lifetime of Britney Spears: the country must move beyond nuclear-power phobia and start producing more clean electricity from uranium. As the science writer Gwyneth Cravens argues, "More progress can be made against greenhouse gases in less time by expanding nuclear power than by any other step."[8]

Suppose, for example, the "plug-in hybrid" car, a concept currently exciting interest because it promises the equivalent of 50 m.p.g., is successful. Plug-in hybrids will recharge overnight. The economic drawback of the nuclear power reactor is that for engineering reasons, it must run at the same output all the time, unlike fossil-powered generators, which can crank up during the day then throttle down when most people go to bed. That nuclear reactors must run at full power even when full power isn't needed is the primary reason—not environmental lawsuits, as claimed in political chatter—that nuclear power usually is more costly than fossil power. Aha! Plug-in hybrid cars will draw their power at night, exactly when nuclear generators have excess capacity. The passively safe nuclear power plant and the plug-in hybrid automobile, needing electricity at night, may be a match made in energy-reform heaven.

As for solar power, the electricity value of the sunlight that falls on Earth's surface works out to four thousand times the power now used by humanity; tapping even a fraction of that sunlight could drastically reduce fossil-fuel needs.[9] Capitalism is not conspiring to prevent you from having solar power. It's the other way around: capitalism is trying like crazy to bring solar to your home and office—the first firm able to do this affordably will find El Dorado in profit terms. The key word is *affordable*.

———

"All I need is one percent of this market to become huge," Nanosolar founder Martin Roscheisen shouted above construction of the company's first factory, in San Jose, California. Workers in hard hats bustled in all directions. Pallets of supplies were stacked about—rolls of steel, tanks with bright labels warning of liquid nitrogen. Roscheisen continued, "If my ideas impact just one percent of a seven-trillion-dollar industry, that will be huge, huge." He meant both in dollar terms and in a cultural sense.

Trees and flowers convert sunlight into biological electricity, then use the energy to make carbohydrates; if the lilies of the field can do it, why can't high technology? About a century ago, researchers figured out how to convert sunlight directly to electricity: Albert Einstein's Nobel Prize was not for his two theories of relativity, but for becoming, in 1905, the first person to explain the photoelectric effect. For many decades, engineers have made photocells for special applications such as providing electricity to spacecraft, or in rural locations remote from power lines, but price has always ruled solar cells out for general use. Today the retail price of electricity in the United States is 8 to 20 cents per kilowatt hour. In the 1970s, when the first oil crunch came and futurists began to extol solar, solar power was up to $5 per kilowatt hour, stated in today's money—orders of magnitude higher than conventional power. By the 1990s, solar-cell costs had fallen to perhaps $1 per kilowatt hour—too high to be practical. Right now solar power costs 40 to 60 cents per kilowatt hour—still high, but down enough to make production at Germany's subsidized 70-cent rate an attractive proposition. What's important is the trend: solar costs steadily have declined.

Much of what we take for granted today—television, cell phones, air travel, antibiotics—initially was rare and costly, then became cheap and common. Because solar cells employ silicon, the critical ingredient in electronic chips, there seemed a potential for solar-cell costs to fall as spectacularly as the cost of electronics. By about the year 2000, General Electric, British Petroleum, and a number of venture-funded start-ups were racing to find the affordable solar cell.

Nanosolar's core business idea is to make solar cells using copper indium gallium diselenide—it's about time this book contained a phrase as impressive as "copper indium gallium diselenide"—which is a less expensive formula than that employed in previous kinds of photocells, then to print the solar semiconductors in sheets rather than piece by piece.[10] This concept, which Roscheisen's engineers devised, trades off performance for cost. Solar cells made by Nanosolar convert about 15 percent of the energy value of sunlight into electricity, versus 18 or 19 percent for the best current cells and a theoretical value that's somewhat higher. I visited British Petroleum's facility in Frederick, Maryland, which makes 18-percent-efficient solar cells. Laser engraving and monocrystalline chemistry are involved; workers wearing surgical masks lifted the cells off the production line one by one, touching them delicately. BP's solar cells produce more power than Nanosolar's—but cost more, are shipped in flats that require elaborate handling, and shatter easily. Nanosolar's output is spools of solar cells, similar to big rolls of Scotch tape and designed so that construction workers can install them without special precautions against breakage. They don't provide ideal output, but they don't break easily, and the price is lower than for other solar cells. Even so, power from Nanosolar cells costs at least 40 cents per kilowatt hour, well more than a customer would pay for electricity generated using fossil fuel. That means Nanosolar cells make financial sense only if they are subsidized, or in places where they can be used to generate peak power. California utilities, for example, charge customers more for peak power than for baseline power, and peak demand tends to come on hot sunny days, which is when solar cells function best.

Energy reformers have been rooting for one of the start-up solar companies—Nanosolar, First Solar, SolFocus, there are others—to make a photocell cheap enough that people will want it solely to save on electricity costs, regardless of government action or climate concerns. Once there are solar cells that make economic sense on their own, homeowners and businesses will buy them voluntarily, and no special programs will be needed. Nanosolar seemed as likely to reach the cost breakthrough as any firm, because the company seemed to have everything. The product idea is good. The backing is high-status—Nanosolar was bankrolled by Benchmark, the venture-capital firm that made billions on eBay; by Mohr Davidow, a venture-capital firm with a track record of picking winning ideas; and by Lawrence Page and Sergey Brin, the founders of Google.[11] But pure-commercial solar has not happened yet. Nanosolar's first large orders were shipped to a utility in Germany, drawn there by the country's subsidy. In 2008, California's Pacific Gas & Electric signed contracts, with OptiSolar and SunPower, for the first really big photovoltaic solar facility in the United States—making 800 megawatts of electricity, about the output of a standard coal-fired power plant. The PG&E solar power will cost 40 cents per kilowatt hour, again too high for pure-commercial justification, but also again following the trend of gradually declining cost.

Solar enthusiasts look to the moment when cells are practical and affordable enough to go on the roofs of homes, allowing individual homeowners to "get off the grid" and stop making payments to big central utilities. After all, there's no requirement that a person have power lines attached to a house. If you could make your own watts from sunlight or some other way, you could ring up the utility monopoly and say, "Remove your wires from my property, please." Then you wouldn't be patronizing fossil power and you would be safe against future utility rate increases—because you'd have no monthly electricity bill. Sounds sweet. But in the 1970s and 1980s, many homeowners were burned when they spent huge sums to have first-generation solar roofs installed, only to find the power output poor and the systems failure-prone. Various ideas for storing household energy when the sun was down—banks of car batteries, thermal systems—were nonstop headaches. Someday homes, offices and stores in perpetually sunny areas such as Arizona will power themselves using cost-effective solar roofs, while in cloudy places such as Leipzig or Boston, solar roofs will reduce though not eliminate grid-power needs. But Nanosolar can't make such products cost-effectively yet, and neither can anyone else.

This leaves solar entrepreneurs and inventors with a problem common in the realm of business innovation—if an idea seems promising but resists becoming practical, should you give up or keep losing money in hopes your luck will turn? "The very first entrepreneurs to an idea are often unsuccessful, they burn out trying to make an immature idea work, then a second- or third-generation effort is the one that makes the idea profitable," says Patricia Cloherty, who became a venture capitalist in the late 1960s, when the field was exotic and women were nearly unknown. (Cloherty has a résumé typical of venture-capital life—she backed Apple early, earning herself a small fortune, but passed on ground-floor investing in FedEx, which she thought was a crazy idea that would never work.) What's now Oracle Corporation, which in 1977 had the basic idea for what's now the networked database, struggled for years to make its concepts useful; when in 1984 Sequoia Capital, a venture firm, kept the start-up from folding with an infusion of cash, analysts thought Sequoia poured a large sum of money down the drain. By 2008, Oracle had $22 billion in revenue, and those who held its early stock had become wealthy. Then again, hundreds of millions of dollars were invested from 1994 to 2001 trying to develop the company that, at the end, was called Excite@Home, and which promised to deliver an incredibly revolutionary—well, it was never clear what, exactly. Investors kept pouring capital into Excite@Home even as it foundered, and lost their shirts when the company folded.

So should solar-power entrepreneurs and inventors keep pressing

on, hoping someday to have the product that stands the energy industry on its head? When international markets were less unpredictable,
such decisions were easier to make. Increasingly, such decisions will
be more vexing.

———

Vexing choices are not in short supply. How much, for example, should
policymakers or entrepreneurs invest in wind energy, ethanol, fuel
cells or sci-fi-style power? You probably wouldn't guess that Texas is
America's number-one state for wind power. The Lone Star State has
about 7,000 megawatts of electricity-generation capacity from wind,
about twice the output of Arizona's Palo Verde, the largest U.S. nuclear
reactor station. California and Iowa also produce significant amounts
of wind-generated electricity. California has areas with steady, nearly
year-round winds—including the Altamont Pass region you may have
seen in adventure movies—while Texas and Iowa have large stretches
of pool-table-flat farmland or rangeland, ideal for wind turbines. Many
people complain about the aesthetics of wind towers, and some worry
the turbines kill birds and bats. (Bats are not popular, but are a lynch-
pin species because they control insects.) Farmers love wind turbines,
however, because they generate both power and extra income.

Expect to see more wind farms with each passing year: the Department of Energy has estimated the United States could meet as much
as 20 percent of its electricity needs using wind generation. General
Electric, the leading American manufacturer of wind turbines, has
opened factories in Iowa and South Dakota to make wind-turbine
components; a Danish company called Glasfiber is building an
Arkansas factory to make wind-turbine blades. Denmark is the country most committed to wind energy, and has already probably maxed
out its wind potential, not quite reaching 20 percent of its electricity
baseload.

In 2005, the United States made a commitment for a fivefold increase in ethanol production; if this happens, America will pass Brazil
as the world's leading ethanol producer. Rising demand for corn to
convert into ethanol caused food prices to spike for a while in 2008,
while many investors, including the billionaire Bill Gates, put money

into ethanol start-ups. Don't be surprised if ethanol has a short life span as everyone's favorite green energy solution. Corn-based ethanol is heavily subsidized by payments to farmers, tax exemptions to oil companies that blend ethanol into fuel, and trade barriers against cheaper imported ethanol.[12] Corn requires substantial inputs of petroleum (as fuel and fertilizer) to grow. The point is hotly disputed by specialists, but at least some studies suggest that corn-based ethanol is a net loser for energy—more energy is used in creating a gallon of ethanol than is released when the ethanol is burned as fuel. The economics of sugar-based ethanol as grown in Brazil are better than the economics of corn-based ethanol, but most nations have a limited amount of territory on which sugar grows, if any. Land, in turn, may be the ultimate worry about ethanol. Topsoil in farm regions is a precious resource that may deplete faster than fossil fuels. Making corn ethanol effectively trades topsoil for small reductions in petroleum imports. That may not be a smart trade.

If ethanol can be made from dwarf trees or perhaps from the perennial grass *Miscanthus giganteus,* that's a different story, as both grow without any petroleum input. The promise of a biofuel grown from something other than corn or sugar has in recent years caused politicians of all stripes to stumble to pronounce the tongue-twister "cellulosic ethanol." Researchers and entrepreneurs are trying to develop enzymes that will convert trees or tall grasses into ethanol. After cellulose, lignin is the next most common polymer in the plant kingdom, and some researchers are pursuing ethanol made from lignin. If there's a breakthrough, a tree-based biofuel might be greenhouse-neutral, as new trees while growing would subtract from the atmosphere the same amount of carbon dioxide as would be added when a tree-based biofuel burns.

In theory a benign energy economy could be structured around hydrogen, the cleanest fuel—in a "fuel cell," hydrogen and oxygen combine to release electricity and water, with no other by-products. Today hydrogen is made from fossil fuels and the fuel cells themselves are fantastically expensive, leaving a hydrogen economy a blue-sky idea. But someone may invent an affordable fuel cell, and in theory lots of nuclear reactors, or wide desert areas covered with solar cells, could make so much extra electricity that generating hydrogen from water would become practical, and then hydrogen could be used as a fuel in cars or buildings. A major increase in electricity availability would be needed for hydrogen to be a common fuel, as it takes a lot of wattage to split the two Hs in H_2O away from the one O. As this book was headed to press, researchers at the Massachusetts Institute of Technology reported they had found a catalyst that lowers the power requirement for splitting hydrogen out of water.[13] If hydrogen could be made from water relatively cheaply, the hydrogen-powered vehicle might someday happen. And if cars ran on hydrogen, at that point the traffic jam would become a permanent feature of the human experience, since there would no longer be any environmental objection to cars.

Even if an affordable hydrogen-based economy becomes possible, it would require hundreds of billions of dollars to build the infrastructure of a hydrogen-energy economy. Very large amounts of capital would also be needed if ocean-current or deep-thermal power production becomes practical. Waves slap endlessly; their motions can be used to spin a turbine, and thus converted into electricity. Warmth from the heated rock found two to three miles below Earth's surface in many parts of the world could drive turbines. Both these fossil-fuel-free, greenhouse-gas-free energy options work on paper, though tremendous capital costs would be entailed in bringing them to common use.

Within your lifetime, hot-fusion energy production may become possible, and potentially breathtaking capital costs would be entailed in constructing a fusion economy. However expensive, such an investment could solve society's energy needs on a permanent basis, as no uranium is needed by a fusion reactor.[14] Within your lifetime, space solar power may become practical. The energy value of sunlight in space is thirty times higher than for sunlight that has passed through the atmosphere and reached the ground. Giant solar collectors in orbit might beam energy to Earth's surface, probably as microwaves. Like hot fusion, space solar would be tremendously expensive to put into operation—construction of a space solar electricity economy would be the most expensive public-works project ever. But if it worked, once the system was built, again society's energy needs would be solved on a permanent basis with no greenhouse gases, no smog, no use of fossil resources.[15] Someday children might ask, "Mommy, why did people worry about energy?" Someday the descendants of contemporary oil sheiks may wish their ancestors had sold every last drop of crude while someone still wanted the stuff.

———

Another prospect for a new energy economy sounds spooky, but could be welcome—"synthetic biology." Every college chemistry student at some point has marveled that carbohydrates are similar to hydrocarbons. Plants use photosynthesis to convert sunlight, water and carbon dioxide into carbohydrates; imagine if that process could be tweaked just a bit, and hydrocarbons made instead. Richard Newton, who died in 2007, was for years the dean of engineering at the University of California at Berkeley, a school that is among the world's leading sources of engineering innovations. Shortly before his death, Newton told me, "Synthetic biology will be the most important advance since silicon chips. Manipulating microorganisms to make them produce desired compounds will enable antimalaria doses that cost ten cents instead of ten dollars, so antimalarial drugs become affordable throughout Africa. And synthetic biology may allow society to use microorganisms to make fuels and petrochemical products at a fraction of the cost and environmental consequences of today."

Researchers at Berkeley are working on plants whose cellulose or lignin would break down easily into ethanol. The hydrocarbons in gasoline are medium-length by the standards of molecules, whereas ethanol molecules are short-chain—Berkeley researchers are trying to engineer yeast that will make ethanol with longer molecules, so ethanol performs more like gasoline. (Today's ethanol has only about two thirds the energy value of petroleum fuel.) Beyond this it is conceivable, though far from certain, that plants could be altered so that they grow hydrocarbons directly: fuel would then become a crop.

And why does electricity need to originate in a giant generation facility many miles from the user, then shipped through miles of costly, unsightly overhead lines? Why not electricity cooked at home? A cen-

tury ago, steam for home and office heating was made at central facilities and piped to customers: the advent of the safe, affordable furnace
rendered at-home and at-office heating more efficient, as users made
only the amount of heat they actually needed. Originally only central
steam boilers had been practical; once individual furnaces were practical, building heating became cheaper and less wasteful. The central-
power-station concept arose because a century ago, electricity was
practical only when generated by very large spinning devices. Should
the "fuel cell" become affordable, that would change. Natural gas or
hydrogen would be piped or delivered to homes, offices or schools; end
users would generate only as much electricity as they actually needed.
Don't be surprised if, within a few decades, new homes and other
structures kiss the power grid good-bye, using a combination of roof
solar cells and on-site generation of their own electricity. This could
lead to significant economic dislocation—workers laid off at power
plants combined with job growth in the on-site fuel-cell maintenance
profession. There would be change and insecurity. And society would
become better off.

————

If it's really true that $45 trillion will be invested in energy infrastruc-
ture by 2050, then it is hard to imagine how there could be more incentive for inventors, engineers, entrepreneurs, venture capitalists and
business thinkers to charge into this sector. Cut a 0.001 percent slice
from a $45 trillion pie and you will be as rich as Croesus! Neverthe-
less, despite the incredible incentives already built into the energy sector, there are calls for a "new Manhattan Project" of energy research
funded by tax subsidies.

Even if the swelling federal deficit were not an issue, public subsidies for energy investment are neither needed nor wise. Imagine if,
in the year 1990, the government had decided on a "new Manhattan
Project" to devise portable telephones. Today no one would have a
portable phone because the project would be behind schedule and
over budget; the prototype portable phone would weigh 20 pounds and
be designed to bounce signals off supersonic jets circling over cities;
and applying for a portable phone number would be a five-year

process. The reason the inexpensive cell phone went from nonexistent to ubiquitous in a mere decade is that the government had nothing to do with it—cell technology and marketing were driven by inventors, entrepreneurs and financial backers seeking profit. Government should protect the country, the environment and the poor, and enforce rights: these are valid, important roles. Engineers and businesspeople should be the ones to solve technical and economic problems, such as energy reform.

The less the federal government spends on energy research subsidies, the higher the chances green energy will succeed! But even assuming green energy does succeed, more upheaval is coming, because we will be reinventing the energy sector at the same time climate change and Sonic Boom economic change are happening.

Six

ARLINGTON

Though Washington, D.C., the Rome of our era, sits within view on the opposite bank of the Potomac River, the downtown of Arlington, Virginia, manages to be nondescript. The office-tower streets of Arlington are the kind of generic business zone that can be found in any metropolitan area. One of the many nondescript offices of Arlington houses the National Venture Capital Association, representing perhaps the largest and most important economic interest group of which few are aware. The NVCA's headquarters look out not onto the Jefferson Monument or the U.S. Capitol but onto an ordinary traffic-clogged road. Venture-backed companies generate about $2.3 trillion in annual revenue, almost the size of the federal budget, yet probably most people who work in the building where the National Venture Capital Association is located don't even know it is there. Most likely not one Washington power broker, media pundit or member of Congress in a hundred could tell you what NVCA stands for or who runs the organization. Yet if the global economy is to continue to grow, the "venture sector"—independent funds that back new ideas—must be important.

In 2007, companies founded by entrepreneurs backed by venture capitalists provided 10.4 million U.S. jobs, about a tenth of private-sector employment that year.[1] Venture-backed Home Depot had 355,000 U.S. employees, venture-backed FedEx had 275,000 U.S. employees, other venture-backed firms such as Google, Cisco and Apple employed tens of thousands in the United States and elsewhere. The $2.3 trillion generated in the United States by venture-backed companies in 2007 was about 18 percent of the country's GDP; the sum exceeded the entire GDP of France. Between 2003 and 2006, sales by venture-backed U.S. firms rose by 12 percent, compared to an overall sales rise by U.S. firms of 7 percent in that period; jobs created by venture-backed firms rose by 4 percent, compared to a 1 percent rise in job creation by all firms combined. California, America's cutting-edge state in practically every category, is also the top state for entrepreneurs and venture capitalism—with the most new business start-ups, the most venture-capital firms, and in 2007, 2.4 million jobs in companies that were in their formation stage backed by venture capital. In addition to fostering growth and job creation, the venture sector backs little-guy firms, and we all love to hear of little guys running rings around big guys. A generation ago, only a slight fraction of the research and development conducted in the United States was conducted by companies of fifty or fewer employees. Today more than 20 percent of R&D happens at small independent firms. That shift of basic thinking away from giant corporations or government agencies, toward nimble little companies (invariably with zoomy names) where everyone on the payroll knows everyone else, has benefited economic growth, and could not have happened without nimble little venture-capital firms.

The acceleration of economic change has numerous underpinnings, including modern communication and personal freedom that allow ever more brains worldwide to work on economic questions, and advances in technology that make it ever cheaper and ever faster for electronics-based ideas to copy and distribute themselves. But another factor is that in recent decades it has become easier for someone with an invention or an innovative business concept to find backing from investors who are willing to gamble on losing their entire stake in return for the chance of a spectacular payday. As the Sonic Boom arrives and the world grows more prosperous, there will be more capital that investors (whether individuals or pension funds and endowments) can put behind new ideas; the more new ideas that are funded, the higher the chance of developments that benefit everyone.

"After World War II the United States needed a new model for how to start entrepreneurial companies," says Franklin Johnson, a venture capitalist who made his fortune in the 1980s by helping found the biotech giant Amgen. "The old system was that someone with a business idea went to wealthy families—the Rockefeller family supplied the capital used to start Eastern Airlines, for instance. But after the war, the country was expanding and things were changing too fast to think the wealthy families could play more than a small role in reviving the economy. At the time, banks did not like to lend to start-ups— they wanted to lend to established firms or for real estate because, unlike start-ups, land never became worthless. Yet the United States needed to move away from the idea that big companies and big banks should run everything. The country needed a way for the individual to strike out on his own in business and even overcome a big company."

Enter Georges Doriot, born in France, who emigrated to the United States to attend business school, then became a U.S. Army officer during World War II and worked in the quartermaster corps, where he acquired considerable firsthand experience in what is needed to bring products into existence. Taking a faculty job at Harvard in 1946, he wanted to find a way to help people who weren't insiders start businesses. Rather than let inventors and entrepreneurs come to him—until then it had always been the custom than an entrepreneur's first task was to locate a backer—Doriot hired business-school graduates and told them to look for ideas worth financing. Doriot sought to fund basic concepts that might become new business categories. In 1957, he struck gold. Two engineering professors quit M.I.T. in a dispute over something called the TX2, a transistor-based calculating engine with what was then called "core memory" and is now called random-access memory: that is, memory that can be read and written to quickly. Doriot invested $70,000 in the TX2 idea, the equivalent of about half a million dollars today. The two engineers used the money to found Digital Equipment Corporation, which would build some of the most successful corporate computers of the 1960s and 1970s. In 1968, Doriot's investment fund sold its stake in Digital Equipment for $450 million—not too shabby a return on $70,000—then distributed this profit to its investors, based on how much each had contributed initially. Doriot, generally viewed as the grandfather of venture investing, also helped found INSEAD, a Paris business school that is a leading advocate of globalization. Doriot's 1950s dictum about business sounds strikingly up-to-date: "Somewhere, someone is designing a product that will make your product obsolete."

Outcomes such as $70,000 growing into $450 million got the attention of the business community—though, of course, some of the ideas Doriot backed were duds on which no money was made. In 1972, the archetype of the contemporary venture-capital company, Kleiner Perkins Caulfield Byers, opened its doors. Among the things that distinguished Kleiner Perkins were that its founders, Eugene Kleiner and Tom Perkins, were engineers rather than MBAs. Kleiner had worked for Fairchild Semiconductor, which produced the first commercially useful integrated circuit, while Perkins came from Hewlett Packard. The two had noses for what was up and coming in technology. Rather than the traditional financier capitals of New York, Boston, Philadelphia or Chicago, Kleiner Perkins set up shop on then-remote Sand Hill Road in Menlo Park, California. They wanted the California lifestyle, and to be close to Stanford and Cal Berkeley; they also thought a nearby large land basin, then used mainly for agriculture, would be a good place to site factories someday. Today Sand Hill Road in Menlo Park is the Mecca of risk capital, and what was once an agricultural land basin is known as Silicon Valley.

Kleiner Perkins employed what was at the time a quirky financial structure, but has since become standard. The company would assemble an investment pool by soliciting money from endowments, pension funds and well-off investors. Those who ponied up would be "limited partners," limited in the sense that they would share the risks and profits, but have no say in where their money was allocated. Offi-cers of the venture firm would be "general partners," making the deci-sions about what start-ups or entrepreneurs to back, and also receiving personal stakes in the fund's equity growth. Typically a fund would run for five to ten years; at the end of that span, the venture-capital firm would sell its positions. If the net was a loss, the limited partners would get hammered; if the net was profit, both the limited and the general partners would receive slices. From the venture firms' per-spective, the beauty of the arrangement was that investors put up all the capital, and stood to lose if things went south; the firms put up nothing, and stood to gain if things went north. Whatever else this arrangement might have been, it was a keen incentive for the firms to pick winning business ideas.

Still, the total amount of capital flowing into the venture sector was modest, only a few hundred million dollars per year in the early 1970s. Money realized from venture investments generally is taxed at the cap-ital gains rate, and in the 1960s and 1970s, the U.S. capital gains tax rate was nearly as high as the regular income tax rate. That meant a safe return in something like corporate bonds made more sense than a risky play that would just be taxed away; why invest in a start-up com-pany that might fail, zeroing out the investment, when any profits from one that succeeded would be taxed as if you'd played it safe?

Since it is commonly said that having capital gains tax rates lower than income tax rates represents a gift to the moneyed class at the ex-pense of average taxpayers, it's useful to understand how reducing the capital-gains rate helped spur innovation and job creation. In the 1970s, one of the leading venture capitalists was a man named Reid Dennis, who tirelessly argued to Congress that cutting the capital-gains tax would help invigorate the stalled economy of that decade. Dennis, today retired, maintains an informal exhibit of early Silicon Valley technology. His prize possession is the very first Seagate ST-412 hard drive to come off the assembly line in 1980—the Seagate hard drive being what made the desktop PC practical. Readers under thirty, don't be shocked, that historic Seagate drive held 10 megabytes of memory: today a bargain-priced home desktop has 500 gigabytes of memory, about fifty thousand times as much.[2]

In 1978, Dennis convinced Congress to cut the capital gains rate. The rate fell that year and again in 1981, declining to 20 percent. "Suddenly it made sense to investors to back inventors and entrepreneurs with risky ideas," Dennis says. "The capital gains tax cuts also made it attractive for talented people at big companies to go out on their own. Many entrepreneurs had their basic ideas in big companies, but could not convince their corporate bureaucracies to take any chances. Once money was flowing into the venture sector, a person could leave the safety of a gigantic corporation and get backing to start a new enterprise. Talented people started founding small businesses, which is always good for the economy, since small businesses create more jobs than large businesses." The American economy of the 1970s was mired in "stagflation," which culminated in the deep recession of 1981–1982. From 1983 until late 2008, the American economy boomed almost every year. Lowering capital gains tax rates must have been a factor, drawing money and talent into new business ideas.

In the early 1980s, Apple took off, both ushering in the concept of comprehensible computing (prior to Apple, computer users had to memorize dozens of recondite codes; Apple's graphic interface led to click-based computing) and creating windfalls for its initial venture backers, including Sequoia Capital, which would eventually become the juggernaut of Sand Hill Road. After Apple's 1984 initial public offering returned several billion dollars to early investors who had put up relatively small amounts, suddenly lots of investors wanted to buy into venture funds. Venture firms proliferated, their rise both assisting and roughly paralleling the rise of Silicon Valley. From the Apple IPO until the tech bubble burst in 2000, venture capitalists and their investors made delightful sums while enabling the development of numerous companies now important to the United States economy. Sometimes the numbers were breathtaking. In 1999, Kleiner Perkins and Sequoia each invested $12.5 million in Google, in return for a share of its equity. At that point Google had existed for a year but was running low on cash and needed to improve to win the battle against several other now-forgotten search engines. By the point of Google's IPO in 2004, the Sequoia and Kleiner Perkins stakes had risen to about $2 billion in value, a phenomenal return. That wasn't all—from the 2004 IPO to

2006, Google shares quintupled in price; taking into account that Sequoia and Kleiner Perkins sold their shares in Google over a period of
several years, it is believed each firm realized $4 billion to $5 billion
from a $12.5 million stake, roughly a 300- to 400-fold gain. Obviously
there only needed to be a few deals like that to get substantial capital
flowing into the venture sector, and that happened. In 2005, for example, $22 billion was invested in start-up firms.

The explosion of valuable technology developed by small start-ups
funded by quirky venture-capital firms was not something any expert
saw coming. John Maynard Keynes, who died in 1946—Keynesian
economics, which holds that government spending should be used to
regulate business cycles, is named for him—thought Western capitalism had already grown so slow-moving and overdeveloped, the best
that could be hoped for was to manage a long phase of sputtering. As
Carl J. Schramm has written, roughly from the 1950s until the late
1970s mainstream economists believed "industrial capitalism had ma-
tured to a state of sluggish growth"[3] in which breakthroughs would be
few, new firms would rise only on rare occasions, and incremental improvement of existing industries would be the best-case outcome.
Cars and television sets might get slightly better, but no new entire
product categories were in store, nor was there much risk of Fortune
500–class firms driven out of business by agile smaller competitors. By
the 1960s, "managed capitalism" had become the watchphrase of
economists and policy makers, the phrase suggesting a dull future. In
"managed capitalism," it was assumed change would come slowly, if
at all.

Instead by the early 1980s free-flowing venture capital entered the
scene, encouraging inventors to try crazy ideas and entrepreneurs to
strike out on their own. Especially on the West Coast, Americans
began to think it was fine, even fun, to work for a small business in
constant turmoil rather than for an enormous firm with an organizational chart that looks like a map of the London Underground system.
And sure enough, as venture capital and the entrepreneurial spirit
worked its way into the economy in the 1980s, there was a burst of
economic growth.

In a world where most products slowly evolve from existing products—the world economists and experts thought we'd be living in—big companies will have the upper hand and big banks that own skyscrapers will dominate financial decision-making. But in a world where a new product can go from unknown to omnipresent very rapidly—in an iPod reality—lone-wolf entrepreneurs and investors who work from small, nondescript offices can be players. And while established companies and big banks usually prefer to perpetuate the status quo, protecting their existing product lines, entrepreneurs and venture capitalists want disruption. *Disruptive* is, to them, a good word. "To succeed in the globalized era, you can be the lowest-cost producer for an established product or you can have a fundamentally new innovation that disrupts the marketplace," says Harry Rein, who once ran the venture division of General Electric, then ran a venture firm called Canaan Partners, and now dabbles as a private investor. "How many American companies are going to be the lowest-cost producer? A few, but not many. That means disruptive innovation will be essential to future U.S. economic growth. And you'd better have a steady supply of disruptive ideas, because even many good ones won't last long." The original desktop PC, from IBM in 1981, was a disruptive idea; so was the first truly portable laptop, from IBM in 1992.[4] By about 2000 the affordable, lightweight laptop, from Dell, Apple and other producers, disrupted IBM's market; in 2005, IBM sold its PC business to the Chinese manufacturer Lenovo. IBM had one of the most important, most successful and most disruptive ideas in business history, the PC, and the idea lasted twenty-four years, until the company sold off the remains of that business. IBM disrupted a market, only to be counterattacked by more disruption.

The pace of the search for disruptive ideas goes approximately like this. First, venture capitalists raise a fund from investors who are willing to accept that their money may be lost by a start-up failure, in return for a decent chance of outsized returns. Then the fund managers listen to pitches from entrepreneurs and inventors, trying to sift out the ones with business potential. Generally, venture capitalists are fearful of the very first product in a new field, as the first often paves the way while the second or third makes the money: the first afford-able video-recording system, the Betamax, was a commercial disaster, while the second, the VCR, was a home run. "To me, the word *pioneer* sounds like the word *poison*," says Michael Moritz of Sequoia, who be-came a billionaire by investing early in Google, Yahoo, Cisco, Apple, YouTube and other tech standouts. Venture firms listen to everything from elaborate presentations to "elevator pitches," meaning a super-condensed spiel short enough for an elevator ride. They pick firms to invest in, negotiating how much of the firms' stock they will receive in return. At that moment the entrepreneur or inventor is handed a bag of money that ultimately comes from the investors, not from the ven-ture capitalists. If the start-up fails, that money is lost. If it succeeds, eventually the new firm will either offer itself to the public through an IPO, or sell itself to a larger existing entity. At that point the entrepre-neurs become rich while the venture capitalists sell their positions and distribute the gains to investors, after taking a cut.

If all goes well, the venture capitalists have served as the filtering mechanism between the entrepreneur and the marketplace. In many instances, big companies watch to see which venture-backed ideas pan out, and then buy whatever new company proved the idea. Here's a fairly typical example. A biotech start-up called Sirtris Pharmaceuti-cals began looking into sirtuins, a class of body chemicals they may have something to do with aging. (Resveratrol, the red-wine ingredient believed to slow aging, is a sirtuin.) Sirtris signed up a Harvard Med-ical School ace as its chief researcher, and raised about $67 million in venture capital, including from Polaris, the firm that has helped revive Waltham, Massachusetts. In 2006, Sirtris held an IPO of stock—expertly timed to occur one week after the company was featured in *Fortune* magazine.[5] By 2008, Sirtris had at least some indication its work would lead to practical age-retarding drugs.[6] At that point, pharma giant GlaxoSmithKlein bought Sirtris for $720 million, making those on the company's ground floor—its initial researchers and initial backers such as Polaris—very happy. Big Pharma, especially, now gets many of its new ideas and patents by purchasing start-ups. This shifts the capital risk away from the pharma firms and onto individual in-vestors, while shielding the Big Pharma company from liability if a trial goes wrong. Meanwhile Amgen, itself once a venture-supported start-up, has since become so big, with 17,000 employees, that it is too bureaucratic to perform innovative research; instead, Amgen buys other biotech start-ups.

It might be comforting to think that venture capitalists and similar backers of early-stage businesses are employing incredibly sophisticated insider knowledge, but often as not, Lady Luck is their muse. "Investing in start-ups is like buying lottery tickets, and praising venture capitalists as business geniuses is like saying a lottery winner was a genius at selecting tickets," says Jay Watkins, a California venture capitalist. For example: in the mid-1990s, the venture firm Benchmark Capital backed the start-up of eBay, which became a wild success. Benchmark put $6.7 million into the ground floor of eBay and the stake grew to $4.2 billion, an amazing return.[7] Each of Benchmark's top personnel realized about $300 million from that success. At the same time Benchmark helped found eBay, its other big project was a direct-to-your-door grocery delivery service called Webvan, which has since become something of a poster child for Internet-bubble fiascoes. The grocery business is low-margin to begin with, so spending a huge amount to jump in never made much sense. Webvan burned through $350 million of investors' money before folding in 2001; as its business plan was going down in flames, Webvan spent $100,000 of investors' money to purchase $900 Aeron chairs for office personnel. Benchmark investors in the fund that backed Webvan were wiped out.

Thus the same venture capitalists at Benchmark who spectacularly guessed right on eBay also spectacularly guessed wrong on Webvan. Kleiner Perkins guessed spectacularly right on Google, but the same officials at the same firm passed on a chance to back the Palm Pilot, which they thought would never work. Other investors sank $280 million into the start-up of Kozmo, a Web-based company that promised to deliver anything in sixty minutes with no service charge. Kozmo got a lot of press—so did cold fusion!—and never came close to covering its costs, folding in 2001. My favorite from the Internet boom-and-bust: in 2005, eBay spent $4 billion to purchase Skype, the cheap-calling service.[8] Two years later, eBay would "write down" or declare as worthless $1.4 billion of Skype, which was losing money—eBay had been taken in by the very sort of unrealistic expectations that accompanied the IPO of eBay!

Google, eBay, Webvan, Kozmo—they were all lottery tickets. The sense of accelerating disruptive change—that economic ideas can quickly become a big success and just as quickly a huge flop—is likely to get worse during the Sonic Boom, making economic decisions seem more like wagering and less like rational planning. Consider a company called CMGI, which came out of nowhere in the early 1990s, offering promises of vague but advanced-sounding Web technology for corporate marketing. The firm's 1994 IPO went so well that CMGI started a venture-fund division to invest in other start-ups, including an Internet search engine called Lycos. Just before the Internet bubble burst in 2000, CMGI was, on paper, worth $40 billion—more than Alcoa was worth that year.[9] In early 2000, Lycos was sold to the Spanish communications conglomerate Telefonica for $5.4 billion. Flush with cash, CMGI bought the naming rights to the new stadium the New England Patriots were building; on the day of the transaction CMGI was, on paper, worth fifty times as much as the Patriots. Had the deal stood, CMGI Stadium would have been the first pro sports facility to sound like it was named after a blood protein.[10] But in just a few dizzy months after the tech bubble burst in 2000, CMGI's on-paper worth dropped by 99 percent, while its share price fell to under a dollar. The company canceled the naming-rights agreement with the Patriots, having no hope of paying the fee. (The Patriots now play at Gillette Field.) In 2004, Telefonica sold off Lycos—defeated in the search-engine wars by Google, Yahoo and Ask—to a South Korean firm for $95 million, accepting a 98 percent loss.[11] Today Lycos still exists as an Internet portal and CMGI still exists, now called ModusLink Global Solutions, as a firm that contracts to solve technical problems for big corporations.[12] Neither is worth a fraction of its value less than a decade ago. Spectacular rise followed by rapid fall once was the exception in economics. Increasingly it's a ho-hum story.

Why are people with money so prone to make foolish decisions? This was among the questions of the 2008 financial scandals. People with money make foolish decisions on a regular basis—investing eagerly in 1990s dot-com start-ups that not only had no revenue but no plans for revenue, believing that Enron and WorldCom really could have ten times more income than seemed possible if you checked their number of customers, believing that housing prices could rise by 15 percent annually forever, believing Lehman Brothers and AIG and Fannie Mae executives would never dream of lying to investors to justify their bonuses, believing Bernard Madoff had an incredible secret that would ensure wealth without risk.[13] Madoff had a secret, all right; his secret was that he was a criminal. As the sense of Sonic Boom expands and new ideas grow more important and more lucrative, a next wave of foolish decisions may involve investors believing that merely getting a piece of a new-idea company is a sure path to wealth. It's not. Nine out of ten start-ups fail. One of the mistakes many of Madoff's marks made was giving their life savings to a man who claimed he was running a supersophisticated hedge fund. *Even if he'd been telling the truth,* a hedge fund is no place for retirement money, because hedge funds are inherently risky. *If Madoff had been telling the truth,* he could have wiped out people's life savings perfectly legitimately and respectably.[14] Similarly, your retirement savings don't belong anywhere near venture funds or new-business start-ups. Economically, both are wagers: they can wipe you out perfectly legitimately. Only wager what you can afford to lose.

Many start-up business deals are structured so the venture capitalists themselves make out handsomely even if investors get hammered; if you're interested, see a complex example at the footnote.[15] Pets.com, Flooz.com and other improbable Web firms once collectively satirized as TieClasp.com were among many enthusiastically hyped by venture firms and investment bankers, in deals that produced substantial profits for those who did the hyping while individual investors, and in some cases pension funds, took losses.[16] If global growth reignites, there may be another round of temptation among investors to engage in wishful thinking about start-up businesses: always bear in mind that the promoters and venture capitalists behind such deals may have a financial incentive to hoodwink investors.

Susan Woodward, a former Securities and Exchange Commission

economist who runs a firm called Sand Hill Econometrics, which studies private-equity flows, estimates that Sequoia Capital's 2000 fund raised $695 million from investors and ultimately returned to them $700 million—worse than putting the money in a savings account. Yet Sequoia claimed about $175 million in fees and commissions on the fund, Woodward estimates, profiting handsomely while investors took a setback. The economic research firm Cambridge Associates has estimated that venture funds begun in 1995, just as the tech bubble was inflating, produced median returns to investors of 45 percent per annum, obviously excellent; but that venture funds begun from 1999 to 2005 have median losses of 14 percent per year. Woodward says her studies show that over the long term, venture investing offers only a slightly better return than simply putting your money into blue-chip stocks. A slightly better return is not all that impressive considering investments in start-up businesses are "illiquid"—you can't take your money out for years—while most stocks can be converted back into cash whenever you wish.

Fear of sounding like the next Madoff or Lehman Brothers is a reason most involved in risk capital keep their heads low. Most forms of start-up capital are unregulated;[17] publicity might only bring in prosecutors. "The venture sector discloses nothing to the Securities and Exchange Commission, does no public reporting to anybody," says Mark Heesen, head of the National Venture Capital Association—he is the person not one Washington power broker in a hundred would recognize. "Why would we want to raise our profile? That could only lead to federal reporting requirements." A generation ago, mutual funds were unregulated and in most cases faced no requirement to disclose data. Mutual-fund managers fought like demons against disclosure, because it removed the illusion that they were financial masterminds using incredible insider knowledge. Also, services such as Morningstar began to rate the performance of mutual funds; such improved access to information benefited the public by driving down costs, as mutual funds reduced their fees to remain competitive. Right now hedge funds and private equity funds—which are similar to venture-capital funds, but invest mainly in businesses that are already established—are fighting like demons against public disclosure, because they don't want scrutiny, don't want competitive pressures on their fees, and don't want to lose the aura of being secretive geniuses. Venture capitalists are likely to fight public disclosure, too. They, too, have cultivated a perception of being secretive geniuses. They certainly don't want the public to know they are claiming enormous bonuses for buying lottery tickets.

———

But let's assume a world in which investment advisers and fund managers are all honest, wanting nothing more than to help entrepreneurs start useful businesses. Here is the sort of story that may result, and it's one that will become more common with the passage of time.

Loren Burnett is a "serial entrepreneur"—the kind of person who likes to be around the founding of companies, then once the firm either succeeds or fails, moves on, seeking a fresh challenge. To be a serial entrepreneur is not an easy way to make a living. There is considerable ambiguity involved in this kind of life, long hours, income boom-and-bust, and even if all goes well, a lot of moving and refinancing of mortgages. But as the pace of economic change accelerates, the world increasingly will value the kind of people who are eager to jump in and help start new companies. Anyway, if you think there has been uncertainty in your job-hunting, consider Burnett's.

His first white-collar employment was at the accounting firm Coopers & Lybrand. Burnett hated it. "I would have gone mad if I spent forty years reviewing audits," he says. Burnett quit, and in 1983 found a job with MCI Communications, a daring young company offering low long-distance calling rates that challenged then-mighty AT&T's stifling dominance of the telephone business. Readers under age thirty may not believe this either, but at one time AT&T had a federal monopoly on long-distance service and charged three dollars a minute, in today's money, for a call from New York to Los Angeles.

MCI was one of the great maverick firms of free-enterprise lore. The company began, in the 1960s, building microwave relay towers intended to make possible long-range two-way radio communication for construction crews; portable two-way radios of the time worked only over short distances. The radio-relay idea flopped, as the initial plans of start-up businesses often flop, though perhaps you have already said to yourself, "That sounds a lot like the idea for a phone network based on cellular antennas." Often successful economic ideas are improvements upon what was originally a bust. Initial photocopiers of the 1950s were nearly useless and widely ridiculed. The arrival, in 1959, of the first practical plain-paper copier, the Xerox 914, started the awash-in-paperwork society we inhabit today. MCI came under the sway of a celebrated entrepreneur named Bill McGowan, who raised some venture capital and decided to go after AT&T. During the 1980s, anyone who was cool switched to MCI long-distance service; meanwhile, the company's engineers were the first to commercialize a cool idea called e-mail. McGowan died young, and the company was acquired by Bernard Ebbers, who changed MCI's name to WorldCom and began lying about the books to rationalize lavish bonuses for himself; in 2006, Ebbers was sentenced to twenty-five years' imprisonment for fraud. After Ebbers, the flaming remains of WorldCom were bought by Verizon. Today the name MCI is forgotten, though Verizon's MCI-derived division remains home to some of the world's top telecom engineering.

In any event, Loren Burnett was hooked by his years spent with McGowan at the original MCI. "I loved the informal entrepreneurial environment where you could try ideas, went full speed, nobody cared about rank, and nobody cared if most of your ideas failed as long as you came up with something that worked," he said. "As opposed to being a middle manager at a gigantic corporation where you spend months preparing for five minutes sitting with the CEO, and exist in complete terror of anything other than very slow incremental change." After six years with MCI, Burnett left to work as an executive at a software start-up firm that later was acquired by a larger firm. Burnett then became chief financial officer of another start-up, one hoping to compete with PeopleSoft, which in the 1990s was a red-hot provider of corporate software, though by 2005 was defunct. Burnett's new company was bought up by a larger firm, giving him a nice payday when he cashed out his stock. Then he helped found a company with the perfect globalized name FutureNext, which would provide the same kind of business services as the corporate giant Oracle.

By 2000, FutureNext had five hundred employees and nearly $100 million in annual sales. Burnett and the other founders decided to place the company into the public arena via an IPO. They went to Manhattan for a day of meetings with investment bankers who were competing to be the FutureNext underwriters. Bankers at the first meeting, over breakfast, said the IPO should be priced at $550 million, which would have made Burnett quite wealthy. The second investment group, which met in mid-morning, said $300 million. The third investment group, over lunch, said they would not underwrite the sale. It turned out that FutureNext had decided to conduct rounds with investment banking houses on the very day that the Internet bubble burst and NASDAQ, the stock exchange for high-tech firms, went bust. Soon FutureNext was worthless. Rather than wealth, Burnett was left with nothing but Manhattan hotel bills.

Burnett persevered, taking at top job at another start-up, Riptech, which was funded by an establishment firm called Columbia Capital, but whose software writers were all in their twenties. In 2002, Symantec bought Riptech for $145 million; Burnett received a substantial share of the price, and after two decades of nonstop entrepreneurship, finally was a rags-to-riches case. He took some time to travel the world, but itched to create another business, and was hired as CEO of a start-up called Celcorp, which was backed by a single wealthy investor: an "angel," in entrepreneurial slang.[18] Burnett did not get along with the angel, and they parted ways; Celcorp became Teradact, which "provides clients with an integrated delivery of information intelligence solutions," whatever that means. Burnett then was hired as CEO of Astral Brands, which specialized in acquiring niche products that had not been profitable in stores, then repositioning them for marketing using infomercials or on shopping channels such as QVC. Astral's big hit was Chesapeake Bay Crab Cakes & More, which direct-markets high-end seafood. Six four-ounce crab cakes from CBCC&M were at this writing $58, plus shipping—or $39 per pound.[19] There's a considerable markup in that number, and the crab-cake firm did well. But Burnett tired of commuting to Astral's headquarters in Atlanta, so he took a buyout.

Then Burnett heard from a venture capitalist named Roger Novak about two professors who had an idea for "self-healing" software. If you've slaved in a big office with networked computers, you know that once every few days the system freezes owing to a malfunction or virus, and an hour or two passes as techies isolate the problem and write a "patch" that repairs the defect. The professors' idea was a software system that would isolate problems on an automated basis, write its own patches, and repair networks without the users ever knowing anything was amiss. In 2006, Novak's firm, Novak Biddle, handed Burnett $2 million to start Revive Systems, which would develop and sell self-healing network software.

When I first met Burnett, he had just leased an office for Revive. Most of the office was empty, with the company's new chief information officer lying under a desk wiring up phones. By the end of the year, Burnett had several dozen people working for him and an impressive software "beta" that, in tests, did in fact automatically diagnose and patch computer systems. Then the company's sales force discovered that the number of large corporations willing to put their computer networks into the hands of an independent automated system was—zero. No one trusted computer programs to fix computers, even though computers have been designing their own chips for more than a decade. Once the "Dilbert" comic strip featured a subplot of an office spam filter that became self-aware and started running the company. This is roughly how potential buyers saw the Revive idea.

So Burnett relaunched the company as StackSafe, to build "virtualized stacks" in which corporate clients can test new computer networks without worrying about crashing their main systems. Through 2008, StackSafe was making progress, and hoping to sell itself to a large corporation—"the exit," in entrepreneurs' slang. At the exit, the entrepreneurs, creative people and early investors leave with their rewards while the MBAs, marketers and bankers take control. The two groups have a symbiotic relationship in business: neither could exist without the other, and each thinks of itself as the real source of economic growth. Things at StackSafe seemed to be going well—the company was signing up customers—and in early autumn 2008, Burnett began to seek fresh investment capital to expand the firm and ready it for a lucrative exit. September 2008 was the moment of the credit crunch; no bank or equity fund would lend to StackSafe, which went out of business in early 2009. Burnett helped clean out the office, then immediately began casting around for other ideas to back. He'd heard about some professors with an idea for making complicated transmissions require less bandwidth.

Burnett's bottom line on his experiences jumping from start-up to start-up: "The word *fun* is never used in large organizations. Starting a business is fun. It's satisfying. It's almost artistic. It can make you wealthy or cause you to lose your shirt, but most of all, it's fun."

Fun. Fun is unlikely to be a huge factor in the Sonic Boom. For most people, work is not about fun: it's about earning a wage, with perhaps a sense of satisfaction added, if you enjoy what you do for a living. Fun happens far, far from the workplace. But in an interconnected economy that produces a lot of prosperity but also constantly reshuffles the deck with old firms failing and new firms coming into existence, it might help us all to think there is a bit of fun to be had in helping start a business. Not that we may have much choice in the matter.

Seven

CHIPPEWA FALLS

Chippewa Falls, Wisconsin, is an eight-hour drive from Chicago, northwest toward the Canadian border. Driving there, you pass near Oshkosh, where the denim firm began in 1895, and Ripon, where in 1854 abolitionists founded the Republican Party. Arriving, you discover a lovely old town along the Chippewa River, an idyllic place whose architecture and wooded character evoke the paper mills and shoe manufacturing that dominated the central Wisconsin economy of the past.[1] Because the appearance of the town calls to mind a previous century, one might assume the technology-crazed hullabaloo of our age has passed Chippewa Falls by. Hardly: Seymour Cray grew up there, and built the first commercial super-computer in an improvised laboratory in his hometown.[2] Today Silicon Graphics, which makes advanced electronics, does its manufacturing in Chippewa Falls. Originally, however, Silicon Graphics was in Silicon Valley—and why the company moved from the center of the technology universe to a quiet town in rural Wisconsin contains an object lesson in how even a successful modern business must innovate continuously.

Silicon Graphics was among the red-hot growth firms of the 1980s, the decade when the forces that would eventually cause the Sonic Boom were just becoming tangible. That was the decade the personal computer began to arrive in the home, and also when a PC's "graphics card" was a constant source of frustration. Readers under thirty years of age, accustomed to reliable computers whose components set themselves up and that display cinema-quality images, may not know that long, long ago—in the 1980s—computer graphics were unstable and fault-prone, while connecting the graphics processor to the rest of the computer was a time-consuming hassle that even people who like electronics found exasperating. Silicon Graphics made the first really successful graphics processors for the PC, using you-don't-need-to-know-the-details concepts such as floating-point accelerators. By around the time the elder George Bush was being elected president, graphics cards from Silicon Graphics were all the rage for most computers, and the company was rolling in money. Silicon Graphics built for itself a vast, modernistic headquarters complex in Mountain View, California, on the main highway leading into Silicon Valley. Admired by techies and on Wall Street, the company capped its rise to prominence by designing systems for the lifelike computer-generated special effects of the 1993 movie *Jurassic Park*.

By 2006, Silicon Graphics was bankrupt.

Silicon Graphics' key achievement was to figure out how semiconducting chips could process large streams of data to create high-fidelity moving images on screens. As everyone knows from today's inexpensive video games, which look as realistic as movies of the 1950s, the solutions worked. But many of Silicon Graphics' solutions were general ideas as opposed to the sort of specific design that could be protected legally. By the late 1990s, just a few years after the company had enjoyed strong profits, its concepts about how to handle computer graphics had been "commoditized" and were being made in knockoff form, at lower prices, by competitors from Texas to Asia.

A generation or two ago, a company that came up with a novel product might have decades of a business to itself, even if the underlying approach could not be patented, because it would take that long for other companies to hear about the idea, gear up to copy it, then learn to produce facsimiles close enough in quality that buyers would be happy with them. With each passing year, this process speeds up.

Free-flowing information makes it easier for other businesses to find out what is being done successfully, and to imitate that success. Companies with an innovative approach face quick-rising competitors not just from their region or nation but from the entire world. In commodity markets, price governs most decisions—if competing products are about the same, why not pick the cheapest? Commoditization happens faster and faster, and not just in electronics. In 1998, for instance, a company called Great Wolf Resorts began franchising family vacation destinations in which a hotel is built around an elaborate indoor water park; kids walk barefoot from their rooms to the water. Initially the Great Wolf destinations were fully booked, and some had waiting lists; the firm's stock soared. It took just five years for another firm, Kalahari Resorts, to match and improve the concept, offering family lodges with larger enclosed water parks. The Great Wolf innovation was commoditized amazingly fast, considering this wasn't just copying software—heavy construction was involved—and the company's stock nosedived. Today's rocket-propelled movement of information enabled Great Wolf's potential competitors to figure out what the firm was doing, and to imitate its ideas, faster than could have happened in the past. Because valuable business ideas tend to originate in developed nations then be copied in developing nations, the increasing speed and ease of commoditization will tend to make American and European growth and employment even more turbulent—while broadly benefiting everyone, by driving down prices. This is the kind of bittersweet effect likely to increase during the Sonic Boom. Broadly, prosperity will rise and prices will fall as the world gets ever more efficient at making products people want at prices they can afford, while large numbers of new jobs are created. But existing firms will become more likely to fail and existing jobs more likely to disappear, owing to the same forces causing general prosperity.

Seemingly taken by surprise by how rapidly its computer-graphics business was assailed by competitors, Silicon Graphics tried to respond with a new line of business, manufacturing networked workstations of the type found in offices. The product flopped and the firm, which grew from nothing to 25,000 employees in about a decade, began to fall as fast as it had climbed. Successful innovation made Silicon Graphics big; failure to continue innovating caused it to shrink. Through a chain of events the company ended up owning Cray's old supercomputer facility in Chippewa Falls, where a remnant of Silicon Graphics emerged from Chapter 11 protection and now, with about 1,500 employees, designs the kinds of advanced electronics that sell in small batches, and thus does not attract the attention of commoditizers. On the way out of California, Silicon Graphics sold its futuristic headquarters complex to Google—the tech darling of the early twenty-first century taking over the stronghold of a tech darling of the late twentieth century. Google seems today invincible as a corporation—great products, great people, great positioning, plenty of cash. In a booming globalized world, will any company ever be invincible?

———

Standing at the center of the Googleplex, as employees call the Mountain View, California, headquarters that Google bought from Silicon Graphics, I wondered what an industrialist of the nineteenth century, if transported to that location in the present day, might think of the place. He would be disoriented, of course, by the appearance of Google's avant-garde campus—large, bright, angular modern-art touches everywhere; bright purple, lime green, and bright pink in the halls of a place of business; a funky impression made by what appear to be heat pipes and pressure lines along the ceilings, but are actually just visual touches lacking functionality. A nineteenth-century business leader would be baffled by a prominent business run mostly by young people, few wearing ties, and scandalized by women everywhere not just as secretaries but as engineers and executives, some dressed in short skirts, many of them *not married*!

A nineteenth-century industrialist also would be astounded by the scale of money Google deals with. In 1890, when the Standard Oil monopoly was at its peak with control of 90 percent of the American petroleum trade—inspiring Congress, in that year, to pass the Sherman Anti-Trust Act—Standard Oil had a capital value of around $4 billion, stated in today's dollars. As I write this sentence, Google has a capital value of $120 billion—and that's after the big stock-market decline that began in mid-2008. Global prosperity is way up and population is way up; there is far more wealth in the world than in 1890. Still, to think that in adjusted terms, an Internet company is today worth thirty times as much as the most notorious Gilded Age trust! Innovation is the key to all this, allowing prosperity to increase by orders of magnitude, based on entire new categories of goods and services, rather than by gradual improvement in whatever already exists. In 2007, the National Academy of Sciences estimated that in the last century, 85 percent of global economic growth has come from new technology and innovation, with all other positives—labor productivity improvements, discoveries of natural resources, rising education levels and capital growth—accounting for just 15 percent.[3]

But if snatched from 1890 and transported to the Googleplex, what really would dumbfound a nineteenth-century business leader would be: What does this company do? Even a business leader from the 1950s might be stumped by that question. Desktop screens linked to other screens across the world using invisible mechanisms hardly anyone can explain—do you even know where the servers that manage the Internet are physically located?—all for the purpose of searching masses of electrons held on miniature wafers. Why, someone from the relatively recent past might have asked, does anyone care about this, let alone consider it highly valuable? If told, "Google devised a fundamentally new way of selling advertising," our time-traveling guest might be somewhat mollified, thinking in response, "Well, at least they are selling something. The world hasn't gone entirely mad." Otherwise Google, one of the most important economic innovations of the twenty-first century, would be mystifying to the nineteenth century, and even to a representative of the Eisenhower period. The ability to store and access video images in common forums; instant news updates by keyword; satellite photos that show individual homes from space; maps that can tell a pedestrian what street she is on and which direction to turn to find the closest bank or restaurant; devices that scan books, patents and scholarly journals without the user ever having to enter a library or even know where the library being used is located: you don't have to go particularly far back into the past to find a point when these innovations would have been viewed either as impossible or nonsensical. Yet here they are, and are elements in rising international prosperity.

I went to the Googleplex to meet Google's CEO, Eric Schmidt, and how I met him would have flummoxed a business person of the 1950s, too. First I checked in at a computer station; to get a visitor's badge, I was required to click ACCEPT to an extremely long disclaimer that, most likely, no one has ever read before accepting.[4] Then I was shown to a conference room. Silicon Valley enterprises, and California-style businesses in general, have lots of conference rooms because people are encouraged to meet and brainstorm, in contrast to East Coast–style businesses, where people tend to toil alone in individual offices. Anecdotal evidence is what it is, but my impression is that in fast-moving industries, such as one finds in California, staff members spend a lot of time in ad hoc get-togethers in conference rooms, whereas in stodgier businesses such as one finds on the East Coast, conference rooms are used mainly for formal meetings. At any rate I sat down in the conference room and a moment later Schmidt walked in. He wasn't accompanied by a flurry of aides and flunkies, as high corporate and government officials customarily are. He just walked in by himself, said hi, and asked what I wanted to talk about. He was wearing khakis and a denim work shirt, and runs a $120 billion company.

"One hundred years ago, people worried that we didn't have enough wood," Schmidt said. "New ideas made the use of wood for fuel no longer necessary. Now we worry about not having enough petroleum, or the environmental consequences of using what we do have. In another hundred years, people will wonder what the fuss with oil was all about, because we will innovate away from fossil fuels. The role of the idea is completely unappreciated in daily life. Ideas aren't just academic abstractions. Our lives depend on them."

There are no panaceas; we should not be confident something new will be invented to solve whatever plagues us. Still, the history of ideas is that in almost every case, something new was invented to replace what had become outdated, or ceased to serve. Google was born in new ideas about the new medium of the Web, made its initial reputation on a combination of search quality and memorably odd name, and today is crammed with complicated technical features invisible to the user. You don't need to know how Google's internal algorithms work, but you might consider that hundreds of engineers, mathematicians and whiz kids spent about two years on the firm's initial offering, software that enables anyone to scan the entire content of the Internet in the time required to snap your fingers. Software is perhaps the fastest-evolving, most innovation-intense product in modern commerce—pharmaceuticals are similar in complexity, but don't innovate as fast—and the United States dominates this speed-thinking-based field. Nathan Myhrvold, one of the founders of the software colossus Microsoft, now runs a firm called Intellectual Ventures, which searches for new economic ideas; he notes, "For the last few decades I've bought Japanese or German cars but no Japanese or German software. Only the United States can handle the thinking speed of the software field." Some specialized software used in defense, medical research or communication might be viewed as the highest achievements of this new industrial art, but Google is its highest achievement in daily use by large numbers of people.

In a complex and noisy age, Google's rise was aided by a dash of simplicity—its nearly blank white opening page, which when first broadcast to the world seemed shocking, in a pleasant way, in contrast to the screaming, flashing, color-pumped appearance of most software products. Google's monetary success owes to an innovation involving an old idea, advertising. Newspapers, television and other media traditionally sell ads based on a fixed charge, and the better the placement—back cover of a magazine, during a hit TV show—the higher the price. Google's idea was, first, to allow advertisers to determine their own placement via auction, and second, to charge advertisers only when a customer actually looks at the ad, by clicking. "This means I run a business where the customer sets the prices," Schmidt notes, an idea that would have befuddled John D. Rockefeller. Commercial radio and then television both began as media that gave away their products (news, music, shows) in order to get customers to watch or listen to ads. Today Google gives away its products (search results, maps, indexing, document storage) in order to induce customers to click on advertising. This is a novel twist on an existing concept, which is the most common form of innovation.

Because of the accelerating velocity of technical change, Google has been able to create an impressive range of business in only somewhat more than a decade of existence. Consider Google Earth, which allows anyone with a broadband connection to inspect astonishingly detailed satellite or aircraft images of much of the surface of the planet. Using Google Earth, I was able not only to see in fair detail my house, but also to see the lawn chairs on my patio. A generation ago, Google Earth would have been considered something so fantastic and mysterious it would have been classified and available only to Pentagon and White House officials. Indeed, the 1992 cult novel *Snow Crash,* which imagined the year 2025 and anticipated the "avatar" reality now found in virtual worlds such as Second Life, had a subplot involving a future CIA computer network called Earth, which allowed the user to call up detailed photos of any point on the surface of the planet. In the 1992 novel, the Earth program is phenomenally expensive and available only to big corporations or the super-rich. Less than a generation after a science-fiction writer imagined a costly, exclusive Earth program possessed solely by elites, Google Earth is free to everyone, though you can opt to pay four hundred dollars for a version with more features. Soon Google Earth may also show my dog on the patio, complete with his perplexed look.

While many Web-based businesses seek ways to charge users for their content, Google clings to the model that helped radio and television blossom—providing almost everything at no charge. "Generally, the more abundant something becomes, the less it costs," Schmidt says. "If the product is free, then it is impossible to undercut the price." This is an important point in a global economy. Surely tech types in India or Estonia could at this point build a product similar to Google—but they couldn't offer it any cheaper, which helps secure Google's position.

Despite size, resources, breathtaking share price—$372, at this writing—and presence in everyday culture, Google is all too aware that even though most of its product is given away, the company remains subject to the basic threat overhanging the Sonic Boom economy: that every year it gets easier for someone with a superior idea to come along and put an established firm out of business. Google relentlessly innovates, hoping to forestall that day. The company adds minor features to its Web sites so often that most users have given up trying to keep track of them, and has averaged one major new feature (such as Gmail, the best Web-based e-mail service) per year. Google is also innovating the physical part of its business, completing, in central Oregon, an advanced server farm that has the technical capability to fulfill the company's seemingly impossible promise of making all public information in the world available to all people in the world. The server farm involves an attempt to build computers with even more speed than today (though a standard Google message such as "found 184,354 references in 0.39 seconds" seems sufficiently swift to me) while allowing each server to use far less electricity than current systems. Just a decade ago, to declare a goal of making all public information in the world available to all people in the world would have seemed either absurdly pretentious, or something for an enormous century-long project requiring sprawling government-run installations on multiple continents. Now there seems a good chance Google will achieve this goal relatively soon, at no charge to users, without government involvement (whew!), and reducing its resource consumption in the process.

The universal information portal Google hopes to create will accelerate progress and freedom. As billions of people worldwide acquire the ability to know what's going on and where, this will bring more brainpower to bear on issues of all kinds—replacing the previous restrictive arrangement in which only a few hundred million people in Western nations had full access to knowledge, with a new and much better arrangement in which several billion people have knowledge access. In turn, Google may be knocked off by the forces Google sets in motion. There is no guarantee Google will be able to stay in its imposing Googleplex. The company may someday sell the keys to whatever up-and-coming firm is the talk of some future decade, and retire to some pleasing locale such as Chippewa Falls.

Now suppose it is one hundred years in the future. Eric Schmidt steps out of a time machine in Mountain View, California, where the

Googleplex once stood. His company is long gone, the collapse of Google having become a business-school cautionary tale. ("Can you believe they put all that capital into trying to develop teleportation?" the Wharton professor asks, rolling his eyes, then adding, "At least it was supposed to be free.") Schmidt looks around and sees a new corporate complex, built in whatever style will be considered futuristic in the early twenty-second century. People walking about the campus of the new company seem, to Schmidt, scandalously attired. Luminous mood-sensitive hair, that year's fashion fad, seems to him ridiculous. Objects are floating past—packages delivering themselves. They change course if he steps into their path. A jetliner arcs overhead on descent into San Francisco International Airport; Schmidt does a double-take when he realizes the plane's engines make no noise at all. People wandering the campus occasionally pay attention to small devices they take from their pockets, though do not speak to the devices or type anything in. When Schmidt looks at one he just sees a softly glowing flat surface suggesting finely polished stone: there are no keys, screens or switches of any kind. Fortunately, Schmidt does spy someone carrying a book.

Here's the big question about what would happen if Eric Schmidt took a time machine to the Googleplex a hundred years into the future—would he have any clue what the company there was doing or why people cared about its product? Probably not. Too much economic change will have happened by then. Even someone right at the top of driving today's transformations may not be able to follow future change.

———

Everything in economics is going to change, and sooner than you may think, including factories themselves. From high-level policy discussions to chatter in store aisles, attention focuses on the things we buy—what do they do, what do they cost, what colors do they come in? Yet the factory that builds the product can be as important. A well-designed factory can produce a quality product at low cost; a poorly designed factory may drive up costs or drive down quality. Factory designers, who generally work in an industrial subspecialty called A&E—architecture and engineering—will rise in importance owing to the

Sonic Boom. Traditionally, factories have been built to manufacture one specific product that is not expected to change much for years or decades. Increasingly, flexible factories will be designed to produce a range of products with ever-changing features. The factory will build whatever customers want that year, that month, or even that week. Flexible factories employ more automation than traditional factories, and because of this, require fewer workers. Flexible manufacturing centers on devices usually called "robots," but these are nothing like the robots of science fiction; rather, they are automated arms that lift, place and weld. Because factory robots are driven by software, they are adaptable: to change from making SUVs to making sedans, or from making washing machines to making dryers, engineers just turn off the software for one type of product and insert software that tells the robot arm where parts for the next type of product need to go. Commentators, and labor unions, tend not to like flexible factories, because software-controlled mechanisms reduce factory jobs. But innovation involving factory-floor automation not only helps society generally, by holding down prices: such innovation could be stopped only by establishment of a centrally planned economy, and perhaps you remember how things turned out when the old Soviet Union tried that. So better a profitable flexible factory with a few hundred workers than an old-fashioned facility that would have employed thousands—if it hadn't gone out of business.

Toyota and Honda have been building flexible factories for two decades: the high quality of the factories' output, combined with the speed with which Toyota and Honda can switch among models according to consumer demand, is a reason these companies began showing their taillights to the Detroit Big Three. American automakers, and the United Auto Workers, have resisted the flexible-factory concept—a reason inflexible General Motors, Ford and Chrysler kept declining relative to Honda and Toyota. During the 2008 petroleum price crunch, Honda was the sole major automaker whose U.S. sales were better than in the previous year. The obvious reason was Honda's long-standing commitment to reasonable fuel efficiency; the less apparent reason was manufacturing flexibility. Honda's East Liberty, Ohio, factory was designed to make either high-mileage Civics or mid-sized CRVs. When gasoline prices started to increase in early 2008, it took the East Liberty factory only a week to begin supplying extra Civics to dealers; at the same time, Chrysler, Ford and General Motors dealers continued to receive truckloads of low-mileage vehicles they couldn't sell, because the Big Three lacked the ability to switch production in response to unexpected events. Honda's and Toyota's flexible factories in Alabama, Indiana, Kentucky, Ohio and elsewhere in the United States are staffed by American workers doing excellent work and earning excellent pay; it's just that there are fewer such workers per car produced, a reality U.S. automaker executives and unions have resisted.

Of course U.S. automakers, and other American manufacturers, are not ignorant of the flexible factory. In 2006, Chrysler invested millions of dollars to convert its Belvidere, Illinois, assembly plant into the company's first flexible production facility. When gasoline pump prices shot to four dollars a gallon in the spring of 2008, the Belvidere factory required just a week to convert from making large low-mileage vehicles to producing the smaller cars that were selling. In a bad year for Detroit sales, the Belvidere plant ran double shifts to meet demand for its cars. Contrast this to what happened the same year, when Ford Motors decided to stop making SUVs at its Wayne, Michigan, factory and convert the facility to producing high-mileage cars. Because the Wayne plant is not a flexible factory, Ford said it would take two years, and a $75 million capital infusion, to produce a different product type there. Needless to say, a factory that needs two years to adjust to consumer demand is a factory whose long-term prospects are not good.

Flexible manufacturing also increasingly will result in companies that don't have an intended consumer product at all; rather, they will simply make things for other firms. One of the first major Silicon Valley enterprises, unknown to the public, called Flextronics, was founded in 1969. Flextronics built flexible factories that would produce whatever the nascent computer industry needed: many of the early computer game devices, sold under a variety of brand names, actually were built by Flextronics. In 1981, the company anticipated trends again by shifting production from California to Singapore, becoming the first major U.S. manufacturer to offshore. Today Flextronics employs more than 100,000 people and has annual revenues of nearly $20 billion: all for a company with no product, just factories that can build whatever someone else wants built. Most likely there are Flextronics-produced items in your home or office—the company makes the Xbox series game-platform device for Microsoft, for example, and also makes Lego toys—though you will never see a Flextronics brand. Flextronics-like firms have sprung up in China and the Asian Tiger countries, competing for contracts to manufacture whatever is wanted at the moment. It is far from inconceivable that in your lifetime, most places that build specific product categories will be replaced by flexible facilities that manufacture a broad range of product types. The same facility might manufacture laundry detergent, or tennis rackets, or car parts, or cell phones, or furniture or practically anything, depending on what is needed at that moment. Some people may find working in such facilities interesting—"What are we building today?"—but such work will also be less predictable and feel less permanent than production in the past. Like this or not, it's coming.

It is even possible, in theory at least, that production eventually will shift from big factories with die tools, welders, furnaces and cranes to devices that manipulate chemicals and metals directly into products. A California company called Idealab, which exists to generate business innovations—most of its ideas so far have been Internet or software firms, the best-known being NetZero—has been working for years on a futuristic device that is essentially a three-dimensional printer. Give the device the specifications of a product, say a handbag or a computer component; it "prints" a three-dimensional approximation you can hold in your hand. Right now, the Idealab factory-box thing is a way to spend a million dollars making a bad papier-mâché model. But the initial iterations of many important technologies, such as television, photocopying or silicon chips, were ridiculously expensive and close to worthless in terms of what they could do. If the factory-box thing gradually improves, it may radically redefine what "manufacturing" means, providing a way to convert raw materials into finished products using a fraction of the manpower, energy or space of existing factories. It is even conceivable—

far-fetched, but conceivable—that someday homes will have a Mr. Factory device in the basement. If you want to buy a shirt or a coffeemaker, you won't go to a store or place a home-delivery order. You will use the Internet to purchase the schematics as a packet of code, paying a rights fee; manufacturing instructions then will be beamed to your household Mr. Factory, which will produce the product.

This seems incredible today—how could a small device have the ability to manipulate metals and other materials into a sophisticated product? Only gargantuan factories with stamping presses can do that! Bear in mind that ENIAC, the first general-purpose computer, completed in 1946 at the University of Pennsylvania, weighed thirty tons, contained more than 100,000 parts and needed as much electricity as a good-size apartment building. A marvel of its age, ENIAC had less processing power than a smart phone does today. If you went backward in time to 1946 and told the designers of ENIAC—one of them, Betty Holberton, decades ago defying the stereotype that women have no flair for science—that someday far more power than their machine had could be shrunk into a postage-stamp-size chip with no moving parts and requiring fewer watts than a night-light, they would have said, "That's impossible! You need a huge device and vast amounts of electricity to do even the simplest electronic computing!"

As factories becoming more flexible, while wasting less material and needing less energy, the quality and quantity of consumer products should improve anew, while prices are held down. That's the good part. The bad part is that it will become ever easier to put someone else out of business—by using improved cheap communication to get the company's idea, then commoditizing that idea and flooding the market with copies. Consumers will benefit, because the commoditized copies will cost less than the originals. Firms will need to generate new ideas faster and faster just to run in place, while factory jobs will become even less secure.

———

Maybe we shouldn't worry, though, because there is too much emphasis on manufacturing as a foundation economic activity. One reason there's too much emphasis is that factory jobs are the most expensive kind to generate. For example, in 2006, General Motors invested $118 million in its White Marsh, Maryland, transmission plant, retooling to build fuel-efficient transmissions. So far, so good. But the investment added only about eighty-five jobs to the facility, at $1.4 million per job. With capital costs like those, manufacturing simply won't create enough jobs to fill future needs. The venture capitalist Michael Moritz of Sequoia Capital puts it starkly: "There is tremendous BS about capital and job creation. The real goal of most innovative companies is to create as few jobs as possible, doing the maximum with the minimum of people. Good investments have high return per employee. A lot of useful ideas may be added to the manufacturing base in the future, but not a lot of jobs."

If industrial-production employment will keep declining, then what are most Americans and Europeans going to do, work in the service sector? That is exactly what they are going to do—and it's a good thing. Not only is the service sector here to stay, its growth is a major plus. The reasons are several, including that many service-sector jobs must on a physical basis be done locally, that service-sector jobs cost much less to create than manufacturing-sector employment, and that service-sector productivity isn't rising much, which paradoxically is good for the job picture.

Two hundred years ago, 92 percent of Americans worked in agriculture, 5 percent worked in manufacturing and 3 percent worked in the service sector—which then mainly meant "as household servants." By 1950, agricultural employment had fallen to 18 percent, industrial employment (including mining and construction) had risen to 47 percent and the service sector had grown to 35 percent, even as the prevalence of the household cook or maid diminished fast.[5] By 2007, 2 percent of Americans worked in agriculture, 20 percent in industry (an ever-rising share in construction rather than manufacturing), and fully 78 percent were employed in the service sector. The huge rise in service-sector employment has been coincident with the near-disappearance of the household servant. Service-sector jobs now are mainly hourly or salaried jobs for a company outside the home.

When the term *service sector* is spoken, it invokes minimum-wage cheeseburger preparation. But only a small share of service-sector jobs are dead-end McJobs. Most people in the service sector are professionals—physicians, lawyers, insurance agents, technicians, teachers. Society needs more people in those roles—well, except for lawyers—while many service-sector jobs are highly paid, desirable positions. Service-sector employment moves men and women out of dangerous, debilitating jobs in factories and mines or on farms—statistically, agriculture is among the most dangerous professions—into safe, if stressful, work in office environments. Today more than half of American adults work in circumstances that are white-collar. The United Kingdom changed from a blue-collar to a white-collar nation, and from stodgy to Cool Britannia, in no small part owing to the growth of service employment, much of it professional. Some romanticize blue-collar life but few would wish to live it, considering blue-collar workers often have debilitating health problems as early as their forties, and almost never leave the middle class for the upper-middle in income terms. A philosopher-king would want a nation's manufacturing jobs to yield to service-sector employment.

But don't take my word for it, take China's and India's. Popular commentary in the United States suggests that while America is moving from "real" factory-based jobs to evanescent service-sector employment, China and India are monopolizing the "real" jobs. Actually, China and India show roughly the same progressions toward the service sector as shown in the United States. A generation ago, China's GDP was about 50 percent industrial, 25 percent services and the rest agriculture. Today, following the most spectacular economic growth ever experienced by any nation, China's GDP is 47 percent industrial, 41 percent service sector and 12 percent agriculture, and these percentages were achieved before the downturn that began in 2008. India's service sector has grown from about 30 percent a few decades ago to 53 percent of GDP today, while its industrial sector has held steady at about 25 percent throughout the period of the "Indian miracle" boom.[6] Just like the wealthy, powerful nations they emulate, China and India are converting from factory-based to service-based economies, too.

But why take China's and India's word for it? Stuttgart, the Detroit of Germany, in 1991 had 480,000 manufacturing workers and by 2007 had 325,000. This roughly mirrors Detroit's autoworker decline, though German cars constantly are praised for having the pizzazz American cars lack. Nearly all nations show the trend toward less primary industry and more service employment; absent the arrival of space aliens who place a large order for '58 Chevys, this trend is likely unstoppable. Denmark, which often leads national surveys for quality-of-life satisfaction, draws 72 percent of its GDP from the service sector. Germany draws 70 percent. Brazil and Portugal are at 66 percent. The Czech Republic is at 60 percent.[7] Soon there may not be *any* nation with a factory-centered economy.

Perhaps you fear that a service-based economy is a food chain with nothing at the bottom. The economic food chain has long been conceptualized as having extraction (mines and oil wells), factories and farms as the base, becoming ever more dandified and dependent as one moves upward. Yet services possess tangible, tradable value, just as do silos of grain or hopper cars of potash. The financial sector is essential to economic growth, as we have learned the hard way. Ideas from the tech sector have accelerated progress, depending of course on whether video games count as "progress." Good legal advice is worth substantially more than bad legal advice. Health care is mostly a service sector, indispensable both to life and to the economy, and the health-care sector offers strong tangible value in the form of lives saved. In the United States, health care is now about four times larger as an economic sector than national defense—the country's single largest industry, at 15.6 percent of GDP in 2007, versus somewhat under 4 percent for national defense.[8] A world in which most people are gainfully employed in some form of service to other people sounds good, not bad, and that is the economic world that is evolving.

Service-sector employment is, in turn, less prone to being wiped out by fast-moving economic forces—because in services, automation cannot achieve as much as in goods. William Baumol, an economist at New York University, has noted that exactly the same number of musicians are today employed to perform a Beethoven string quartet as when the composer lived. The same rehearsal time is needed, the same type of rehearsal hall, the same type of instruments; the same type of performance space is also required to experience the music properly. Thus the manufacturing of Beethoven string quartets has not become any more "productive" in centuries! Copying music has grown dramatically more productive—first the phonograph album, then the cassette, then the CD, now the MP3 file that can be e-mailed anywhere. But making Beethoven music is just as expensive and time-consuming as when Archduke Rudolf convinced Ludwig to stay in Vienna by offering him a pension of 4,000 florins a year. In many service-sector areas, a similar dynamic holds. Today's complex surgical procedures, for instance, may require more personnel in the operating room than surgeries of the past.

That productivity doesn't rise much in services has a larger significance. As Baumol and Sue Anne Blackman have noted, there are important areas of life where we do not *want* productivity to rise.[9] Classroom teaching, physician-patient relationships, sports coaching, voice lessons—activities such as these will always be best if done the slow, time-consuming way, focused on person-to-person relationships. Rising manufacturing, mining and farming productivity generate the wealth that allows society to devote greater resources to "inefficient" needs such as teaching and caring for the sick. A farmer who drives a tractor and a teacher who instructs a child are both important to society, but the former works with machines and crops, the latter works with people. A future economy in which almost everyone works with people, rather than with machines, sounds good to me, if only as a hedge against automation. It's a lot easier to imagine a robot that farms than a robot that runs a school.

———

The shift toward service employment has happened at the same time health care has become the fastest-growing sector of the Western economy. Most nations have a rising median age—already China is worried about its aging population, and the health-care and pension-burden consequences. As life spans continue to be extended, it is likely the shift toward ever older populations will continue globally. This raises two issues—the service need in health care and the innovation need.

Health care is service-intensive. As Megan McArdle has written, "The time required to produce an automobile in the United States fell from about 150 hours in 1987 to about 100 hours in 2002. Yet it still takes about the same amount of time as it always did to drive a senior to a doctor's appointment or to help an older person bathe and dress. Productivity growth is faster in the things that kids consume, like electronics, than in the things the elderly need."[10] Every year cars, computers, music players and practically every device in your home or office improves in quality while declining in inflation-adjusted cost. Most years health-care costs increase, in inflation-adjusted dollars. And with an aging population and rising health-care needs, service-employment opportunities are shifting toward work that isn't much fun. Most teachers and coaches, for example, enjoy working with children—they remind you of your own childhood, and usually children improve under your care, so you are rewarded with an annual sense of accomplishment. Working with the old, by contrast, can be dreary, as inevitably seniors decline, in the process reminding you that you are powerless against your own mortality.

The innovation challenge is to control costs. Health care eats up more and more of the GDP each year. This isn't "waste," as some contend—we can think of a lot worse ways to spend money than helping people live longer, with more vitality and less pain. The reduction of debilitation from injuries, disease and aging numbers among the unappreciated achievements of modern medicine. And in most cases, people shouldn't be outraged about paying for advanced treatments or pharmaceuticals, whose benefits usually exceed their costs. A standing complaint of many of today's senior citizens is the price of the prescription drugs they take. Often the pills are the reason they are alive to complain!

But if we are insufficiently appreciative of modern medicine, price remains a clear problem. Median household income keeps rising, though only slightly. Since the prices of most goods and services are in long-term real-dollar decline, a slightly rising median family income ought to be sufficient to cause most people to be better off. But health-care costs have risen so much that they've wiped out income gains for Americans except the top 10 percent, and this is true even for many with health insurance. Health-care costs have risen ahead of wages by about 2 percent per year for about a decade; premiums and copays have increased the typical family's spending on health care by 78 percent since 2001, according to the Kaiser Family Foundation.[11]

Whether or not the financial nature of U.S. health care is re-formed, there must be significant cost-control innovation. In an age when teenagers carry in their pockets the data-storage equivalent of Oxford University's library in Shakespeare's day, nearly all medical in-formation in the United States is still kept on handwritten paper files, often in cryptic shorthand that has meaning to some medical offices but not others. That drives up costs and pushes down quality of care, by making it hard for physicians and nurses to exchange information. If medical information were standardized and made portable in elec-tronic formats, health-care costs would decline. Infuriatingly, legisla-tion to standardize the formats of health records has been opposed by the lobbies of for-profit hospitals and makers of proprietary medical devices, both of which fear standardization. Today it is close to impos-sible to compare hospitals, in part because two equally good facilities may use completely different terminology for care. Standardization would allow comparison shopping, and some in the medical-industrial complex do not want that to come about.

Microsoft has spent years trying to create a standard electronic-format medical file that can be e-mailed. The potential benefits are many. Any car built in the last five years has a data-storage feature that records engine malfunctions; when the car comes into the shop, the first thing the mechanic does is check the reader to see what's wrong. Imagine if we all carried small health-info storage chips, and an am-bulance team arriving to help someone who's sick or injured, or a doc-tor examining a new patient, could in seconds learn what treatments, medications and problems he or she has had during life. "The Veterans Administration has standardized its data, and provides lower-cost care that is often superior to commercial care," notes Peter Neupert, a Mi-crosoft executive on the medical-records project.[12] "We've put too much effort into protecting medical privacy and lost track that often you don't want medical privacy—when you're injured at an auto-wreck scene you don't want your medical history private, you want everyone treating you to know everything about you as fast as possible." Innova-tion that results in a standardized electronic medical-record format, with reasonable privacy protection, is an important cost-containment goal. Standard-format medical information would, Neupert notes, es-

pecially help the developing world, where today millions of sick patients arrive at clinics with no personal medical information at all.

Beyond that, the whole way we think about health care needs innovation. As Dr. Peter Bach of the Memorial Sloan-Kettering Cancer
Center in New York has pointed out, since almost all health-insurance
plans including Medicare pay generously for high-tech procedures and
tests but only token amounts for a physician to see a patient, "the best
way for a doctor to make money is not to spend time with patients but
to use equipment as much as possible."[13] No one likes this arrangement, which results in higher costs and lower quality of care—but because procedures and tests are what the system rewards, that's what
we get. Many studies, including by the Congressional Budget Office,
have shown there is no relationship between increased use of medical
procedures and better health-care outcomes. Physicians who own
their own CT scanners and thus benefit by having patients scanned,
Bach notes, order up to eight times as many scans as physicians seeing
similar patients but having no financial interest in CT billing.

Regardless of what happens to health-care financing, the way doctors and clinics are paid needs to be reformed to reward spending time
with patients and improving outcomes, rather than reward procedures
and tests—which is rather like rewarding farmers based on the
amount of diesel fuel and pesticides they use, rather than on the food
they produce. Nearly all medical plans today, for instance, won't pay a
physician anything for speaking to a patient on the phone or answering
an e-mail about basic symptoms. Yet a phone or e-mail consultation
often quickly pinpoints basic health problems, allowing faster and
cheaper treatment with less inconvenience to patients. The French
national health-care system, whose doctors are salaried, in effect does
pay for phone and e-mail consultation, since a salaried physician's pay
is the same regardless of how his or her time is used. France's health-
care outcomes are about the same or slightly better than America's, at
a price that works out to about a third less per citizen per year.

We think of innovation as clever new gizmos, but innovation can as
much be the way something is done, either procedurally or in the business sense. As recently as two decades ago, moviegoers had to drive to
the theater to find out if they could get in to see a popular film; now

you can check online and print your ticket at home. The innovation is not the mysterious ink-shooting nozzles inside the printer, rather the ability to know on a moment's notice which theater has seats for what showing: now the information comes to you, rather than you having to go to the information. That's an improved way of doing things. To cite a more serious example, twenty years ago acid rain was a major threat to Appalachian forests. Congress enacted a new way of doing things— a permit system that allowed power plants to trade emissions allowances among themselves. Acid rain is rarely discussed today, because since 1992 emissions have declined by nearly 50 percent: the key was the innovative way of doing things (free trading of permits), rather than the technology installed at power plants. Innovation in the way goods are moved and sold can be just as important as innovation in the goods themselves: distributing milk while it's fresh, for instance, is a bigger challenge than producing the milk. Innovation in how we orient cities and suburbs—changing from car-centric sprawl to walkable neighborhoods—is a bigger challenge than building houses.

In no area is innovation in the way services are delivered, how they are priced and how it is decided what's best more important than in health care. This is especially true as the human life span is likely to continue extending—good for everyone, but leading to ever-higher demand for health-care services. At the beginning of the twentieth century, the global average life span was forty-six years. At the beginning of the twenty-first century, the average life span was sixty-six years. Suppose life span extends again by the same proportion. At the beginning of the twenty-second century, the global average life span will be ninety-four years—which means that in countries like the United States, there will be huge numbers of men and women who are still vital and active past the age of one hundred. If health-care delivery continues on its present course while life expectancy rises in such a manner, the system will crash. Innovation is the only choice.

———

Across the economy, innovation is our only choice. We not only should change the ways we use energy, or deliver health care, or organize our living spaces; we must. Baumol, the economist who loves string music played the centuries-old way, thinks "innovative activity may be more important than productive activity."

Ponder a fundamental innovation that may occur in your, or your children's, lifetime: products that are grown rather than fabricated. Nature builds astonishingly complicated mechanisms (pandas, people) using relatively low levels of resources. Nature's organisms are in most cases impressively energy-efficient. A whale heart, for example, uses about 12 volts per beat, and that amount pushes about 250 gallons of blood through the equivalent of 100 miles of arteries and veins. Suppose engineers can find out how to induce biology to make the types of things we use. This has already happened in a few cases. The selectively bred, domesticated cow is essentially a food processor for people: cows chew plants and concentrate the plants' food value into milk and meat for people's use.[14] If biological-based production can be spread to many substances or even products, economics may be revolutionized, while resource needs and pollution decline even as global prosperity rises. Innovation of this or other kinds could make the future global economy far wealthier than today's, yet not choked on pollution and garbage. Two generations ago, most communication required heavy, resource-intensive copper wires; then over-the-air communication became possible, but high levels of energy were required; today, communication by wireless phones, Internet and satellite relay uses steadily smaller amounts of resources and energy, even as the numbers of people benefiting shoot way up.[15] It is not out of the question that many forms of economics will follow this model, requiring lower resource levels and less energy.

That sounds great! But think of the turmoil and job dislocations. The Yale University economist William Nordhaus estimates that 70 percent of goods and services of the year 2000 did not exist in the year 1900. It is hardly a wild guess to suppose that 70 percent of what will be common in the year 2100 does not exist today. Huge amounts of innovation are a necessity, and most will make the material aspects of life better; many prosperity-causing innovations have barely gotten started. But the same innovations that may cause a pleasing Sonic Boom may also bring disorienting turmoil.

Eight

CAMDEN

Camden, South Carolina, site of important Revolutionary War battles, was chartered by King George II in 1730. Through the early nineteenth century, Camden had a thriving gristmilling industry plus many prosperous plantations, all with wealth grounded in slavery. During the Civil War—still called the War Between the States in Camden—much of the town was burned down, local fortunes not recovering until the railroad boom brought a train line through in the 1880s. Camden has been the birthplace of figures as diverse as the AFL-CIO president Lane Kirkland and the storied Confederate general Joseph Kershaw. A steamy locale characterized by historic architecture and a celebrated annual steeplechase, its Southernness—broad-porch houses, hanging vines, meeting points that bear centuries-old family names—is deep. In a world rapidly turning into a frenetic miasma, Camden retains a small-town sensibility: there is just one high school, and everyone seems to know hallmarks of the town's past, such as that after Kershaw became a famous figure, then rose high in politics, late in life he wanted nothing else but to come home to Camden, where he spent his final days as the postmaster.

These things make Camden an unlikely location to play an important role in the international economy: the city is the North American headquarters for Haier, a Chinese maker of home appliances. Though you may never have heard of Haier, each year it manufactures twice as many refrigerators and washing machines as Whirlpool. Haier represents an essential part of China's evolution from indigent dictatorship to crazed capitalism. That a standard-bearer of Chinese economic empowerment would find its way to a conservative Old South town known for mint juleps and horseracing is the kind of story we should find remarkable now, because as the Sonic Boom progresses, such stories will become too routine to remark upon.

What is now Haier began as Qingdao Refrigerator Collective, a classical old-Communist enterprise that accomplished the trifecta of old Chinese economics: it had a monopoly, treated workers terribly and still managed to lose money. In 1984, a man named Zhang Ruimin was named director of the factory, and was horrified to realize the shoddiness of its products. In the 1980s, China was taking baby steps toward liberalization; at the same time, Japanese-style management was at its height of business-school chic. Zhang decided to try Japanese methods in the factory. One day he walked in, glared at workers completing its poorly made pre–World War II–design refrigerators, then wielded a sledgehammer to smash everything that had just come off the assembly line. Never again, Zhang told workers, would the company ship an inferior product.[1] Later renamed Haier, the company began selling improved "white goods"—home appliances—to the domestic Chinese market, and acquired a reputation for making reliable wares. Zhang came to believe Haier could compete in the international marketplace. The company's first product line offered in the United States consisted of small refrigerators intended for college dorms: basically, a refrigerator that in China would serve an entire family was repositioned as a cooler for a Western college student's Gatorade, diet soda and beer. When the dorm fridges sold, Haier began adding other simple appliances, such as low-cost washers and dryers, to its U.S. line.

The company's products were well made but lacked the opulent touches of appliances common in U.S. homes—in-door crushed ice, multiple drying cycles, those sorts of things. Haier's first dryer had just one control—an on/off switch. Zhang wanted a product that would establish Haier's brand. The company's American engineering division took a flier on a clever idea, a freestanding wine-storage unit designed for a kitchen or den shelf. Previously there were the simple wooden wine racks of the kind found in the apartment of every young bachelor and bachelorette, or the imposing Sub-Zero wine snob's chillers that cost thousands of dollars, but nothing in between. Haier's unit sold for $300, allowing anyone to store wine properly, and created a midrange market where none had existed before. The affordable wine chiller was a hit and won Haier salespeople a foot in the door with U.S. appliance retailers—don't blame China that Western manufacturers failed to have this good idea! Once U.S. appliance retailers began to place orders with Haier, the firm's leadership became determined to compete against Whirlpool, Maytag, General Electric and other Western appliance brands. Companies like those made both standard appliances and high-end wares. There's a lot more markup in a $2,000 double-door aluminum-front fridge than in an economy model, and Haier wanted markup. The company's research showed that high-end U.S. buyers thought foreign-built appliances would be undersized and incapable of the five-loads-of-wash-daily U.S. suburban lifestyle. Also, Haier felt it should demonstrate a commitment to the American market by creating employment for U.S. manufacturing workers. So Haier decided to open a U.S. factory, choosing Camden as the location. There, the company builds fancy appliances it can sell as made in the United States—positioning them against U.S. brands that manufacture their products in Mexico or Indonesia.

The arrival of Chinese washing-machine manufacturing in a sleepy historical Carolinas town had the unintended consequence of triggering a consolidation of the appliance business. Faced with fresh international competition, Whirlpool closed factories in Iowa and Indiana, but also purchased Maytag, hoping to consolidate the two into a single, stronger firm. By the time you read this, General Electric may have exited the appliance business, perhaps selling its white-goods division to Haier, which jockeyed with Whirlpool to buy Maytag. Today Whirlpool employs fewer appliance workers in the Midwest, while

Haier has created appliance-industry jobs in the South: sometimes the company ships refrigerators from the Carolinas to China, the reverse of outsourcing. (American origin connotes prestige to Chinese consumers.) Assuming Haier remains in the United States, another generation hence, Camden, South Carolina, may offer a mix of antebellum Scarlett O'Hara customs and Chinese social influences—and what an Old South/Chinese cultural intersection will be like is anybody's guess. Plus, Camden may transition from history buff's tour destination to nerve center of globalized commerce.

None of this was planned. No person, committee or agency said, "Let's blend together China and South Carolina, then see what happens." No leader or academic predicted that an Asian refrigerator manufacturer would set up shop at a Revolutionary War site, or that a Carolinas factory would today use communication relayed off satellites in geostationary orbit to receive production specifications and monitor market trends across the world. No one had the slightest idea that these or other Sonic Boom twists would happen—because in practically all aspects of free economics, no one is in charge. That reality is central to understanding both why the global economy is getting so much more productive, and why the global economy is causing so much more anxiety. Today Haier has an excellent reputation, and often appears on lists of the world's best-run companies. But you won't want to hear Zhang's personal business motto: "Run scared always."

———

Slavoj Žižek, a Marxist philosopher from Ljubljana, recently noted, "Capitalism is the sole social organizing structure in world history that is rendered stronger by its own instability. This is part of the genius of capitalism. Instability does not cause it to collapse." In 2009, the international economic system was under all manner of pressure, but did not fall to pieces. Bank problems, high unemployment, chaotic changes such as Chinese firms building products in the United States to ship back to China—rather than cause the free-market system to stop functioning, this kind of instability, as Žižek notes, only seemed to make the system stronger. But we're getting ahead of ourselves: Quick, where is Ljubljana? Globalization has begun, so you'd better know!

The AutoCorrect feature of my Microsoft Word program contained the accurate spelling of Ljubljana. In the Sonic Boom era, any nation or city whose correct spelling is recognized by Microsoft Word is a place that may cause economic commotion by, oh, tomorrow morning.

Needless to say, you knew that Ljubljana is the capital of Slovenia. Or if you didn't know, you found out in 0.39 seconds using Google. Bear in mind, that is how long it now takes anyone in Slovenia to find out about your hometown.

Žižek, a contemporary Marxist, was enunciating a view very different from that held by Karl Marx. Some 140 years ago, in his book *Capital,* Marx declared capitalism about to implode because it was inherently volatile. Market systems, he believed, were incapable of stability and, left to their own devices, sure to fail. For history's leading critic of capitalism to be wrong in his central prediction is a bit of a complication. Then again, maybe capitalism will fail someday: just because a prediction of doom has not yet come true is no guarantee the prediction never will. The world did not end on October 22, 1844, as William Miller elaborately predicted, but do not feel overconfident this means the world will not end. Be Marx's failed predictions as they may, what in his day was called capitalism is now better called market economics: in our decentralized world, there is *less* concentration of capital than when Marx toiled at his desk in the British Museum. But whatever you call the global economic system, its core assumptions really haven't changed that much since Marx predicted their imminent short-circuit. Puzzlingly, the instability of the system continues to give it strength.

Though Marx's big prediction has fizzled so far, many of his other concerns sound surprisingly up-to-date. Marx worried that free movement of capital among nations would cause businesses to flee from one country to another, seeking the lowest production cost. He worried that immigration would cause downward pressure on wages. He fretted that "commoditization," the rapid copying of ideas, would become steadily easier, robbing labor and inventors of their due by enabling anyone to duplicate value initially created by others. And though history generally depicts Marx as eagerly awaiting the anarchy that would accompany implosion of the free market, Marx not only hated disorder—he wanted "rebels" arrested—more important, he worried that a breakdown of capitalism would cause average men and women to suffer, because production would not be maintained. Marx's reputation is stained because his theories were expropriated by Lenin and Stalin and others who, unlike Marx, did not care about the suffering of average people. If Marx were here today, it is not a stretch to suppose his concerns might be similar to modern American and European concerns: too much economic instability, too much job turmoil, uncertain health care and pensions, too much income at the top, privileged people playing one group of workers against another to drive down wages. Except that today, Marx might say "employees" rather than "workers," and "salary and benefits" rather than "wages."

Go back and examine Marx's *Communist Manifesto* and, once the anachronistic wording is adjusted, you'll find its concerns are surprisingly current. This is not an argument for communism, an awful system; rather, another of the many indications that the kinds of economic tensions and uncertainties today widely viewed as new and unprecedented are in reality familiar and recurring. Let's look at the ten points of Marx's manifesto, published in London in 1848.

One—Abolish private ownership of land, and apply all rents of land to public purposes. Marx is commonly misunderstood to have wanted to abolish private property; rather, he wanted to abolish private ownership of land. There's a considerable difference. In Europe in the nineteenth century, huge tracts of land were held by rich families—that's where the phrase *landed gentry* originates—who lived in luxury based on no productive labor. When employment was mainly agricultural, and before high-yield farming had been developed, large tracts of land were needed for farming: but the landed-family stranglehold made it hard for an average person to get ahead. Each new generation of farmers had little hope of living better than the previous generation, while the landed lords and ladies were assured of their grand estate regardless of effort. Gradually this problem eased in the developed nations as the economy became less based on agriculture, and high-yield crops broke the vise hold of the large-tract owners—and next as the opening of the United States, Canada and Australia dramatically increased the supply of land available to Europeans. Today the landed-families problem remains in feudal nations, especially Pakistan and parts of Africa.

In turn, today zoning laws, environmental rules, labor regulations and the eminent-domain concept mean it is no longer true that "no one can tell me what I can do with my land." All Western societies now impose limitations on privately held land. When Marx lived, landed families could get away with anything on their property, including treating tenant farmers as sharecroppers; now you can't get away with anything on your land, while private land is if anything too easy for government to condemn and seize. Finally, most land ownership is now taxed, as was not the case in the nineteenth century.

Thus in a sense, Marx's first goal has been achieved in the Western nations, though not using the political mechanisms, to say nothing of the terminology, he would have liked. As for rents, Marx did not mean the monthly charge for living in an apartment. Postwar economic theory, including the market-oriented theory associated with Milton Friedman and the University of Chicago, denounces "rent-seeking" as unproductive and bad for society. In postwar economic theory, "rent-seeking" is any activity in which a person or organization manipulates law or circumstances to impose charges for producing nothing of value—lobbyists for government-sanctioned monopolies are engaged in rent-seeking, for example. The landed gentry of bygone days were classic rent-seekers, collecting payments for making no value. Now that most privately owned land is taxed, this problem is diminished. Marx and Friedman were not far apart in their feelings about rents.

Two—A progressive income tax. Marx wanted tax rates to rise as income rose. They did not in his day; they have in the United States and in most European nations since the 1920s. Marx perhaps would have placed the top-rate bracket higher than it is today in the United States, between 36 percent and 39 percent for federal income taxation,[2] but he would have applauded the extent to which changes in the U.S. tax code have shifted the federal income-tax burden toward the best off. Congress, at the behest of President George W. Bush, in 2001 cut the top-rate income tax on the rich, but it is little understood that taxes on average people were cut even more by the same legislation. Since

2001, 40 percent of Americans—the working class and lower middle class—have paid no federal income taxes at all, that tax burden being eliminated, though this group still pays Social Security and Medicare taxes. An initiative by President Barack Obama being debated as this book went to press would extend the tax break, so that 50 percent of Americans would pay no federal income taxes. Congressional Budget Office figures show that in 2005, the top 10 percent of Americans paid 72 percent of federal income taxes, with the remaining 90 percent of Americans paying only 28 percent.

Demographics shifted in a way Marx never would have anticipated—there is now such a large block of Americans earning $100,000 or more per year that taxing them at 36 percent to 39 percent generates more revenue than would taxing the super-rich at confiscatory rates. Roughly the same is true in most European Union nations. Americans, especially, seem ill informed that since the 2001 tax legislation, the well-off have paid a far larger proportion of federal taxes than any other group. One reason America's debt is piling high is that government spending and federally funded benefits keep escalating, yet the working class and much of the middle class pay no federal income taxes. Soaking the rich would close some of this gap, but unfortunately, the math shows that higher taxation on the rich cannot alone solve federal debt problems.[3]

Three—Abolition of inheritance. This has not happened, though nearly all nations now tax inheritance, which was not the case in Marx's day. Inheritance allows land and assets to accumulate across generations, subsidizing an idle rich who use resources but produce nothing, and have little incentive to create economic value. As the social critic Michael Kinsley has noted, a distressing proportion of the Forbes 400, the annual index of America's richest four hundred men and women, inherited their money, rather than earning it by work, invention or any socially beneficial act.[4] Some conservatives want to end estate taxation; as practiced in the United States, the estate tax serves mainly to slow the calculus of wealth accumulation, rather than to fund government.[5]

Four—Confiscation of the property of all emigrants and rebels.
Marx, a leftist, if alive today would fit right in with the anti-
immigration sentiment on Fox News. Marx didn't like immigrants because they drive down wages, exactly the complaint heard about
immigrants today. Marx further disliked immigrants because they tend
to leave nations with troubled economies and travel to places where
the economy is good, rather than remaining in their home nations and
fixing their home economies. Doesn't this sound exactly like a Fox
News anti-immigrant complaint? Imagine *Karl's Korner,* a daily news
and comment show on Fox, on which Marx—beard neatly trimmed by
the makeup lady—fulminates against the menace of illegals sneaking
across the Texas-Mexico border. As for "rebels," Marx meant what we
would now call terrorists. In his day, anarchists plagued Europe, setting bombs for no clear reason other than rage. Marx found anarchists
repulsive, to say nothing of empty-headed, and detested their lack of
respect for the institution of high culture, such as museums and opera
houses. He wanted their property seized—which sounds a lot like
freezing the bank accounts of Al Qaeda. Though Marx longed for an
entirely new system of social organization, he understood that terrorists simply destroy, accomplishing nothing. Alive today, he surely
would say, "The United States does not negotiate with rebels."

*Five—Centralized credit, in the hands of the state, via a national
bank.* The United States has a national bank in the Federal Reserve,
and all other developed nations have similar money-supply gover-
nance. Centralized credit? This was approximately the response of the
United States, the United Kingdom and several other major nations to
the financial markets freeze-up of the last few years.

Six—Centrally controlled communication and transportation. Until
cable television and broadcast deregulation, both beginning in earnest
in the 1970s, most communication in the United States was tightly
regulated by government. The result was very high telephone calling
rates and a four-network monopoly that provided little variety and no
opinion on television. Until airline and truck deregulation, also begin-

ning in the 1970s, there was a moderate amount of central control of transportation, and the result was that only the well-off and business executives could afford to fly, while overnight package delivery was prohibitively expensive. Centrally controlled communication and transportation proved really bad ideas. So Marx was way off here. For, however, a list of 150-year-old proposals, so far Marx's batting average isn't bad.

Seven—Extension of factories owned by the state, cultivation of barren lands, improvement of the soil. "Extension of factories" means increased industrial capacity, which has happened in a dramatic way. Most factories in free nations are not owned by the state; some are in Europe ("crown corporations"), and in 2009, the United States essentially nationalized much of its auto industry. As for soil and cultivation, Marx was intensely concerned that agriculture would not be able to keep pace with food demand caused by population growth. Since the Green Revolution of the early twentieth century, agricultural yields have skyrocketed throughout the world due to fertilizer and irrigation. Barren land has been made to flower in the American southwest, in Israel, in India, in the Brazilian Cerrado and elsewhere. In the second half of the nineteenth century, the United States created the "land-grant" system of colleges, whose initial objective was to teach farmers how to cultivate barren acreage and improve the soil.

Eight—Equal liability to labor, and the establishment of armies for agriculture. "Equal liability" is an antiquated way of saying fair-labor laws and labor unions. Today's labor movement is troubled, but its legal safeguards are sound. A standard view is that the primary reason capitalism overcame the forces Marx thought would destroy it is that the labor-union movement protected workers while giving them a stake, however small, in the profit-making process. Marx thought it inconceivable that factory owners and the super-rich would ever agree to any arrangements that shared wealth. "Armies for agriculture" is an anachronistic concern—Marx believed huge numbers of workers would be needed to grow enough food for a rising population. He died before high-yield farming mooted this concern.

Nine—Combination of agriculture and manufacturing; gradual abolition of the distinction between city and countryside. For good or ill, agribusiness has indeed combined farming and manufacturing. For good or ill, sprawl and exurbia are gradually merging urban, suburban and country living, while the Internet, cell phones, and other new communications media put densely populated and sparsely populated areas in constant contact. Marx worried that people living in the countryside did not know what was going on in the cities and therefore could not become sophisticated—obviously, no longer an issue. The merging of country and city is happening all over the world, on a grander scale than Marx could have imagined.

Ten—Free public education for all children, and abolition of child labor. Done and done, though child labor continues to be a scourge in developing nations.

Marx believed that if his ten planks were ever achieved, market economics would fade away, prosperity would rise, extreme inequality would end, war would cease and society would become content as most of the stresses of human existence would be resolved. Marx's goals have been achieved to a greater extent than one might have thought possible, though the very forces he thought would oppose them have in fact in some cases been their sponsor. Prosperity has risen, and while all are far from equal, the development of the vast middle class has made North America, the European Union and Japan significantly more equal than any society that existed in Marx's day. But happy? Content? Serene? Marx's preconditions for industrial utopia have not made us any of these. If Karl Marx were alive today, he'd be worried about job security, concerned over losing his health benefits, spooked by too many immigrants and scared that globalization will undo labor and environmental protections. Plus he'd be writing books with titles like *Lose Weight Fast Using the Astonishing Secret of Dialectics,* and the books would be printed in China.

Marx was just one in a long line of people who tried to predict the course of economics. Many thinkers have believed that scientific reasoning could be applied to economics, that the movements of markets for goods and labor could be understood in the same way that the courses of spacecraft bound for other planets can be understood. Many thinkers have believed there must be sciencelike "laws" underlying economics, dictating how economies change, in the same way that laws of gravity and motion dictate where a space probe ends up. Many have believed economics must be predictably deterministic—A causes B causes C with no other outcome possible. And boy, has anyone who has ever thought this sort of thing been wrong.

Economists have attempted to explain the movements of the modern global economy based on how central banks manipulate the money supply ("monetary policy"), how governments impose taxes and spend revenue ("fiscal policy"), types of regulations and tariffs, and the relative strengths of currencies and stand-ins for currency, such as gold. Stock analysts seek relationships among rising and falling economic indicators in vain, and have never found one that reliably forecasts whether the stock market is about to rise, fall or stay the same. (Studies show that highly paid Wall Street analysts and economists "outperform" the market, guessing better than simply placing money into index funds, only about one third of the time.[6]) Market psychologists have elaborately studied consumers, using focus groups and other means, and never found a satisfactory means for predicting which products will be popular and which will languish on shelves. Complex computer models of the economy have been constructed by very smart men and women, and the models don't do a good job of predicting the economy—no model foresaw the late-1990s tech boom, the 2007 subprime bust or the 2008 credit-default-swap fiasco, for instance.[7] Countless economic conspiracy theories have been proposed, and they don't explain the economy either. For example, if secret councils of international bankers are controlling global markets, how come so many banks are in financial trouble? That's not much of a conspiracy.

The roster of winners of the Nobel Prize for economics includes many who have skillfully dissected some aspect of economics—but no Nobel Prize economist can be said to have "explained" the global economy, except in the most rudimentary sense, such as that it's good to buy low and sell high. No Nobel Prize winner in economics has ever successfully predicted what would happen the following year, let alone predicted a generation-long economic pattern, except in the most rudimentary sense, along the lines of predicting that "markets will remain volatile." The mathematician Stanislaw Ulam once challenged the economist Paul Samuelson, who won the Nobel Prize for economics for mathematical models that are fascinating to specialists but have no predictive power, to name one finding of economics that is "both true and nontrivial." Samuelson had to think about that for several years before proposing David Ricardo's theory of comparative advantage—that when two nations trade, it is possible for both to end up better off. Comparative advantage is a powerful intellectual notion and an important positive force in world events.[8] But if even Nobel economists have trouble naming economic theories that matter to anyone other than specialists, small wonder average people find the movements of the economy inexplicable.

The history of global economic change is one surprise after another. All technological and scientific changes by definition come as a surprise, since before a discovery or invention is made, the knowledge involved does not exist and therefore cannot be anticipated. Countless major global economic trends of the past, and of the moment, came as surprises. No one, including Chinese economists, could have guessed how rapidly China would develop. No one could have guessed that India's economy would expand so reliably—in 2008, as most of the world knew recession, India continued growing economically. (Just a generation ago, entire books were devoted to the premise that everyone in India was about to starve to death.[9]) The great political economist Jane Jacobs, who died in 2006, in the 1970s predicted the world would fragment into hundreds of autonomous, self-supporting regional mini-economies; instead we're more interconnected by the day. In the 1970s, the wonderful economist Lester Thurow of the Massachusetts Institute of Technology predicted "industrial policy," in which government makes major decisions for big business, would take over the free nations; under industrial policy, politicians rather than the marketplace decide what products should be built. Instead privatization and customer-focused marketing are now the rule practically everywhere. In the one place industrial policy was tried, Japan, the result was the infamous "Lost Decade" of stagnation as the government kept propping up moribund but politically connected firms.

There are sophisticated economists and highly paid investment advisers who will tell you the signs of the savings-and-loan fiasco of the 1980s were obvious all along; or that the signs of the Internet bubble of the late 1990s were obvious all along; or that the signs of the early-2000s accounting-scandal outbreak at Enron, WorldCom, Cendant and the rest were obvious all along; or that the signs of the 2008 credit-institution meltdown were obvious all along. But how many of them said this *before* these events happened? The economist Robert Shiller of Yale University achieved fame for calling the 2000 stock market overvalued just before that market went bust, while the economist Nouriel Roubini of New York University is known for warning in 2006 that the housing market was overvalued: these are the leading contemporary examples of economists forecasting an important economic movement before that movement occurred, rather than retroactively. But while Shiller and Roubini are highly accomplished—Shiller's academic work established that the stock market swings more widely than can be explained by any rational analysis of the underlying value of corporations, while Roubini's academic work showed that emerging market economies are especially sensitive to credit bubbles—both have almost always predicted negative trends. If you almost always predict the negative, you're sure to be right occasionally: Shiller and Roubini failed to predict the 2002–2006 global growth surge; indeed, both were totally wrong about those years. Chief economist Abby Joseph Cohen of Goldman Sachs almost always predicts a bull market, and she's right occasionally too, then totally wrong about down years. The economy trends both up and down. Is there an economist who reliably predicts both the upward and downward movements? Perhaps. But to my knowledge, there are always-rosy predictors who are sometimes right and always-gloomy predictors who are sometimes right. This alone shows how the economy resists forecasting.

Of course if you or I made economic predictions, we'd be wrong, too. What is revealing is that experts in economics often seem to have so little to say about where the economy is headed—in contrast to, say, medicine, aeronautics or physics, where most specialists could present a reasonably accurate forecast of what's likely to happen in the next decade or two.

Consider John Kenneth Galbraith, one of the leading postwar economists, and the primary economic celebrity of the 1950s, whose major works are *The Affluent Society* and *The New Industrial State*. In *The Affluent Society*, published in 1958, Galbraith contended that American standards of living had already risen about as high as they would ever rise. Fifty years later, inflation-adjusted per-capita income is three times what it was when Galbraith said income had peaked; the average 1,100-square-foot American house of the 1950s has become a 2,400-square-foot house; the average one-car family has become a three-car family; by many other measures, living standards are much higher than when Galbraith said they had peaked. *The Affluent Society* further supposed that U.S. society should be revamped to discourage consumption, otherwise raw materials would be exhausted and pollution would overwhelm everyone. Today nearly all resources, including petroleum, are in ample supply, while government planners are almost pleading with the public to increase consumption; and in the United States and Europe, all forms of pollution except greenhouse gases have been declining for a generation or longer. Galbraith used his 1958 book to argue that in order to prevent resource depletion, government should seize control of the economy, going so far as to regulate what people are allowed to buy.[10] At the time, the idea of government regulation of individual purchases was embraced by many intellectuals. Today nearly everyone would agree the idea is disastrously bad, even if, in a free market, people make foolish decisions (gimmick mortgages) or buy wasteful and offensive products (large SUVs). Be these things as they may, practically everything predicted in *The Affluent Society* turned out to be wrong.

Writing in 1967 in *The New Industrial State*, Galbraith said giant multinational corporations were going to steamroll everything on the economic landscape, flattening all small- and medium-size firms other than perhaps mom-and-pop groceries and family-run Italian restaurants. This would happen, he thought, not so much because huge firms had advantages of scale but because in a technology era, huge firms could monopolize innovation: "There is no more pleasant fiction than that technological change is the product of the matchless ingenuity of the small man forced by competition to employ his wits." Galbraith's view was rooted in the transformative experience of the U.S. economy during World War II. Before the war, most Americans were self-employed, or worked for small local businesses; the military was comparatively small. In order to win the war, the United States embraced a vast hierarchy of huge organizations—big industrial enterprises to build tanks and planes, an enormous and tightly structured armed forces, and everything administered from the newly raised Pentagon, the world's largest building. When the war ended, that large-hierarchy structure continued to dominate American life. Galbraith thought only such large hierarchies could face the complex technical challenges of future innovation, and only big firms of national scope could generate jobs.

This turned out to be completely wrong. Since the mid-1970s, small business and start-up firms have created more net U.S. jobs than big business.[11] Far from complicated technology becoming the exclusive realm of huge organizations, fundamental advances increasingly are made at entrepreneurial start-ups or small, nonbureaucratic research labs. Many of today's major biomedical breakthroughs come from small start-ups. For instance, several cancer drugs now sold by Pfizer were not developed by the company, rather by a small California start-up called Sugen, which Pfizer acquired in 2003. In 2005, Microsoft bought twenty-two small start-ups while IBM purchased sixteen. The seed corn of the contemporary international economy continues to be planted by small businesses, not by huge firms. Galbraith in 1967 could not have known how communications breakthroughs such as the Internet would enable small businesses or even individuals to run rings around huge, bureaucratic corporations. So his failed predictions don't tarnish his stature, they simply indicate how easy it is to be wrong about where the economy is headed.

———

There's no shame in being wrong, especially if, as is traditional, experts are always wrong about the economy. Consider the financial spin-out of September 2008. The general view among famous and well-paid economists was that financial markets had become safely self-regulating—this was Federal Reserve chairman Alan Greenspan's core contention—while any problems caused by reckless subprime-mortgage lending had already been resolved in 2007. The economist Edmund Phelps of Columbia University was awarded the Nobel Prize for economics in 2006; by late September 2008, he wrote that to economists, "it came as a surprise the banking industry, and indeed the financial sector, was so devoted to houses . . . and we didn't foresee that a trillion or two dollars of losses in an economy with $40 trillion of financial wealth could bring high anxiety."[12] You didn't foresee it—no kidding! As September 2008 arrived, presidential candidates Barack Obama and John McCain were duking it out around the clock, hurling every charge and accusation the mind can imagine, yet neither had said a thing about any approaching Wall Street or banking distress because neither candidate had any inkling it was approaching, nor did any of their prestigious, highly paid advisers. Even those steeped in Wall Street and banking culture were in denial about the signs. In June 2008, the investment analyst Michelle Meyer issued a strongly worded warning that real estate prices and credit markets would fall hard. Meyer's alarm was ignored—by her own bosses at Lehman Brothers, where she worked at the time. Lehman Brothers went out of business in September 2008, brought down by bad securities based on mortgage debt and by ill-considered transactions involving credit swaps. Lehman's many extremely well-paid, elegantly dressed, management-school-trained executives had failed to notice a freight train barreling directly toward them. This wasn't a weird turn of events. In economics, this is a normal turn of events.

But if economic experts have no idea what will happen next, how do the president and other top officials run the economy? Here is a vital point that you may not like—*no one* runs the economy. The media-shorthand view that the president controls the economy—"I want to be commander in chief of the United States economy," more than one candidate declared when campaigning for the most recent presidential nominations[13]—is Hollywood thinking, serving the need to create storylines and narratives based on personalities. A good presidency is a plus for the economy, a bad presidency is a negative, but in the main the economy operates independently of the White House: the president gets too much credit when things go well, too much blame when things go poorly. Beyond that, the idea that powerful Washington officials such as the chair of the Federal Reserve sit in some kind of James Bond–style master control room, turning dials and controlling economic trends, bears no relation to actual events, although more than a few top Washington officials, looking ahead to their future speechmaking fees and as-told-to book advances, have been happy to encourage this bit of mythology.[14] Nor do top officials in the European Union or Japan in any sense control their nations' economies. Just ask any citizen of Japan how much "control" his or her government has over the economy! Ask any Russian citizen about the masterful "control" his or her government exerts over the economy! Government policy-making is important: whether governments chose wisely or foolishly about new regulatory controls on financial markets will, for example, have much to do with the pace of recovery in the coming decade. But if it hadn't been shown a hundred times before, the financial-world events of the last two years proved that even the most powerful officials have little clue what the economy is about to do, and only a mild, limited ability to influence economic events once they commence.

Yet the international economy functions reasonably smoothly: for all its problems, it was not brought down by the Cold War, or the two 1970s oil shocks, or the savings-and-loan debacle, or currency gyrations in Asia, or September 11. Most likely the international economy will not be brought down by its current tribulations: most likely, it will rebound with a glittering Sonic Boom.

———

If no one can predict the economy and no one is in charge, how does the international economy function reasonably smoothly? Perhaps the economy functions reasonably smoothly *because* no one is in charge. That is, the economy "is rendered stronger by its own instability." With no one in charge, there is no person who can make a fatal economic blunder. Think of all the crazed conflicting statements about the U.S. economy that were offered by high government officials, Democrat and Republican alike, in the fall of 2008 and winter of 2009, as economic grand plans changed on a daily or even hourly basis. Imagine if any one of them had actually been *in charge* of the economy—surely he or she would have dashed through hallways issuing dramatic orders that caused the situation to become considerably worse.

Many companies, institutions or sports teams have a single person in charge, and that person is in a position to make a catastrophic error that brings down the company, institution or team. We know from the sad chronicles of history that placing one single person in unchecked charge of a nation nearly guarantees a catastrophic result. On the other hand, when no one is in charge, blunders by individuals are diluted. Errors count, but cannot be fatal (in system terms) because no one has sufficient clout to commit a fatal error. In the Sonic Boom global economy, the topmost individuals in terms of power—OPEC's chief oil minister, the CEO of the largest bank, the Google engineer who at this moment is saying, "Hey, I just thought of . . ."—can have some bearing on economic events. Perhaps each could cause a 1 or 2 percent swing up or down. Nobody goes beyond that, not the Fed chairperson, not the economic minister of the government of Singapore, not the secretary-general of the United Nations or the president of the United States, not even the CEO of Wal-Mart.

Perhaps we are entering an era of uncommanded institutions, in which more and more aspects of our lives will be influenced by truly huge numbers of people at home and abroad, yet no one is in charge. Think of Wikipedia, which in just a few years has gone from a quirky project to an invaluable global database in more than a dozen languages—without anyone ever being in charge. Its founders, Jimmy Wales and Lawrence Singer, have more influence over Wikipedia than others, but they do not control it and could not control it even if they tried. Wikipedia operates uncommanded, and is terrific. Many trends point in the same direction.[15] Most institutions in most nations are growing more democratic, and thus considering a range of views. Today practically all the world's governments, even the remaining dictatorships, worry about public opinion. Internet connections and other network effects make it ever easier for large numbers of people to have input into decisions, while ever harder for those who aspire to single-individual power to deceive the public.

Traditionally institutions have had kings, presidents, prime ministers, bishops, colonels and the like. Perhaps it could be argued that until roughly our era this was a necessity, because the majority of men and women lacked the education and access to information necessary to govern themselves. Today education is expanding rapidly, with universal global literacy likely soon; access to information is expanding rapidly and declining in cost; belief in human dignity is spreading, with almost all people of almost all circumstances now demanding the natural-law right to determine their own fates. Under these circumstances, the uncommanded institution becomes more practical. Eventually it may be understood that market economics, functioning reasonably well without anyone in charge, lit the way for a new model of social interactions, in which no one is in charge, yet things go well. Experts won't like this, because their predictions will fare even more poorly than now. Overall, the world might be better off.

If the coming sonic boom global economy will function uncommanded, with no one in charge, and if economic incentives are inherently heartless—neither helpful nor harmful, simply lacking sentiment— what will prevent the system from spiraling toward its own demise? This is, in the end, everyone's big fear about a market economy. It's certainly my big fear: that the system will methodically destroy itself, of course without intending to. This fear is *collapse anxiety,* and men and women throughout the Western nations, if not the world, felt collapse anxiety at some level long before the physical collapse of the World Trade Centers made the fear palpable.

Fears of collapse underline our economic thinking because the economy is conceptualized as a Hobbesian war of all against all. A generation ago, every company in a particular line of business in the United States was trying to wipe out every other company in the United States, but at least the conflict stopped at the border. Today every company in a line of business everywhere in the world is trying to wipe out every other company, and working on this 24/7. Just as, in nature, competing species are struggling to render each other extinct, in economics, competing firms, countries and groups of workers struggle for each other's extinction. Someday they'll succeed, and everything will crumble. Don't you fear this at some level? You should, because it is a rational fear. Constant low-level collapse anxiety accompanies all our thoughts about the economy, jobs and moneymaking, causing worry even when events seem to be going fine. And though our distant ancestors grew their own food and made their own clothes, that's about all they ever did. In order to experience a decent life—physical security, health care, education—we need a productive modern economy.

But what if the above view of economics as a war of all against all is wrong? What if economics is mainly a benign force, not just able to produce nicer stereos and more groceries but to push the world toward social betterment? What if the benign aspects of economics have been masked by centuries of political tyranny, which held back everything good about the human spirit: and now that the world is mainly becoming democratic, benefits brought to society by economics will accelerate?

Benjamin Friedman, an economist at Harvard University, has in recent years begun to argue that the sort of rapid, disorienting, often infuriating economic growth fostered by free-market forces brings not just goods and services but "greater opportunity, tolerance of diversity, social mobility, commitment to fairness and dedication to democracy."[16] Citing many examples from the last three hundred years of history, such as the liberalization of social programs in nineteenth-century Britain, Friedman argues that during times of economic expansion, nations tend to liberalize—increasing individual rights, reducing restrictions, expanding aid to the needy. During times of economic stagnation, such as during the Great Depression, nations veer toward authoritarianism, as happened in Germany and Italy. Further, economic growth not only raises living standards and makes possible generous social policies, it causes people to be optimistic about the future, which improves human happiness. "It is simply not true that moral considerations argue against economic growth," Friedman contends. Instead, moral considerations argue that large-scale free-market economic expansion will make the world a better place for all, with most of the positive change in the next few decades felt where it is needed most, in the developing nations.

If Friedman is right, the caffeine-amped, headlong economic change associated with the Sonic Boom will, in addition to leaving us all stressed-out, nervous and overworked, help bring about social changes that nearly everyone longs for—especially a world where most nations are democratic, most people are treated fairly and most human rights are honored. The web of relationships among free economics and political freedom seems clear in the United States, the European Union, Japan, Canada, Australia and New Zealand—why shouldn't the same relationships apply everywhere on Earth?

Beyond this, what if it is ultimately understood that cooperation is a larger theme of economics than competition? The standard view of Darwinian evolution—that in the natural world, all competing species are attempting to render one another extinct—has some defenders, but increasingly, biologists find species existing at least somewhat co-operatively with other species. Sugar maple trees, for example, have deep roots that pull up more groundwater than the sugar maple re-quires, then discharge the water into the surrounding soil, allowing plants such as goldenrod, which lack deep roots, to live nearby. Pres-ence of the goldenrod, in turn, holds soil in place around the sugar maple. The two living things are not attempting to render each other extinct—rather, cooperating to assist each other in overcoming the ob-stacles of the found world. We human beings witness the spectacular exception of the tiger that gores the antelope, and imitate this behav-ior in everything from business to statecraft to our love lives. It may be that the deeper message of nature is enlightened cooperation. This is what was thought by the Framers of the U.S. Constitution, most of whom advocated natural law (that is, law modeled on the natural world) because they believed all truths and first principles are "self-evident" (encoded in nature, so that they may be observed by any per-son). And the Framers have been proven right on practically every count.

Eric Beinhocker, a researcher with the flashy international consulting firm McKinsey & Company, has become convinced that neoclassical economics, the mainstream view that dominates Western academia and government, is mostly off base. He's written a fine book[17] that lays out his reasoning, and I will save you a marathon session with a highlighter by summarizing the book for you. Beinhocker contends economists are obsessed with mathematical models, game theory and hypotheticals because these are supersimplified and can be understood. When economists "model" behavior mathematically, the models float in a vacuum. From the models that float in vacuums but are entirely unlikely in real life, neoclassical economists conclude that men and women are machinelike income maximizers who always seek the most of everything: from this, the economists reach fairly bleak conclusions about human nature and about the chances that people will ever establish a cheerful world. Not for nothing is the traditional form of economics known as the "dismal science."

What if, Beinhocker asks, the strongest underlying force in economics is cooperation? After all, I can't sell to you unless you've earned the money necessary to buy. My business won't remain prosperous for long unless your business does, too. Ideally, we'd all want one another's economic situations to be good, and ideally we'd all work together to help one another succeed—personally, locally, internationally. The same forces that are currently globalizing the world and accelerating economic change at head-spinning velocity may also eventually allow the world to adopt cooperative economics, aided by universal communication, universal democracy and universal education. Then there might be a form of economics that has the productive success and allocative efficiency of market theory, coupled to a more humane pace of life.

Nine

LOS ANGELES

n the University Park district of Los Angeles, just after Thanksgiving Day 2008, some 94,000 people gathered to watch a football game between the Notre Dame Fighting Irish and the University of Southern California Trojans. A national television audience looked on as well, while the American Forces' Network beamed the contest not only to U.S. air and ground units fighting in Iraq and Afghanistan but also to the 820 overseas military bases or facilities the United States had, in thirty-nine nations, in that year.

Spectators approaching the game drove or walked past a mélange of cultures and histories, from the bodegas of the city's Mexican-born population to the stamped-out fast-food and big-box marketing of the corporate world to stately homes built a century before in the American Craftsman architectural form that was California's answer to Frank Lloyd Wright. Above the stadium where the contest was staged, orbiting blimps advertised tires, life insurance and photo-printing services; the blimps had to watch out for a latticework of police helicopters also circling and shining spotlights, "projecting presence," as law-enforcement officers say. Thousands of people lacking tickets to the event milled around outside the stadium, some offering to sell or buy various items, some drinking beer from paper sacks, many present merely to soak up the atmosphere. Inside the stadium, scantily clad cheerbabes danced provocatively. Two marching bands took turns belting out brass numbers; drum lines twirled and spun; when the drummers, cheerleaders and sousaphones were not performing, over-amped rock and hormone-soaked rap music blared from speaker towers at the decibel level of jet-fighter afterburners. Before kickoff, actual jet fighters from the naval air station in San Diego roared above the field, making the air crackle.

Dozens of television production vans the size of tractor-trailer trucks were lined up outside the stadium, many with huge dish antennas pointed heavenward toward satellites. Amid the TV trucks were power trucks—loud, muscular-looking portable generators that handle the extra juice demands of television. From broadcast booths of the network carrying the game, announcers mumbled cliché after empty cliché, declaring players were "giving 110 percent" or "taking it to another level" or "came to play," as if sometimes football athletes came to games not to play but to deliver Shakespearean soliloquies. Within the coliseum during the contest, spectators placed phone calls or sent text messages or checked the Web to find out what was going on in places other than the place they'd just spent a considerable amount of money to enter. On the field, a spectacular performance was staged by ostensible "college students," some of whom would not recognize the interior of a classroom. Hollywood and music-world celebrities came to be present at the event, hoping to catch a network camera's attention. The moment the game ended, local sportscasters and radio hosts began to talk agitatedly about what had happened, going directly to the upper boundary of exaggeration. Staging of the event required hundreds of pages of complex legal agreements involving the universities, the network, the state of California (owner of the stadium, where two Olympics games have been held) and various food, cleaning and security contractors. On the backs of the tickets, printed in extremely small type, were disclaimers warning that attending the game could lead to dismemberment or death.

If the victor and the final score mattered only to alumni of the schools and to those who wagered on the game, the event serves as a window into constantly accelerating American culture. On display that glorious late-autumn evening in Los Angeles was everything that makes America wacky—noise, materialism, superficial sexuality, overemphasis on sports and entertainment, legalism, celebrity worship and loud music, all powered by fossil fuels and underwritten by debt. Contemporary American culture is plagued by too much consumerism, too many lawyers, too many celebrities, too much television, too many booty-shaking bimbos and airheaded studs, too many machines, too much horsepower: at times the country can seem a blur of jabber. Yet the United States functions extremely well as a productive nation, as a pluralistic democracy and as a place of opportunity. For all its shallow wackiness, the United States also leads the world in science, in medical research, in aviation, in advanced-degree education, and possesses the strongest and most efficient military in the history of the world: arguably, one more powerful than all other militaries past and present combined. It could even be argued that America leads the world in serious art.[1] The United States is silly and mighty both at once.

Could it be that America is rich, strong and free *because* of celebrities, lawyers, bimbos, athletes, noise and materialism? More to the point, as the Sonic Boom gathers momentum, are these cultural features that much of the rest of the world will embrace?

———

Noise will not be defended in this volume, nor will popular music. But let's consider some other factors on display in the Notre Dame–USC football game of 2008, and ask whether those factors tell us something about the evolving international culture, and how we will work and think in the near future.

Start with sports fixation. Most of Europe, Africa and South America is wild for soccer, with matches drawing mammoth crowds. India loves cricket—and in keeping with the quickening pace of contemporary life is embracing "short-form" cricket, a game that can be completed in a few hours, as opposed to customary "test match" cricket, which lasts five days. Ice hockey is king in Russia and Scandinavia, baseball is queen in Japan, while China, the Mediterranean nations and what was once the Warsaw Pact cannot get enough basketball. Love of sports is worldwide, cutting across all societies.

But no nation takes sports obsession to the extreme observed in the United States. Not just one or two but numerous sports are followed obsessively, on television and in attendance: football, baseball, basketball, ice hockey, tennis. Sportslike competitions such as golf and racecar driving have substantial followings. Most colleges field a full spread of sporting teams, while major universities spend lavishly on sports facilities and athletes. (In much of the world, collegiate athletics is modest, if it exists at all.) Most of the sixteen thousand high schools in the United States offer a dozen or more athletic teams, and many emphasize the most popular high school sport, football. (Most high schools outside the United States and a few other nations do not treat team sports as integral to education; in many nations, what to the United States would be a high school team is a private athletic club not affiliated with the school.) Each Friday night in the autumn in the United States, an estimated twenty million people attend high school football games—among the highest routine attendance for any sport in the world.[2]

Is the American mania for team sports a byproduct of success—Americans lavish money and attention on sports because they can afford to—or a force in that success? Perhaps you know the aphorism "Waterloo was won on the playing fields of Eton." Attributed to the Duke of Wellington after the 1815 battle that ended Napoleon Bonaparte's reign, and also ended military conflict between the United Kingdom and France, the saying means the cooperative team spirit that the British officer class learned playing sports at a fancy school allowed them to stand together and not fold on a day of horrible danger. By the same token, Americans might say that World War II was won on the sandlot baseball diamonds of the agricultural Midwest and on the high school football fields of the northeast, southeast and California. During athletic contests, the "greatest generation" learned how to cooperate under pressure, while those who watched learned the value of teamwork.

In America's case, love of sports and universal public education arose roughly together, which is an important clue to developing nations: they should expect to place more emphasis on sports as they place more emphasis on education. In his book *The Meaning of Sports,* the historian Michael Mandelbaum noted that the obsession with team athletics began to blossom during the late 1800s, exactly as the universal public education movement went into high gear. The new secondary schools being built across the United States, particularly, formed sports teams both to generate school spirit and to inspire Tom Sawyer–style boys to want to come to school. By playing organized sports rather than traditional street games such as stickball, students learned teamwork within a formal rules structure—which would become essential in the twentieth century, when large organizations supplanted sole-proprietor businesses at the center of the economy. In sports, Americans found common ground—no matter how many arguments you may have with your neighbors, everyone agrees on hoping the local high school or college wins the Big Game. Those who play sports learn to get along with others unlike themselves, and getting along with people who aren't like you makes big, complex societies run better. Even those who merely watch team sports on television, never attending games or participating in a local school's programs, find an outlet for blowing off steam in an arena that, ultimately, doesn't matter. Life is full of issues—war and peace, economics and health, freedom and diversity—where the outcomes matter intensely. Whether the Forty Niners or Red Sox win is an exciting question, but ultimately, the answer does not matter. Thus the escalating status of American sports allowed the country a shared obsession that broke down barriers, but could never result in anything bad.

Most of all, sports and schools go together. It may well be that the Ohio State University athletic budget, at $112 million, is too high compared to other needs at the college. But all across the Midwest, large numbers of teens are excited about the idea of going to Ohio State University, and high-profile sports is a major reason. The same can be said of many other schools. There are a few dozen elite colleges that would generate excitement and "admission lust" among high school students even if no game played by chasing a ball had ever been invented, but collegiate sports have been integral to increasing interest in hundreds of other colleges and universities, and thus to raising attendance and education levels. Sports helps confer prestige on colleges, making them seem like places that eighteen-year-olds should want to go, while raising awareness of schools. Probably, most people had never heard of Boise State before it installed a blue football field. Now Boise State is a popular destination for students. No one would argue that sports is always good for higher education: some top college athletes set a bad example by making no pretense of attending class, many college athletic programs soak up alumni donations that might otherwise go to the school's general operating fund, and in an egregious case, since 2005, Rutgers University has canceled classes and raised tuition in order to funnel money to a football program that, according to a New Jersey state investigative commission, cannot account for the whereabouts of millions of dollars.[3]

But in the main, high-profile sports has been a good thing for colleges. Two generations ago, only a fifth of graduating high school seniors went on to attend at least some college: now 65 percent do. The next-best fraction in the world, enjoyed by Britain, is 40 percent of high school students advancing to at least some college attendance. America's high fraction of graduates advancing to college is partly a result, of course, of its affluence. But wealth-measurement statistics aren't all that different in the United States than in the western European Union nations, yet a higher percentage of American children advance to college than children in any E.U. state. One reason is that big-deal sports makes American kids want to be part of the college experience; sports causes college to seem glamorous and exciting in a way that not even the very best lecture on Proust ever will.

Greater sports obsession at the high school level has also occurred in tandem with better results in the classroom. Several studies have shown that boys who participate in high school sports tend to have higher grades and a higher likelihood of attending college than secondary students as a whole. That is, while there are surely dumb jocks, jocks as a group do better in the classroom than students who aren't jocks. But is this "self-selection"—are the kinds of boys who accept the discipline of sports practice also the kind who do their homework?

An opportunity to study this question was inadvertently created in 1972, when the federal Title IX program in effect required most high schools and colleges to make a significant increase in sports opportunities for girls and women. Betsey Stevenson, a professor at Wharton, the business school of the University of Pennsylvania, has found that every 10 percent increase in participation in girls' high school athletics leads to a 1 percent increase in girls' college attendance and a 2 percent increase in women's workforce presence.[4] Also, she found that "greater opportunities to play sports leads to greater female participation in previously male-dominated occupations, particularly for high-skill occupations." Thus, it wasn't just that girls who were likely to be good students anyway tried out for the field hockey team: playing high school sports *improved* their college and career prospects. Sports made them better students and more successful in the workplace.

The more that nations need better students and better professionals, the more they will need sports.[5] Football has in recent decades leapfrogged other team games in importance in American life. Maybe this is just a fad, but maybe this has happened because the structure of football reflects the modern economic era.[6] Like big corporations, football requires large numbers of people from diverse backgrounds to cooperate. The players on the field are hardly the only ones who must cooperate. For every boy, and occasionally girl,[7] who steps onto the high school football field, at least two people—coaches, parents, teachers—worked behind the scenes to make it possible. In big colleges and the pros, it's more like five or six behind the scenes for each one on the field. In order for football games to happen, large numbers of people who otherwise would have nothing to do with one another must make a commitment to get along. Now consider the direction in which global society is headed. In a globalized world, communication and interpersonal skills grow ever more important. The explosion in communication, especially, means that people in coming decades will have to be able to cooperate not only with those in their immediate field of vision, but also with people around the country and around the world. Team sports teach such interpersonal cooperative skills, in a way most school subjects do not. Working on a term paper alone in the library, or on a science project with one or two other people in the lab, is clearly important, but teaches little about interpersonal relations. Working under pressure with a hundred other people of widely differing backgrounds, groups and ages to stage a football game teaches lessons about how to get along and cooperate.

The audience at a football game sees pumped fists and bumping chests among the players, and may think of football as no more than constrained conflict. But before the game starts come extraordinary periods of cooperative work. In football there are perhaps a thousand hours of preparation for each hour of play, and almost all the preparation must be done jointly. Tennis or basketball players can practice alone; football players can only practice in groups. Football players and coaches spend more hours together, in complex social settings, than players and coaches of any other sport, making the ability to get along with others more important to football than to any other sport. The world will become more white-collar with each passing year. This means interpersonal skills will keep rising in value—employers will want the sort of women and men who show they can get along with others in a cooperative atmosphere. Sports are hardly the only way to learn teamwork, of course—others include volunteer organizations, clubs, political groups, faith-based activity, theater or musical societies. But of the teamwork-teaching activities, athletics has the broadest appeal and scope. Owing to this, expect all team sports to become progressively more important than today. Sick of football? It's going to get bigger and more important! You should view that as good, even if you don't care for athletics. There is an element of pragmatic logic to America's preoccupation with team sports.

What about America's preoccupation with education—is there also a lesson there for the larger Sonic Boom world? Typically, commentators say that America's great strengths are its size and resources, its protection by two oceans, its melting-pot culture and its mastery of technology. What if the greatest strength of the United States is its college-centered philosophy of education? Even leading nations such as France or Japan have only a few colleges and universities that are viewed as top quality, while the United States has dozens upon dozens. This may tell us the world needs to make a substantial commitment to expanding college quality and access—and think how economic growth might accelerate if a substantial number of high-quality colleges were added to the global landscape.

Consider the sheer number of superb colleges and universities in the United States: Amherst, Berkeley, Bowdoin, Brown, Caltech, Carleton, the University of Chicago, Claremont McKenna, Columbia, Cornell University, Dartmouth, Davidson, Duke, Georgetown University, Harvard, Johns Hopkins, Middlebury, MIT, Northwestern, Penn, Pomona, Princeton, Smith, Stanford, Swarthmore, Washington University in St. Louis, Wellesley, Williams and Yale. Then consider how many U.S. colleges and universities are in the near-elite tier: Bard, Barnard, Bates, Boston College, Brandeis, Bryn Mawr, Bucknell, Carnegie Mellon, Case Western, Colby, Colgate, Colorado College, Dickinson, Emory, George Washington, Georgia Tech, Grinnell, Hamilton, Harvey Mudd, Haverford, Holy Cross, Howard, Kenyon, Lafayette, Lehigh, Macalester, Mount Holyoke, Notre Dame, Oberlin, Occidental, Reed, Rensselaer, Rice, Rochester, Sarah Lawrence, Scripps, Skidmore, St. John's of Annapolis, Texas Christian, Tulane, Trinity of Connecticut, Tufts, Vanderbilt, Vassar, Washington and Lee, Wesleyan, Whitman, William and Mary; the main campuses of the universities of Illinois, Michigan, North Carolina, Texas, Virginia and Wisconsin; and the University of California campuses at Davis, Irvine, Los Angeles and San Diego. (Alums, please don't write if I neglected your school; obviously this listing is unscientific.) That's nearly a hundred outstanding colleges and universities in the United States. Equivalent institutions in the rest of the world combined: Cambridge, Ecole Polytechnique (France), the Indian Institutes of Technology, the London School of Economics, Imperial College (England), National University of Singapore, Oxford, SciencesPo (France), Trinity College (Ireland), Tsinghua University (China) and Technion University (Israel). Technology, science, military power, movies, resources, space exploration, traffic jams—the United States leads in many arenas. But in no arena is the U.S. lead as high as 10:1, roughly the American advantage, compared to the rest of the world, in first-quality colleges.

This must have something to do with America's position in the universal public education movement—which in turn suggests a pattern most of the world should copy. Prussia had the first universal primary education system, beginning in the late eighteenth century: it was the United States, during the nineteenth century, that first offered universal public education to age sixteen.[8] America was the first nation to expect the average teen to remain in the education system long enough to graduate from high school; today America is the first nation to expect the average eighteen-year-old to enroll in a college, whether four-year or community. As the sociologist Ruy Teixeira has noted, "In the 1940s, the typical young American was a high school dropout. Today the typical young American has at least some college." The United States is the first nation in which to attend at least a year of college is "typical."

There is a clear economic benefit to higher education. According to Census Bureau figures, in 2006 the median income for Americans with only a high school diploma or a GED was $21,000; the median for those with a bachelor's degree was $40,000; for holders of a master's, $51,000; for holders of doctorates, $70,000; and for holders of professional degrees, $77,000. Households headed by those with bachelor's degrees had four times the net worth of households headed by those with only high school diplomas, and their net worth was increasing at a much faster rate. Statistics like these are sometimes presented as indication of a plot to hold back those whose families can't afford to send them to college. What the statistics in this paragraph really convey is that the United States must work harder to make college accessible to everyone, especially the poor and lower working class, so they, too, can enjoy the income benefits of higher education. Otherwise, the numbers are admirable. They show that the United States not only preaches education but rewards education. Generations of teachers have fretted that they were spending their lives drilling into students' heads knowledge that would never be used. Knowledge turns out to be really useful! People who have studied and learned tend to go far in the United States. In the next phase of global growth, people who have studied and learned will tend to go far in almost any nation.

Don't think the rest of the world has not noticed. Today there is a thriving business in American colleges starting affiliates in Asia, the Persian Gulf and elsewhere, or in Asian and other colleges hiring American professors and administrators to bring both American educational quality and American can-do attitude to their campuses. New York University, for example, has an affiliated branch in the United Arab Emirates; Michigan State and the Rochester Institute of Technology have branches in Dubai. Qatar is building an entire new town called Education City, roughly a shopping mall where the brands are American colleges (Carnegie Mellon, Cornell, Texas A&M) and the goods for sale are knowledge.[9] Traditionally, nations advance economically by first learning to imitate products from developed countries. Over the next few decades, much of the world will learn to imitate how America runs colleges. This will be good for international equity and equality, but also cause more economic turmoil, as much of the world achieves a position to enter the knowledge-based industries that the United States and the European Union now dominate.

America's incredible emphasis on higher education is sometimes seen as if this were an indulgence—kids spend four years holding keggers in dorms. As Robert Grady, a former White House official and now a venture capitalist, notes, "Universities are far more important to modern economics than generally realized. Universities produce new ideas and people that employers want to hire." College emphasis is central to American economic power and even to American military power. Advancement in the modern officer corps of the U.S. armed forces is unlikely without a bachelor's degree, advancement to flag rank unlikely without a master's or more. Wherever American forces dig ditches and pour concrete for runaways, they also build a continuing-education branch for soldiers. For instance, at Bagram Air Base in the wild mountain plateaus of Afghanistan, there are not only four thousand service men and women but a local center for the University of Maryland, allowing soldiers and air crews to work on credit hours.[10] America has the strongest military in the history of the world, and also has the smartest and best-educated—and often, the education is just as important as the hardware.

If I could found a country that had either good colleges or vast reserves of oil, I'd pick colleges in a heartbeat.

We should not fear an education-based ordering of global society, even if it erodes some of the competitive advantages now enjoyed by the United States and Europe. Indeed, we should welcome an education-based global economy, as such an ordering substantially will increase the sum of brainpower directed to creating more prosperity and solving the world's problems. But there are major concerns with the American way of education, including its cost, and spreading American-style college education across much of the world inevitably also will spread American-style costs.

Since 1982, and adjusting for inflation, median family income in the United States has risen by about 150 percent, while the full cost of private college in the United States has risen by about 440 percent, according to the National Center for Public Policy and Higher Education.[11] Averaging out for financial-aid awards, the effective cost of attending a private U.S. college has gone up by about 350 percent in the last quarter-century—worse than the worst price spike for petroleum, and a more enduring cost increase.[12] Public universities would seem to be the solution for most families, but in the United States, costs are rising there, too. As Kevin Carey of the think tank Education Sector said in 2008, "The average price of attending a public university more than doubled over the last two decades, even adjusting for inflation, with the steepest increase coming in the last five years."[13] In 2008, for example, the Consumer Price Index rose by less than 1 percent, but tuition for Virginia's public colleges and universities rose by 7 percent. Taking into account financial aid, during the 1990s, sending a child to a four-year U.S. public college cost the typical middle-class family 18 percent of its income, a difficult enough pill to swallow: now the cost is 25 percent of family income. As public-university costs rise, state support declines. A generation ago, California paid 42 percent of the cost of its state university system, but today pays only 17 percent; as a result, in-state tuition has more than doubled, in inflation-adjusted terms. States including Florida have begun to impose admission caps for the freshmen classes at public universities, turning away high school graduates in order to hold down the numbers on campus, and thereby restrain costs. Some 15.4 million men and women attended four-year undergraduate colleges in the United States in 2007, a spectacularly positive figure. Nearly 80 percent of them attended public universities—which will need more resources, not budget cuts, to continue performing well enough to keep up with the Sonic Boom.

Meanwhile the schools at the top continue to hoard tremendous sums needed elsewhere. In 2008, Harvard had a $37 billion endowment—that figure exceeding the GDP of Iceland and Honduras combined.[14] By contrast, Appalachian State University, a school that serves typical students, had an endowment of $52 million—meaning Harvard possessed $720 for every $1 held by Appalachian State. Yet money kept flowing where it wasn't needed. In 2008, a billionaire named Hansjorg Wyss gave $125 million to Harvard. That sum might have transformed the lives of students at, say, Lenoir-Rhyne College, endowment $58 million. But the glamour is at Harvard, so that's where the money flows. Among the many ways in which the rich consistently let America down is by giving money where the gift buffs their egos, rather than where the money helps typical people. If more of the world imitates the American college system, this problem will be imitated too.

———

Schools at all levels today struggle to compete for students' attention against video games, excruciatingly trivialized entertainment culture, the temptations of drugs, and of course all those fabulous sporting events touted above. The same international forces that will make an increased emphasis on education more important will make that emphasis more challenging, because they will cause the distractions to get more appealing. Studies consistently show that coming from a stable home with both parents present and a stable income is the best predictor of school success: that is, a minority child from a stable home of modest income is more likely to succeed than a majority child from a high-income troubled home. In part because so many African-American and Hispanic students live in troubled home environments, as groups African Americans and Hispanics continue to do less well in school than whites. As globalized economics makes us better off overall but increases instability, home structures will remain under siege. Economic trends that cause overall prosperity but destabilize individual families will make the children from those families less likely to succeed in school. Already most of the dropouts from California high schools are children of first- or second-generation citizens or immigrants with Mexican or Central American backgrounds:[15] that they aren't finishing high school is especially alarming, because taking the next step to college is what they need to swim in the currents of larger economic forces.

And as regards college preparation, here's an issue that ought to be in the public educational debate but is not: How should the curriculum be revised for a Sonic Boom world? Probably you're thinking, "Make kids learn more math and science." What if the answer is *less* math and science, but more economics, technology and cross-cultural studies?

In the last generation there has been a national push for more, more, more math in middle school and high school. In 1994, President Bill Clinton challenged American schools to teach algebra in eighth grade, which was then rare, in order to make it possible for high school students to advance to calculus, which a generation ago was a college subject. Today some 31 percent of eighth-graders in the United States take algebra,[16] and about the same fraction of high school students take calculus; California plans to mandate that by 2011, all eighth-graders take algebra. Schools in Asian nations emphasize math even more intensely.

Yet unless you enter into the hard sciences or become an actuary, you will likely walk through life without ever once calling on algebra or calculus. Arguably, there should be *less* math emphasis in public schools, since even in a technological society, the majority of adult men and women will never use higher mathematics for any purpose whatsoever. Math is being heavily pushed in political disputes about education, though often it serves primarily to make teens feel stupid.

This isn't a personal gripe. I was good at math in school—so there!—but I knew high school students who were made to feel dumb because they didn't get math, and whose interest in school declined as a result. And I can assure you that since the day I passed my college calculus course, I have never once done a Riemann sum in my adult life. Math education is pushed because people think schools need to become more "traditional," and learning higher math was a tradition—before pocket calculators. Schools do not, however, necessarily need to become more traditional. In many cases what they need is to become more modern.

Most students graduate from U.S. public schools without any instruction in economics. Economics impact every person's life every day, and as globalization spreads and deepens, the impact will increase. One reason people experience so much anxiety about Sonic Boom forces is that many are poorly educated in economics, and public schools are doing nothing about this—while making students stare at Lorenz Transformations. Defenders of advanced math education say it "teaches students how to think." So does economics, and better to learn to think on a subject that will be useful to your future. More than a century ago, Andrew Carnegie scoffed at schools as places that taught Greek and Latin when what students needed to learn was economics. His complaint remains valid today—economics is not required in public high schools, or in many cases even taught. My children's wonderful public high school, Winston Churchill of Potomac, Maryland, has seventeen full-time math teachers and two teachers who offer an economics course as a sideline. (One mainly teaches math, the other mainly teaches history.) At the collegiate level, economics often is seen as a topic strictly for business majors. Economics needs to become central to public education, and a core-curriculum component of college.

By the same token, high school science instruction tends to focus on chemistry and the underlying theories of matter and energy. Most people will never use what they learn in such courses. How about, instead, courses on technology—its good and bad applications, its public-policy implications. Those are areas in which all global citizens need to know more. And what about cultural studies? Most schools have courses in the history of other parts of the world, but what students really need to learn is the contemporary culture of other parts of the world—politics, economics, religion. Just as the structure of high school math teaching is based on the outdated assumption that problems must be solved with slide rules, the structure of high school history teaching is based on the outdated assumption that most students will have little or no personal contact with other nations, except as tourists at historical sites. In the Sonic Boom world, students will grow up to have nearly constant contact with other cultures, yet most public school systems aren't preparing them for this. I worry a lot more that Americans of the future will not understand Chinese society than that they will never have taken Calc II.

Here's another reason the world must invest ever more in education—it pays off! Governments the globe around expend huge amounts in categories where the ideal outcome is waste (ideally, all military spending is for forces that sit unused) or the expense is necessary but not productive (pensions). Education, by contrast, has a fantastic payback. Critics of the American public education system complain that SAT scores have been essentially flat since about 1990, which is true.[17] But in that period the percentage of high school students taking the SAT has shot way up, with most of the new test-takers being foreign-born or from disadvantaged backgrounds. Given that SAT scores would be expected to decline, that they hold strong during the all-time peak for immigration into the United States is a positive sign. More broadly, there is the steady, nearly global rise in IQ scores. Since roughly the 1920s, when widespread administration of intelligence tests began, IQ scores have risen by about 3 percent per decade in almost all nations, adding up to a nearly 25 percent overall increase. This tells us, first, that genetics cannot be the number-one factor in human intelligence, as evolution does not occur nearly fast enough to explain a 25 percent rise in less than a century. If genes were the main explanation for IQ, pretty much the entire world would need to be mutating like mad to get such a big shift in a short time. (Genes must have something to do with IQ, as they must have something to do with height; they are just

not the main factor.) This tells us, second, that on the whole schools
are getting better and access to education is getting better in a substantial, international manner. Better health and better nutrition are
factors in the fast IQ-score rise. Higher living standards are a factor.
Studies show that when a child is taken from an impoverished background and placed into a middle-class home (say, by adoption), the
child's IQ score rises by around 15 percent within a few years. But that
education is improving is almost surely the lead factor in higher IQ
scores. As Nicholas Kristof has written, "Good schooling correlates
particularly closely to higher IQs. One indication of the importance of
school is that children's IQs drop or stagnate over the summer months
when they are on vacation."[18] School not only makes people smart—
it's a smart use of money.

As recently as a few generations ago, most of the world's citizens
had no access to education, while more than half were illiterate. One
generation ago, a quarter of the world was illiterate, most people still
had no access to higher education, and most of those who did manage
to attend a college sat in enormous lecture halls listening to a professor drone on in monotone. A professor droning to a huge lecture hall,
then taking no questions, is still the format in many of the public universities of Europe, Canada and Asia—small wonder America's
challenge-the-professor system is superior! Today 90 percent of the
global population is literate. Educational opportunities are increasing
in most nations, while the seminar method of teaching is proliferating.
Just as whole swaths of the world are finally tasting democracy and
market economics, they are also finally tasting real education. Substantial global increases in the number of men and, notably, women
who are educated, think for themselves and contribute ideas to the
world will accelerate the material and social improvements of the
Sonic Boom.

Ten

SÃO JOSÉ DOS CAMPOS

ecause the powerful Paraíba do Sul, a river of rapids and swirling currents, flows through the city on its way to the sea, and because the local topography includes highlands that drop off rapidly toward the flat infinity of the Atlantic, São José dos Campos is adorned with waterfalls as if an ancient luminist had supervised the design. For centuries, São José dos Campos has been a minor location in a little-noticed part of the world. The Conquistadors took the area from indigenous people, then the Portuguese took the area from Spain, then for a phase São José dos Campos was a jumping-off point for the Brazilian gold craze, then a support center for coffee plantations, then its isolation was employed to make a sanitarium town for tuberculosis victims. When antibiotics were discovered in the 1930s, tuberculosis treatment became possible anywhere, and sanitariums closed. By the 1950s, São José dos Campos, with 40,000 residents and no distinction other than its urban waterfalls, was the sort of town young people dreamed of leaving.

Today São José dos Campos is a metropolis of 625,000, about the same population as Boston. Glistening office towers and high-rises form a skyline that gives modern contrast to the ancient highlands: any product or service the mind can imagine is available in the city's shopping districts. Dams were built on the surging rivers, and low-cost energy from hydropower began an urban development cycle; with each passing year, as petroleum becomes problematic and greenhouse gases accumulate, a city that uses zero-emission flowing water for power seems a better place to be. Anchoring the new economy of São José dos Campos is Embraer, the world's third-largest manufacturer of aircraft. The company's technical design bureaus, manufacturing facilities and corporate offices are the heart of the now-bustling location.

You may not be aware of Embraer, but probably have flown aboard its planes; if not, you will. One generation ago, America's Boeing and Europe's Airbus dominated commercial aircraft manufacturing, with Russia's Ilyushin and Sukhoi, Canada's Bombardier, Germany's Fokker and Sweden's Saab the also-rans. Today Embraer trails only Boeing and Airbus, and Airbus is nervously glancing at its rearview mirror. As an entrepreneurial story, Embraer is a scriptwriter's dream. Originally the firm was a state-owned corporation plagued by corruption and low product quality. In 1994, Embraer became a private enterprise, whose management gambled on an idea that Boeing and Airbus had rejected. The idea—Boeing and Airbus studies said there was no market for this—was high-quality "regional" jets with fifty to one hundred seats, an ideal range of less than fifteen hundred miles, and low purchase cost, but the very latest in propulsion and avionics. The Embraer ERJ series has since become among the aerospace industry's greatest hits. Fuel efficient, comfortable and electronically advanced, ERJs have been snapped up by airlines eager to replace slow-flying, loud, bumpy-ride turboprops on routes such as Atlanta to Austin or San Francisco to Seattle. Embraer's aircraft are well made and reliable. The company buys engines from the United States or the United Kingdom (General Electric or Rolls Royce) and avionics from the United States (Honeywell), but the airplanes that rise off its runways and depart for customers worldwide are designed by Brazilian engineers and built by Brazilian workers.

For Brazil, Embraer represents a source of jobs and national pride. For everyone else, the company represents the next phase of international economics—developing-world companies won't just take orders to produce advanced products designed elsewhere; the developing world will design its own advanced products from scratch. The success of Embraer could not have happened a few decades ago: trade barriers, capital-movement restrictions, information scarcity and above all the rarity of higher education in the developing world confined the "southern" nations to agriculture, mining, unskilled-labor industries such as textiles, and manufacture of products whose research and development was done on another continent. Today a Brazilian or Chinese business may be every bit the equal of an American or German business in technical proficiency, manufacturing quality and market savvy.

This growth of important ideas originating outside the privileged Western nations is sure to keep accelerating. A generation ago, Boeing engineers and machinists did not need to care about what was happening in Brazil; now they do. How long until Brazilian engineers and machinists need to care about what is happening in some other up-and-coming nation? Not far from its headquarters city, Embraer owns a flight-test facility called Unidade Gavião Peixoto, which features one of the longest runaways ever constructed. No flying machine the company currently manufactures needs a runaway anywhere near as long as the one at Unidade Gavião Peixoto. But Embraer is already thinking ahead to a future in which fundamentally new aviation products may be developed.

Maybe Embraer just had good luck with a product idea in an industry of top-heavy, bureaucratic giants that could be outwitted by a more nimble competitor. But Embraer is, itself, huge and resource-intensive—factories, laboratories, many thousands of hourly and salaried workers. Its basic idea, the high-quality regional jet, required years of testing before the first sale, and therefore complex capital financing. This isn't five college kids in a loft.

Embraer's success keys from thinking about not what customers want right now, but what they will want in the future. Every business, school and college across the world needs to focus more on thinking ahead, because as the Sonic Boom takes hold, "the future" is going to arrive sooner and sooner. Once, "the future" was what would happen in your children's lifetime. Currently "the future" is what will happen later in your own lifetime. Soon—and by "soon," I mean "really soon"—the future may arrive with scarcely a moment's notice.

———

The nature of work, business and economic connectedness is fundamentally changing. Soon—meaning "really soon"—examples such as the rapid rise of high-quality manufacturing in Brazil will no longer be worth remarking upon, because they will have become norms. Americans and Europeans will benefit in many ways from a fast-changing Sonic Boom economy, especially in that most consumer goods will cost steadily less and be of steadily higher quality—but more economic turmoil and more competition will be nearly inevitable. Most of the world's nations are acquiring the same core structures (democracy, free-market economics, emphasis on education) that make the United States the current international leader and also the same quirks (loud music, sports obsession, fast food) that make the United States wacky. Many nations or cultures don't want to grow more like the United States, but this is likely regardless, and on balance will be good for most other nations. The more America-like the world becomes, the faster the pace of economic change will be. As Fareed Zakaria pointed out in his 2008 book *The Post-American World,* the United States dominated the twentieth century not only because of its advantages in physical resources, brainpower and protective oceans, but because much of the rest of the world had crippled itself via dictatorship, suppression of free speech and lack of education.[1] As the whole world moves toward democracy, free expression and education, areas previously "not performing," in Zakaria's phrase, will begin to perform. The United States, the European Union and Japan will find that many of what once were automatic advantages are no longer automatic. This is not bad, but we will be forced to adjust. Here are important considerations to keep in mind:

YOU CAN'T STOP GLOBAL CHANGE

Quite literally, no one can—certainly, the governments of the world could not. You might wish the arrival of freedom in many other nations would not cause them to challenge the United States and the European Union in multiple ways, including their business interests. You might wish rain never falls on picnics! Suppose the new international economy had not begun, that free expression and free trade had not spread: that things had remained like the 1960s, with a third of the world feudal or fascist, a third of the world Communist and only a third of the world free. If so, the West could well be mired in long-term economic stagnation that would last not a year or two, but a generation. Fast-changing international economic disruption is simply the world's condition for the time being. For most people in most nations, the result is that material life is better than it has ever been before, though with lots of anxiety added. Regardless, the main forces involved cannot be brought to a halt. To argue against global economic change caused by spreading freedom is about as useful as arguing against the phases of the moon.

As this book was being completed, in France, workers at a construction-equipment factory owned by the American firm Caterpillar had taken over the facility to protest a reduction in total jobs, and in employee benefits, there. The workers contended that international-economy competition was being used as a sledgehammer to force them to accept less-attractive deals—and they were right! That's exactly what was happening. But the same workers staging the protest carried inexpensive cell phones made in Asia, drove to the protest in cars whose petrol came via tanker from other nations, and were using Internet technology and servers developed in other countries to tell the world about their cause. They dreamed that the forces that reduced Caterpillar jobs in France could be stopped, yet that they could continue to enjoy the rest of what international interconnectedness offers. But you can't pick and choose the economic forces that you like—rather, you must live with the whole package, its good and bad. If the borders of France were closed against the rest of the world, certain kinds of stress would immediately decline. But so would French prosperity—it is inconceivable that the typical French citizen would be better off. The same logic applies to almost every nation and situation; regulations should protect the environment and protect workers from unsafe or exploitive conditions, but can't protect anyone from change. We must make our peace with the forces of the present; wishing they would go away is a waste of everyone's time. No clock has ever been turned back.

People in the original industrial nations seem spooked that the Factory Age is winding down, to be supplanted by a Sonic Boom era dominated by desk jobs and education. Yet this transition is positive: better most people should spend years in college, then work at a desk, then go home to watch the NFL or Canal Plus on television,[2] than other possible outcomes. The factory-based era that commentators and politicians romanticize was a period in which most people did not graduate from high school, choking pollution was everywhere, prejudice against women and minority-group members was ubiquitous and living standards were far lower than today. Factories themselves ought not to be romanticized, as most were dangerous places to work and consumed huge quantities of energy, minerals and ore while converting only a tiny fraction into usable products: most of what went into a factory left as waste, either pollution or trash or vented heat. (Heat that simply wafts away from a factory, or from your car's brakes, represents wasted energy.)

The biological approach to manufacturing, in which very little energy is needed to convert resources efficiently into bones or tree trunks and so on, will represent a step forward, assuming this can be accomplished. Spider silk is about as strong as steel, yet is produced with almost no energy input—you've seen photos of the roaring blast furnaces needed for steelmaking, with far more heat wafting away as waste than is utilized by the product—and almost no waste. Spider silk is about as strong as steel yet *contains no metal,* that's how efficiently nature uses materials: Charlotte the spider puts our wasteful factory-based approach to manufacturing to shame. A nature-imitating, knowledge-based approach will entail more desk jobs and fewer factory jobs, and that's good. In 2009, a Korean researcher working at the Max Planck Institute in Germany went nature one better and discovered a way to make spider silk as strong as the kind of titanium alloys used in spacecraft. The technique requires far less energy and lower resource inputs than making any ore-based hard substance. In a few generations, the idea of a vast, hot, dirty place gobbling tremendous amounts of resources and energy to produce metal may seem as quaint as the village smithy's shop seems now.

Nostalgia for old-style industrialism is easy to sympathize with. In the initial postwar era dominated by the factory, across entire regions such as the Ohio Valley and the Ruhr Valley, the global economy was comprehensible. You could see with your own eyes the anchor of the economy: it was the factory, nearby and physically visible. Stresses on factory workers and management have always been present—never put the past on a pedestal—but a generation ago, such stresses were simpler than today, and mainly local in origin. Ronald Reagan once said that the sight of a factory belching smoke made people feel safe, because the smokestack was a symbol of humanity's ability to overcome the natural world: he sounded like he was defending pollution, but he meant something altogether different, which we now sense as gradual disappearance of those smokestacks makes us feel insecure. Not too long ago, if you asked yourself, "Where is the economy?" you could answer, "There, at that factory." That answer doesn't apply today, and won't ever apply again. Not too long ago, if you asked yourself, "Where is the competition?" you could answer, "A hundred miles away, at that other factory." That answer also doesn't apply today, and won't ever apply again.

But you can't argue in favor of sunrises and against sunsets. To have one, you must accept the other. Sonic Boom prosperity and anxiety-inducing personal upheaval are two sides of the same coin. Even as a global boom returns, we'll become sick to death of talking, thinking and worrying about economics; we're going to want this topic to go away. It won't, and this simply cannot be changed.

THIS IS NOT THE FIRST MOMENT OF UPHEAVAL AND WILL NOT BE THE LAST

Human beings tend to overestimate the desirability of the past and underestimate the value of what is occurring in the present. This book offers many examples of past points in which economic and social change have occurred at dizzying rates, leading to forecasts of calamity.

In every case, after the turmoil was over, people considered the new condition superior to the previous one—and then hoped to stop any further change. Turmoil followed by more turmoil with additional turmoil on the horizon is the way of the world, stretching as far back as written records extend. Two thousand four hundred years ago, Plato wrote that the world had been sweetly ordered and serene in his youth, but now was going to hell in a handbasket. He did not actually use a Greek word for *handbasket,* but you get the point. Seventy years ago, George Orwell wrote that Britain had been a prosperous and pleasant place in his youth, but the future held only decay and deprivation.[3] Today every resident of the United Kingdom lives far better than when Orwell predicted decline; the British poor, Orwell's leading concern, enjoy dramatically improved material, political and educational circumstances. People have always extolled the past and feared the future. In nearly every case, the future has turned out the better place to be.

YOUR BOSS WILL BE YOU

Through most of American and European history, most people were self-employed in various trades or worked for small, locally based businesses whose owners they either knew personally or at least occasionally saw in person. This arrangement was not necessarily idyllic—local business owners can be bullies—but at least a person's economic affairs were mainly in his or her own hands. The large-organization life that arrived with World War II drove out many small businesses, becoming the rule for most Americans and Europeans for a half century. Now the trend is back toward smaller firms, self-employment and locally based enterprises. Unlike the local enterprises of past generations, future local enterprises are as likely to trade with other continents as to supply parts for a nearby factory or services to a nearby school. But the general direction will be for gigantic corporations to matter less to people's lives, and what happens locally to matter more. Rather than finding a job, more and more Americans and Europeans will be expected to create a job. It is a standard dream for men and women to say they wish they worked for themselves, rather than for a boss. Ever more people actually will work for themselves. This will bring a sense of freedom, but also new forms of anxiety. You'll never really be away from work. If things go poorly, you will have no one but yourself to blame.

HOME AND WORK WILL MERGE

Until roughly the early twentieth century, significant numbers of people did their wage-earning at home—counting farms as homes—or close to the home, in store/apartment combinations or similar arrangements. Today we think the correct ordering of the economy is to drive a considerable distance to work in a place isolated from the home—indeed, most people assume it's not "work" unless it involves some kind of commuting hassle. American-style suburbs were intended to separate home life from wage-earning, so the home could be a peaceful place (lawns, fresh air) physically removed from the noise and pollution of the workplace. But the sense of peace gained by having a nice setting for the home is now lost to the daily grind of commuting in backed-up traffic, and at any rate, over the course of time, there may be a rebound of the historical pattern of living close to where you work. In the twenty-first century an ever-increasing amount of work will return to the home, and to larger, more comfortable homes than those of the past.

There will be convenience attached to this: but as home and work increasingly blur, getting away from work will grow harder and harder. Already for millions of people, cell phones and texting make escaping the job difficult: and communication technology is about to get much better. It took the fax machine about two decades to transition from cutting-edge to old-fashioned. Today the text message has been around about five years; how soon until it is considered old-fashioned and clumsy compared to whatever comes next?

FALLING BACKWARD WILL BECOME A GREATER RISK

The American national narrative is up-from-nothing, a story embodied by the country's current president, Barack Obama, who came from a modest family with no connections. Americans embraced Obama in part because his life story is their national story—and as feudal economies worldwide yield to open economies in which a hardworking person can better himself or herself, for more and more of the world, up-from-nothing will become a standard dream. In the American version of this story, people must strive hard to enter the middle class, but once there, rarely fall backward. If you study in school and work diligently, you will be rewarded with a decent material existence *and you won't lose it*. Sociological "graduations"—from poverty to working class, from working class to middle class, from middle to upper middle, from upper middle to wealth—are seen as one-way boulevards. Those who leave the working class for the middle class, or leave the middle class for the upper middle, don't return.

That, at least, is the traditional assumption. But as the global economy becomes more volatile, the future may hold as much fear of falling down the economic ladder as promise of climbing up. Carol Graham of the University of Maryland, who was born in Peru, has studied contemporary South America, where incomes, living standards and personal-freedom levels are rising quite nicely. Yet social happiness is declining. Why? Graham's research finds that many people who attain middle-class status in today's South America fall back out of the middle class and end up bitterly unhappy—more so than if they'd never joined the middle class in the first place. Fear of loss, she further finds, plagues even those who are doing fine. Middle-class advancement in today's prosperous South American nations is not seen as a one-way graduation; rather, it is seen as a fragile thing that breaks easily.

Such fear of falling backward is coming to the United States and the European Union, and the fear will prey on our minds even if actual loss is never experienced. We need to prepare for this problem with social strategies. Two generations ago, big corporations offering long-term employment were seen as bringing stability, along with stifling conformity, to the middle class. Now you can act any way you want and say anything you want—but no corporation cares about you. Alternative stabilizing forces are needed.

We'll need to refashion government, community and financial institutions around a new reality in which sudden job loss could happen to anyone—and more than once per lifetime. For houses, some more flexible financing premise may be needed to ensure that those who make responsible purchases of homes they can reasonably afford won't be in danger of losing them every time the global economy undergoes a mood swing. Universal, comprehensive health coverage will be needed to prevent the personal disaster of a catastrophic illness from expelling the entire family from the middle class, as will college-financing plans that take into account that parents' incomes will vary more in the future than they have in the past. Government will need to plan for less-predictable revenues, too, saving in flush years so that money is available to carry the nation through lean years. Just that idea alone—that government should *save* when years are good—will be a major shock to many political systems.

MOST THINGS WILL GET BETTER FOR MOST PEOPLE—BUT UNLESS YOU LIVE IN A POOR NATION, DON'T EXPECT THAT TO MAKE YOU ANY HAPPIER

In poor nations, economic growth is making men and women happier. Since 1981, Ronald Inglehart of the University of Michigan has been the chief investigator for the World Values Survey, which uses polling data to track the sense of well-being in fifty-two nations. For most of its existence the World Values Survey numbers have been static, re-porting little change up or down, which has caused Inglehart to de-velop a number of theories about how people's sense of worth has little to do with their material circumstances. But in the most recent World Values Survey, the "Happiness Index" improved in forty countries, while showing a negative trend in just twelve.[4] The countries where happiness is rising are developing nations that recently switched to open elections and free-market economies. For such nations, which had never known the social structures taken for granted in the West, democracy and free economies are bringing with them a clear rise in social satisfaction. But in the other countries in the World Values Survey—the nations that have long enjoyed free elections and open economies—measures of happiness are either flat or negative.

Many studies, including some by Carol Graham, have shown that except in the case of nations leaving poverty, rising income and higher living standards do not necessarily equate to increased well-being. The things that bring true satisfaction—friendship, family, honor, love, a sense of place in the community, a sense that one's life has purpose—cannot be purchased with money; thus, having money may be unrelated to having happiness. Probably in the Sonic Boom economy, most people's lives will be better than their parents' lives and most of their children's lives will be better in turn. But this may have surprisingly little to do with whether anyone feels happy.[5]

The near future is likely to offer a quicksand of factors that stifle happiness even when national conditions are basically fine. Job insecurity; media-heightened awareness of whatever's going wrong anywhere in the world; 24/7/52 economic competition; exaggerated doomsday alarms; accelerating mixing of peoples, cultures, religions and worldviews; a low-lying haze of uncertainty. If you find yourself experiencing a mild unease about life in general even if you cannot put your finger on any one specific thing that's really wrong—welcome to the club! Nonspecific mild unease about life in general may be much of society's fate for decades to come, if not indefinitely.

HEALTH CARE MUST BECOME ASSURED

We have little choice but to learn to live with the stresses and anxiety associated with constant economic change. But as regards health care, we do have a choice. Society can, and must, end the stress associated with obtaining and paying for health care. In much of Europe this issue is reasonably resolved, but at this writing nowhere in the United States is it. If society asks its citizens to accept regular turmoil in their working lives in order to improve economic efficiency, society must ensure that health does not suffer.

It is ridiculous that the current American health-care system, which is mainly employer-sponsored, expects people to gamble with their health every time they change jobs—to say nothing of expecting men and women to find entire new sets of health-care providers as often as annually, owing to constant change in the fine print of health-care programs, while navigating through hundreds of pages of insurance mumbo-jumbo intended to discourage claims. It is worse than ridiculous that in mid-2009 the current system strongly discourages men and women from becoming self-employed, or from starting small businesses, because individual and small-group health-insurance policies cost far more than large-group policies. Society should be encouraging women and men to start small businesses or become self-employed: increasingly, a leading obstacle is the cost of individual or small-group health insurance. It is worse than ridiculous that in the United States, having a "preexisting condition"—that is, being sick!—makes it far harder, and far more expensive, to obtain health insurance. If you haven't dealt with this awful catch-22, here's what it means. You work for an employer, and develop back pain; the employer's plan pays for your care. You leave this job for any reason, whether bad (laid off) or good (you have an idea and start your own business). Your previous health insurance ends, and you buy a new policy. Because your back condition is "preexisting,"[6] the new insurer refuses to pay for back-pain therapy. Every potential insurer says the same: coverage denied.

Unlike in other aspects of life, where we must be accountable for our choices, in health outcomes men and women are almost always blameless. The social compact must include comprehensive quality protection for all. Yet although the United States extends retirement benefits to 100 percent of its citizens through the Social Security system, whether you receive health insurance is strictly a roll of the dice. Even those who have good health-care plans through their employers increasingly find it's a roll of the dice whether the employer will continue to offer the plan from year to year. Even those who purchase individual plans increasingly find it's a roll of the dice whether the insurer will continue to offer the plan, or raise the rates through the roof if someone in the family becomes seriously ill, or cite fine print to reduce benefits.

Both formal psychological studies and anecdotal evidence say that Western Europeans suffer less from stress than Americans, yet Western Europe is being buffeted by the same Sonic Boom economic forces as the rest of the world. Hanging out in cafés and pubs as the Euros do, while pleasant, can't possibly account for the less-stressful nature of European life. Western Europeans get on average six weeks of vacation per year, versus an average of ten days in the United States: time off is a stress reducer, and Americans should get more time off. But the primary stress differential between the European Union and the United States is that in the former, no one worries about losing health-care coverage. No one skips physician visits because of inability to pay.

European-style health care is far from perfect, and to some extent enjoys a free ride on American health care, which performs much of the expensive research and development that pushes medical science forward. But surely the United States can find a compromise system that preserves the best aspects of American medicine—ready access to care, funding for high-tech research—while removing the personal terror of losing coverage, and the crisis of the costly operation that a family can't afford. America spends $6,700 per capita annually on health care, versus $4,000 annually in Germany or Sweden.[7] Surely making the American health system more efficient, and less focused on wealth for physicians and health-care company executives, would save enough to extend comprehensive coverage to all Americans.

At this writing, newly elected President Barack Obama was promising significant health-care reform in the United States, but few specifics were known. Hoping to head off some kind of nationalization of health care, lobby organizations for the American health-insurance industry offered a little-noticed compromise: that insurers would end the practice of excluding "preexisting" conditions from policies, while adopting standard comprehensive policies with standard prices. Availability of standard-price, no-denials plans would be a tremendous step forward for the United States. At minimum, the U.S. regulatory premise must change so that any company that wants to be in the health-insurance business must sell the same coverage to all customers at the same price. Spreading the risk in this way is the only solution that would transform a job change, or a move into self-employment, from a potential health-care disaster to something with no health-care implications, since your premiums would be the same regardless of what kind of work you do or whether you get sick. Auto insurance ought to cost careless drivers more, in order to reward responsible driving. Most health problems are just bad luck. Health insurance should not penalize those who have bad luck.

The "iatrogenic" condition—a disease or other harm that actually is caused by a physician or a hospital—has long plagued the practice of medicine. The entire U.S. health-care system has become iatrogenic, causing stress, which is medically harmful. Why do Americans subject themselves to health-care-related stress when universal standard coverage is a known cure?

EVERY LIFE MUST INCLUDE SOME COLLEGE

In nineteenth-century America, the greatest reform was abolition of slavery; the second-greatest, mandatory public education. *Mandatory* is a loaded word, yet the mandatory feature of the public-education movement was essential to its wide-ranging success, and very much in the interest of those upon whom the mandate was imposed. That the United States in the last century became the richest, strongest nation the world has ever known was not a deterministic outcome of U.S. advantages in geography and resources. America's success was the linear result of the U.S. educational premise—everybody goes to school, everybody cares about school, and every school tries, at least, to be a quality school.

The next step, both logically and as a matter of necessity, is that everybody goes to college. For two generations in the United States, Canada, Japan and much of the European Union, middle-class families have known that college is essential to their children's prospects. The next step is to extend this premise to *everyone's* children. Universal higher education will be as important to the world's fortunes in the twenty-first century as public high school education was to the West's in the twentieth century. In much of the world and, we may hope, eventually in all of the world, the social standard must change from the current assumption—go to college if you can—to a new standard, that everyone attends. "Attend" may entail living in a dormitory on a leafy New England campus, or taking classes at a community college as a commuter student, or may mean distance learning via computer.[8] America should lead the way by becoming the first society in history in which all adults have attended at least some college: this is a reasonable objective for the next half-century. Once America sets the example, other nations will follow.

Consider the mathematics of life span. In the late 1800s, when mandatory schooling until age sixteen was the great progressive reform, the typical life span in Western nations was less than fifty years. Now it is above seventy-five years, roughly a 50 percent gain. If we're living 50 percent longer and residing in a far more sophisticated society than when the minimum school-attendance age was fixed at sixteen, shouldn't we expect to need 50 percent more schooling? In the late 1800s, a person leaving the educational system at age sixteen, then the age beyond which only the sons and occasionally daughters of the affluent went on to college, had attended ten years of school.[9] Assume today's longevity and social complexity mean we need 50 percent more education—that works out to fifteen years of school. Make fifteen years of school the social norm, and you're in school until your early twenties—the standard age for college graduation. Compared to life expectancy, a twenty-five-year-old of today is younger than was a sixteen-year-old leaving high school in the 1890s. In a reality where people live longer and engage in ever-more-complex tasks dictated by an ever-more-complex world, school until the early twenties merely keeps society at the same relative level of education achieved in the late nineteenth century. Surely we can resolve to do as well as the nineteenth century!

The second reason a mandatory-college aspiration is important is national competitiveness. Critics tend to cite with alarm the higher ratios of science and engineering degrees produced by Chinese and Indian universities, compared to American and European colleges, and suggest the West's students must shift from liberal arts majors to hard science. That's wrong—the future needs more history majors, more literature majors, more philosophy majors. Many vital business and political achievements are made by men and women who did not major in science or engineering. Colleges may also need to reorganize their departments. Mark Taylor, a professor at Columbia University, has proposed that rather than cling to traditional highly stratified academic departments that have little to do with one another—the physics department never talks to the international-relations department—the college of the future should organize coursework around such concepts as Mind, Body, Law and Information.[10] Today most colleges and universities lack the sort of cross-category classes that address issues such as "How do other cultures think?" or "How does law influence business decisions?" or "Should technology be subject to ethical restrictions?" Questions such as these will rise in importance; colleges must learn to teach the answers.

A third reason expanded access to college is important is that educated people are better at looking after themselves. The educated know more; they change professions more easily; they don't have the factory-town mind-set of feeling dependent on whatever the local leading employer is. In cold economic terms, the well educated are more valuable than the undereducated—and in a turbulent economy, we want *everyone* to be valuable. As the world transforms during the Sonic Boom, it may prove cheaper, to say nothing of kinder and fairer, to assure that every adult has the higher education needed to look after himself or herself than to be endlessly trying to identify and subsidize those cast out from industries that change.

Because higher education will be steadily more valuable to society, fundamental reform in college economics is called for. Many states have good-quality public university systems—California, Michigan, New York, Pennsylvania, Texas, others—yet are reducing state support for their colleges. This is penny-wise and pound-foolish, especially since the relatively small sums saved by cutbacks in higher education can lead to higher amounts of tax revenue lost when economic growth does not occur. Some states are taking steps to make it harder for illegal immigrants to attend public colleges. Illegal immigration is a problem to be sure, but what end is served by denying people the education they need to look after themselves? Many nations face similar questions—whether to save a small amount by cutting back on college funding, risking the loss of large amounts in the future. Much of the money spent by government is either subsidy or entitlement; both categories may be necessary, but neither is productive. Money spent on education is an *investment,* improving society's future. A 2009 study by the consulting firm McKinsey & Company estimated the United

States GDP would be at least $1 trillion higher if public education were better;[11] such benefits from improved education should exceed the costs. Nations must learn to view the price of widely available higher education as an investment, and spend more for public colleges and universities, while reducing other kinds of spending.

Eleven.

YOUR TOWN

You live in a place that once was called a town or city, but now is called a "market." Centuries ago, towns and cities were organized around markets; now they *are* markets. The economic aspects of your behavior are elaborately tracked by credit cards, "affinity" cards (the key-chain barcode tags that give you grocery-store discounts also compile a profile of your purchase habits) and demographic analysis that allows merchants to know, block-by-block, what kinds of things people in your market buy, and how often. Every road of the place you live in has GPS coordinates that are easily accessed by children; anyone can access highly detailed aerial views of the places where most people in your town live and work. As you drive and, if you have a newly purchased cell phone, as you walk, satellites in outer space transmit second-by-second updates on your location, with accuracy of about a meter, soon to improve to about a foot. You own at least one device that can communicate essentially instantaneously with any similar device anywhere on the planet, including the ability to send or receive video, a task that once required an entire television studio. A billion people now have such devices, and the number is rising fast. With every passing day, the rest of the world is closer to you, just as you are closer to others who live on other continents. You benefit from the actions of millions of people who live thousands of miles away, and they benefit from your actions. You need them and they need you.

A century ago, when people resided in towns rather than in markets, it was possible to live out a life in which the rest of the world was an abstraction. Unless there was a war, what happened in other nations simply didn't matter much, and you sure did not need experts or international agencies to help you make day-to-day judgments about your life. That phase of existence for the human family is now over, except in parts of Africa and Asia, and it won't last much longer there, either. A new phase has begun—one that will make the world more prosperous and less warlike, but will also bring an enervating sense that nothing is ever permanent.

Even in a new economy where nothing is permanent, a few principles are certain. Education will matter more and more—there is no scenario in which education doesn't ascend in importance. Governments will need to invest both in ever-better public education through the high school years, and in universal college education. Interpersonal skills, particularly the ability to get along with people who aren't like you, will be highly prized. Whether you're looking for a job with a big employer or going into business on your own, the ability to communicate with people different from you, and cooperate in a constructive manner, will be essential. And don't get set in your ways—those who embrace change rather than fearing it will be the winners as decks are endlessly reshuffled.

Not far into the future, globalization will mean more to your daily life than it does now. International ease of trade and ease of communication, which seem advanced today—it can't be repeated enough that both are just getting started. Those seemingly superadvanced devices in your home, car and office? Soon every form of electronics you now rely on will be viewed as rudimentary. The near future holds a greater pace of change than the pace that today makes you crazy. The Sonic Boom is just beginning.

Even if there are no superpower wars or asteroid strikes, changes are likely that will shake society. During the twentieth century, global life expectancy increased dramatically. Suppose that during the twenty-first century, life expectancy increases at the same rate as it did during the twentieth, with life past the age of one hundred a common outcome, rather than a rarity that merits a congratulatory letter from the president or prime minister. Imagine how society will be rocked by another substantial jump in life expectancy.[1] Chip-based electronics have existed for just a few decades, and already computers are designing new computers without direct human input. Suppose self-aware artificial intelligence happens: imagine how society would be rocked by that. Suppose one morning all the world's television screens light up with a message from a distant alien civilization. Even if the message is friendly greetings, imagine how society would be rocked. It's easy to think of a dozen striking developments, unrelated to war or natural disaster, that could happen in the near future. And of course some striking development that is expected by absolutely no one is sure to occur.

Everything you don't like about contemporary social insecurity is going to get worse. Job turmoil, the economic roller-coaster, financial bedlam, media superficiality, celebrity inanity, political blather, targeted advertising, scream-and-shout discourse, the paving over of nature—they're all going to get worse. A lot worse, in some cases. Most likely, global economics will be blamed for whatever about coming decades we don't like. It will become standard for people to claim that everyone's benefiting from globalization except them. That won't be true, but the claim will be ubiquitous.

At the same time, much of what you do like about life will get better. Prosperity will increase, especially in the less-affluent nations where improvement is most needed. Democracy will flourish on five and perhaps six continents, which would have seemed a pipe dream just a generation ago, and seemed entirely impossible in the dark hours of World War II. Information and knowledge will proliferate as never before, while art and culture become available to everyone. Many aspects of the evolving Sonic Boom will be really terrific. The terrific aspects and the anxiety-inducing aspects will be intertwined, and we're just going to have to live with this.

———

Have you ever heard a sonic boom? There is a sharp crack, suggesting an extremely loud slam; the air shudders, windows shake; an instant later, there is a kind of "whap" sound with lots of lesser whaps echoing inside it. Sonic booms are really irritating, and seem unnerving, in the sense that it's hard to believe so much disruption could be caused by the passage of a relatively small object. And sonic booms are stress-inducing. You want to yell at the pilot to slow down and show some consideration. But the pilot can't hear you.

The global Sonic Boom now beginning will cause the kind of clamor associated with actual sonic booms. Relatively small changes throughout the world will result in window-shaking that seems all out of proportion, just as with actual sonic booms. You won't be able to yell at the pilot, because the Sonic Boom has no pilot. You won't be able to complain about navigation, because no one has the slightest idea what destination the international economy is moving toward.

No matter how crazy and chaotic events become, probably things will turn out fine; probably with each passing year the world will, on balance, be a better place than at any point in the past. Whatever comes next, bear in mind the high-tech economic muddle of a Sonic Boom world is a thousand times preferable to military conflict, isolationism or authoritarianism. A chaotic, raucous, unpredictable, stress-inducing, free, prosperous, well-informed and smart future is coming. Just remember to cover your ears.

Acknowledgments

For the realization of this volume, thanks are due to my friends, colleagues and editors Jonathan Alter, Chris Anderson, Timothy Bartlett, Ethan Bassoff, Emily Bazelon, Peter Beinart, James Bennet, Christine Berg, Jackson Bowling, David Bradley, David Brady, Carol Browner, Evan Camfield, Robin Campbell, David Caputi, Michael Carlisle, Erin Carter, Stephen Carter, Richard Celeste, Gina Centrello, Diane Stevens Chandler, Sarah Chilton, James Collins, Matthew Cooper, Kieran Darcy, Katherine DeShaw, Eric Dezenhall, Deborah Fallows, James Fallows, Franklin Foer, Jonathan Fried, William Galston, Michael Gerson, James Gibney, Kukula Glastris, Paul Glastris, Ann Godoff, Bonnie Goldstein, Ed Goldstein, William Goss, Carol Graham, David Gray, Joshua Green, Wendy Guillies, Tedd Habberfield, Pat Hanlon, Toby Harshaw, Bethany Hase, Marjorie Hazen, David Hendrickson, Stephen Hess, Lauren Hovel, Garry Hoyt, Arianna Huffington, Alexis Hurley, Mark Iwry, Kevin Jackson, Jay Jay Jones, John Judis, Lou Kallas, Ron Kaplan, Jonathan Karp, Bill Keller, Elizabeth Kennelly, James Kennelly III, Robert King, Michael Kinsley, Michael Knisley, Dorothy Koch, John Kosner, Robert Krimmer, Timothy Lavin, Emily Lazar, Nicholas Lemann, Toby Lester, Ann Lindgren, Robert Litan, Darrion Locke, Ben Loehnen, Thomas Mann, Tien Mao, Jynne Martin, Jon Meacham, Amy Meeker, Matt Miller, Lesa Mitchell, Jaimie Muehlhausen, Cullen Murphy, Thomas Neumann, Pietro Nivola, Timothy Noah, Joseph Nocera, Lynn Olson, Steve Olson, Sue Parilla, Don Peck, Denise Pellegrini, Charles Peters, Elizabeth Peters, Michael Philbrick, Julia Pilcer, Walter Powell, Jonathan Rauch, Noah Rifkin, Roberta Rifkin, David Roberts, Katy Roberts, Yvonne Rolzhausen, Robert Samuelson, Isabel Sawhill, Aaron Schatz, Kurt Schluntz, David Schoenfield, Carl Schramm, Lindsey Schwoeri, Peter Scoblic, Jack Shafer, Jenn Sides, Allison Silver, John Skipper, Ellie Smith, Barbara Snyder, Albert Song, Samuel Starr, Mark Steinmeyer, Richard Stengel, Patrick Stiegman, Sage Stossel, Scott Stossel, Maria Streshinsky, Strobe Talbott, Michelle Tessler, Nicholas Thompson, Steven Waldman, John Walsh, Jessica Waters, Peter Wehner, Jacob Weisberg, William Whitworth, Leon Wieseltier, Willie Williams, Norby Williamson, Scott Winnette and Claudia Zahn; to my father, George, and stepmother, Donalda; to my brother, Neil, and sister, Nancy; to Daniel Goulding, 1936–2002; to Conrad O'Donnell, 1953–2005; to Marjorie Williams, 1958–2005; to James Kennelly, Jr., 1930–2006; to Whitney Hendrickson, 1990–2009; to my children, Grant, Mara, and Spenser; and to my wife, Nan Kennelly.

I especially thank the Ewing Marion Kauffman Foundation of Kansas City for supporting the research for this book and the Brookings Institution of Washington, D.C., for sponsoring that research.

Notes

Most of the book's quotations from living persons are from interviews with me. The exception is quotations from Presidents Barack Obama and George W. Bush. Throughout the book, all references to amounts of money have been converted into today's dollars.

INTRODUCTION

1. *SIPRI Yearbook 2008.* Stockholm International Peace Research Institute, 2008.

CHAPTER 1: SHENZHEN

1. Dubai is the other contender for this distinction. But this very-fast-rising city mainly contains trade and tourist facilities, plus theme-park-like areas. It's not really a place for typical people to live.
2. Stockholm Institute for International Peace annual survey, 2009.
3. *Peace and Conflict 2008* by J. Joseph Hewitt et al. University of Maryland, Center for International Development and Conflict Management, 2008. According to the 2008 report *Global Burden of Armed Violence,* published by the nonprofit group Geneva Declaration, nearly 4 million people per year died

owing to war or organized violence (the Holocaust, Soviet and Chinese mass murders or mass relocations) in the first half of the twentieth century; in the second half, the number of deaths from war and organized violence declined to about 800,000 per year. Obviously that number remains horrific, but taking into account population growth, in the second half of the twentieth century a person's chance of dying by armed violence was less than one tenth as much as in the first half of the century.

4. I do not pretend to understand why the United States invaded Iraq in 2003, but doubt the underlying reason was to seize oil—it would have been far cheaper to purchase all the oil in Iraq than to invade and occupy the country.

5. *Human Development Report 2007.* United Nations Development Programme, Geneva.

6. *World Development Indicators 2007.* World Bank, Washington, D.C.

7. *The Illusive Quest for Growth* by William Easterly. Cambridge, Massachusetts: MIT Press, 2002.

8. "The Upside of Income Inequality" by Gary Becker and Kevin Murphy. *The American,* May–June 2007.

9. It's easy to be wrong—trust me, I have plenty of experience!—but for landing wide of the mark, few serious works can top *The Atlantic*'s February 1994 cover story by Robert Kaplan, "The Coming Anarchy." This piece basically predicts the world would have ended by now, with developing nations collapsing into postapocalyptic brutality and the West barely functional. *The Atlantic* is America's finest periodical and Kaplan is an accomplished writer. Neither could resist the urge to exaggerate the negative, to a drastic degree. Equally revealing, the article received effusive establishment praise, including from President Bill Clinton.

10. Those in the Western nations are keenly aware of the danger of dictatorship, but forget that feudalism—in which accidents of birth rule a person's life, and the landed lord it over the landless—has been the circumstance for the numerical majority of human beings ever to have lived, including the majority who lived during the twentieth century. The decline of feudalism, being accelerated by globalization and the rising accessibility of international communication, is as important to the fortunes of the world as the decline of dictatorship.

11. Futurism can be profound or silly; if you read up on Raymond Kurzweil, you will find he exhibits both traits. Kurzweil believes humanity is about to "transcend biology," whatever that means. More on his thinking is in *The Singularity Is Near.* New York: Penguin Books, 2006.

12. "You Are What You Spend" by W. Michael Cox and Richard Alm. *The New York Times,* February 10, 2008.

13. Calculated from the *Statistical Abstract of the United States, 2008–2009*. Washington, D.C.: United States Census Bureau.

14. Some studies indicate low-cost physical therapy relieves chronic knee pain just as well as expensive surgery, but that's a topic for another book.

15. *Rising Above the Gathering Storm* from the National Academy of Sciences. Washington, D.C.: National Academy Press, 2007.

16. "Bright Lights Big Cities" by Matthew Quirk. *The Atlantic*, December 2007. See also the United Nations publication *State of the World Population 2007*.

17. *The Starting Gate: Birth Weight and Life Chances* by Dalton Conley et al. Berkeley: University of California Press, 2002.

18. As Sam Paltridge has noted in "The Next Several 'Billion," *OECD Observer*, July 2008, a generation ago only 5 percent of Jamaican citizens possessed telephones; in 1991 the nation switched from a centrally controlled socialist economy to a liberal free-market economy, and now nearly 100 percent of Jamaicans have telephones. Rural farmers in Jamaica and elsewhere "now use mobile phones to track commodity prices they previously knew little about, helping them bypass intermediaries and corruption."

19. "Can America Still Compete?" by Robert Lawrence and Martin Baily. Peterson Institute, Washington, 2006.

20. "The Productivity Revolution" by Brian Wesbury of First Trust Portfolios, an investment firm in Wheaton, Illinois, 2008.

21. Annual Report of the American Iron and Steel Institute, Washington, D.C., 2008.

22. And though automotive fuel efficiency needs to improve, we forget that average m.p.g. has doubled since the late 1970s.

23. For instance, in 2008, before the financial-markets typhoon hit, General Motors was selling four very similar mid-market sedans: the Malibu, Aura, G6 and LaCrosse. Built by separate divisions of the same company, these models advertised against one another, and their dealers price-cut against one another. In the same year Toyota had only one mid-market sedan, the Camry, while Honda had only one, the Accord. In 2008, the Camry and Accord each alone outsold all four G.M. competitors combined. Yet G.M.'s superhighly paid top managers refused to switch to the successful single-model marketing strategy being employed directly in front of their eyes. General Motors did not simplify its model lineup until 2009, when the company went on federal life-support payments and was compelled by Washington to change its ways. Had G.M. changed its ways voluntarily years ago, the company's 2009 shattering might not have happened.

24. Big Three costs per labor hour rise to about $70 when retiree benefits are included.

25. In the same critical years General Motors was doing little about low fuel mileage and low manufacturing quality, the company was investing billions of dollars in an all-new division for its Hummer brand. By 2008, Hummer dealerships were folding, sales had all but stopped, and Hummer was among the worst fiascos in American business history. Even had gasoline prices not risen, the ultrahuge, ugly, unsafe Hummer always would have been a niche product with limited sales potential. After all, there are only so many people who wish to spend $50,000 to broadcast to the world the message "FU," and once these people had purchased Hummers, the market had been saturated. Yet G.M. executives showered capital on the Hummer project while cutting corners on manufacturing quality—though study after study has shown that manufacturing quality is what draws customers to Toyota and Honda.

26. In 2008, Caterpillar had its best year ever, running double shifts at its Aurora, Illinois, factory to meet export demand for industrial equipment. In winter 2009 it laid off many workers owing to the global downturn, but said it expected to resume hiring soon. So would Illinois-area factory workers have been better or worse off if international trade were restricted?

27. The system, operational for just six months from 1975 to 1976, was decommissioned as a consequence of the 1972 ABM Treaty. Though that treaty was negotiated with the former Soviet Union, the Sentinel antimissile missiles themselves had been optimized for use against the small Chinese ICBM force; Moscow had too many nuclear missiles to stop. The 1972 treaty allowed the United States and former Soviet Union each to possess just one ABM site, optimized for defense against China. The United States closed its sole ABM site in 1976; Russia's is still operational, though mainly as a symbolic gesture, as its technical quality is low.

CHAPTER 2: WALTHAM

1. Owing to its association with quality, several watchmakers still use the Waltham name; none is affiliated with the original Waltham Watch.

2. In 2007, Wal-Mart released a study claiming the company's aggressive price-cutting saved the typical American family $2,500 per year. The number is based not on Wal-Mart sales but on all inflation-adjusted reductions in prices of retail goods, regardless of whether sold by Wal-Mart—on the theory that Wal-Mart's pushing its competitors to outsource to other nations caused $2,500 worth of benefits per family broadly through society. Perhaps this claim is true, and if so, you do not need to shop at Wal-Mart to benefit.

3. "Roboburgh Rising" by David Ignatius. *Washington Post,* March 28, 2008.

4. "Export Boom Fuels Factory Town Revival" by Timothy Aeppel. *Wall Street Journal,* July 18, 2008.

5. See Jacob S. Hacker, *The Great Risk Shift.* New York: Oxford University Press, 2006.

6. "Current Employment Statistics," February 2009. Bureau of Labor Statistics, Washington, D.C.

7. My hobby is writing a football column for ESPN. In February 2009, ESPN decided not to fill two hundred new positions originally budgeted for that year. An Associated Press story headlined "200 Laid Off at ESPN" ran across the country. No one had been laid off; the company had decided not to make additional hires. That's hardly good, but nowhere near as bad as media negativism made it seem.

8. "Anxious Workers" by Rob Valletta. Federal Reserve Bank Economic Letter, June 1, 2007.

9. *High Wire* by Peter Gosselin. New York: Basic Books, 2008.

10. *Inside the Middle Class.* Philadelphia: Pew Research Center, 2008.

11. The Pew poll cited above also found that in 2008, 53 percent of Americans thought their future would be better than their present; that's slightly above the average for the 1960s. So Americans are not necessarily any less optimistic than in the past—just more anxious.

12. "Brother, Can You Spare a Billion?" by Stephen Taub. *Institutional Investor Alpha Magazine,* April 2009.

13. The Ponzi-scheme con artist Bernard Madoff was running a hedge fund. He did not call it that, but that's how the fund was registered with the Securities and Exchange Commission.

14. *The State of Working Americans 2007* by Lawrence Mishel et al. Washington, D.C.: Economic Policy Institute.

15. CEOs actually use the word *incentivize* to describe what their bonuses allegedly do for them, and I was dismayed to find that the spell checker of the latest Microsoft Word recognizes *incentivize* as a proper word. CEOs also use *incent* as a verb, and Microsoft Word recognizes that, too. Perhaps Bill Gates at some point told the Microsoft board of directors he would refuse to answer the phone anymore unless he was incented with more money.

16. See "The Inequality Conundrum" by Roger Lowenstein. *The New York Times Magazine,* June 10, 2007.

17. "The Inequality Myth" by Brad Schiller. *Wall Street Journal,* March 10, 2008.

18. Household income for the middle class is up 15 percent after inflation since 1978, but since the average number of people per household has declined, per-capita middle-class income is up 23 percent.

19. *Current Population Survey.* Washington, D.C.: Census Bureau, 2008.

20. *Wealth and Economic Mobility* by Ron Haskins. Washington, D.C.: Brookings Institution Press, 2008.

21. Though high-pressure sales tactics surely were to blame for pushing some buyers toward gimmick mortgages, many put little or nothing down, and thus suffered no out-of-pocket loss. The nothing-down gimmick mortgage was essentially renting with an option to buy; if you never put any down payment into a house, then had to move out, you were very unhappy but had not "lost" the house because you never owned any of it in the first place. When people say "my house," in most cases they mean "the house I live in" rather than "the house I own," because until the mortgage is satisfied, the mortgagee is not the owner. Many housing-crisis news reports of 2008 and 2009 involved people who had never put up any down payment saying "They're taking away my house!" and being treated by a credulous media as victims. If you purchased a car with nothing down then stopped making the payments, you would not be surprised to receive a repossession notice, nor would media outlets treat you as a victim.

   For some reason, Americans can't think clearly when it comes to homes—about who actually holds title to the home and how tenuous the position of the no-equity occupant is. If you default, be glad you don't live in Europe. American mortgages are "no recourse" loans, meaning if you move into a house and then stop making mortgage payments, the most you can lose is physical residence in the house. The mortgage holder can't come after you for your bank account and retirement savings. In most European Union nations, mortgages have recourse clauses—if you stop paying a mortgage, you are sued and your assets seized. Needless to say, the European housing market is considerably more stable than the American housing market. And in Europe, people don't casually lie to lenders.

22. In retrospect, people who bought houses using gimmick mortgages or liars' loans in the 2002–2006 period will appear as lottery winners who were awarded prizes in the form of taxpayer-subsidized homes. Other government actions besides the ones mentioned in the main text will subsidize those already in homes while penalizing young people attempting to buy homes. Allowing bankruptcy judges to "adjust" mortgage terms by eliminating a portion of the debt, for example, will be a prize awarded to current mortgage holders, but an extremely strong disincentive for bankers or investors to make future mortgage loans.

23. "Equity Loans as Next Round in Credit Crisis" by Vikas Bajaj. *The New York Times,* March 27, 2008.

24. That's stating the 1975 national debt in 2008 dollars; stated in the dollars of the time, the 1975 national debt was $540 billion.

25. The portable 401(k) only partly solves the pension problem because many employers impose a three-to-five-year vesting period. If you change jobs before the pension vests you get no matching contributions; worse, the employer may fire you the week before you were about to vest, in order to avoid paying into your 401(k). The solution is legislation requiring employers to make 401(k) donations beginning on the first day of employment, or perhaps after a brief probationary period.

CHAPTER 3: YAKUTSK

1. "Joint Science Academies' Statement: Global Response to Climate Change." http://royalsociety.org/displaypagedoc.asp?id=20742.
2. "Finally Feeling the Heat" by Gregg Easterbrook. *The New York Times,* May 24, 2006. Google this phrase: "Climate Change Science 2007: The Physical Science Basis." That will take you to the encyclopedic summary of current global warming research compiled by the Intergovernmental Panel on Climate Change.
3. Al Gore's movie *An Inconvenient Truth* depicts New York and San Francisco flooded by a twenty-foot sea-level rise. This could happen only if all the world's land ice melted, which the National Academy of Sciences has called extremely unlikely, even over the course of many centuries.
4. The clunky phrase "artificially caused global warming" is needed for precision: natural global warming owing to atmospheric water vapor and naturally emitted carbon dioxide has been around for eons, and is essential to life.
5. Studies by Josefino Comiso of the National Snow and Ice Data Center at the University of Colorado show the north polar ice cover of summer 2007 was the smallest ever recorded.
6. "Shrinking the Carbon Footprint of Metropolitan America" by Marilyn Brown et al. Washington, D.C.: Brookings Institution, 2008.
7. Needless to say, entire books have been written on whether global-warming theory is right or wrong. For the purposes of this book, all that matters is that the scientific consensus now holds that some degree of climate change is likely. For details see my white paper "Case Closed: The Debate on Global Warming Is Over." Washington, D.C.: Brookings Institution, 2006.
8. Some theories have held that freshwater entering the North Atlantic from ice melting could prevent the Gulf Stream from moderating weather in Western Europe, leaving Europe much colder even as the world warms overall. If temperatures fall in Europe, even more disruption will occur. At this writing, the science was shifting back toward thinking that a sudden ocean current collapse is unlikely. But the possibility remains, and at any rate, ocean currents are little understood.

9. Nouriel Roubini of New York University is generally viewed as the sole prominent economist who predicted what became the 2008 meltdown. In 2005, he told a conference of economists that careless mortgage lending, overrated mortgage-backed securities and too much leveraging at investment banking houses would soon cause "an economic breakdown" at least as bad as the S&L crisis of the 1980s. A few months later he warned that the real estate bubble was about to burst and the results would be "nasty all around." He was right. But Roubini was also a top economic adviser to President Bill Clinton and Clinton's Treasury Department when some of the policy decisions that led to the 2008 meltdown were made, and he did not warn against them at that early stage.

10. *Data Smog* by David Shenk. New York: HarperCollins, 1997.

11. Video Consumer Mapping Study, 2009. Washington, D.C.: Council for Research Excellence.

12. In 2007, two news helicopters collided in Phoenix, Arizona, killing four people, as the aircraft jockeyed for position to beam video of police chasing a truck. A total of *five* news helicopters were in the area when the collision occurred, all vying for video of a truck with a police car behind it.

13. There is something similar to my hypothetical *Consensus Today*, a British publication called *Positive News*. This is not a Pollyanna sheet, but a publication devoted to reporting reforms that work. Because there is so little interest in this subject, *Positive News* is a quarterly.

14. The First Amendment bargain, well understood by the Framers, is that for speech and expression, only absolute protection works: government cannot be in the business of choosing what types of expression are good or bad. That means that in books, media, art and religion, the trite and the inane receive the same protection as the profound. Jefferson and Madison knew this would happen, and if it didn't bother them, it shouldn't bother us.

CHAPTER 4: ERIE

1. Transportation canals were the Next New Thing around the year 1800. Many investors backed them, and were wiped out when another innovation, steam locomotives, caused railroads to become more attractive than canals. It turned out that many rail lines of the nineteenth century were built along rights of way originally purchased for canals. Often in economics, an initial failed innovation paves the way for the idea that works.

2. Many Southern states also held out against the standard-gauge movement. When Southern rail lines were destroyed by Union soldiers during the Civil War, they were replaced with standard width.

3. The state's steel industry missed the example of Philadelphia, which at the founding of the United States was the new country's wealthiest city, in part owing to its liberal attitudes about free trade.

4. Getting out of the locomotive business would prove to be one of the many management blunders that drove General Motors to its 2009 bankruptcy.

5. The unducted fan engine, which is odd-looking, offered most of the speed of a jet engine, but lower fuel consumption. In the 1980s, when petroleum was $20 a barrel, airlines chose maximum speed. The unducted fan might make a comeback in an age of expensive oil.

6. Gore also asked college students to practice civil disobedience against coal by blocking roads leading to any sites where coal-combustion facilities are scheduled to be built. From the Edmund Pettus Bridge to the power-plant access road! Gore says so many nutty things about environmental issues that it's hard to tell whether he is exaggerating to get attention or has been enjoying a little too much Tennessee sour mash.

7. In classic boondoggle form, FutureGen was organized as a consortium of eleven companies, all of which spent all their time and government appropriations wrestling for control of the project budget. Absurdly, all eleven companies were either coal-mining concerns or utility firms—neither of which have any experience designing power-generating systems! That is done by the research divisions of companies such as General Electric or Babcock & Wilcox. No such firm was included in the FutureGen consortium. If you wanted a project to be a wasteful failure, you couldn't have come up with a better organizational chart.

8. No hurry to polish your telescope—that will happen in 2061.

9. When you dial a customer-service number and the clerk who answers in an Indian accent identifies herself as "Rachel," there's a good chance you were routed to a call center in Bangalore. The 2009 book *Your Call Is (Not That) Important to Us,* by Emily Yellin, estimates that each customer-service call handled within the United States costs a company $7.50, while one handled in India costs $2.35.

CHAPTER 5: LEIPZIG

1. "The Rooftop Revolution" by Mariah Blake. *The Washington Monthly,* March–April 2009.

2. While brands of gasoline are interchangeable, there is a range of aviation fuels with different chemical properties intended for different altitudes and engine types. See "New Generation of Cleaner Jets Possible If Biofuels Can Be Produced" by Michael Mecham. *Aviation Week & Space Technology,* April 6, 2009.

3. "Assessment of Energy Policy and Practices," World Energy Council, 2008.

4. See "Long Term Fundamental Energy Research" by George Whitesides. *Science,* February 2, 2007.

5. "Stabilization Wedges" by Stephen Pacala and Robert Socolow. *Science,* August 13, 2004.

6. *Energy Technology Perspectives 2008.* Paris: International Energy Agency.

7. Philips Electronics, the first to market compact fluorescents, has done tests in which consumers say they like the quality of CF light if they don't know what kind of bulb it is coming from, then say they dislike the light once the source is revealed.

8. *Power to Save the World* by Gwyneth Cravens. New York: Vintage, 2007.

9. "The Billion Ton Biofuels Vision" by Chris Sommerville. *Science,* June 2, 2006.

10. This idea was not original; a Michigan company called Energy Conversion Devices has been attempting to print solar cells since the 1980s.

11. Even the name is cool, combining solar power with nanotechnology, a buzz term. The nano part is mainly marketing, though. So far, nearly all companies with "nano" in their portfolio only mean "Our products contain molecules, and molecules are really small."

12. Because ethanol has lower energy value than gasoline, there's also a "stealth tax" invisible at the pump. The 2005 law mandated that all gasoline sold in the United States be at least 10 percent ethanol; the 90/10 mix now sold at filling stations contains 3 percent less energy than pure gasoline. That means 3 percent lower m.p.g. performance; a typical driver now has to fill the tank twice more per year to compensate, resulting in an ethanol stealth tax of around $75 per year per car owner.

13. "In Situ Formation of an Oxygen-Evolving Catalyst in Neutral Water Containing Phosphate and Co^{2+}" by Matthew Kanan and Daniel Nocera. *Science,* July 31, 2008.

14. Today's nuclear power relies on fission, or the splitting of heavy atoms, which is only practical using uranium or plutonium. Fusion, the process of the sun, joins light atoms. Fusion releases far more energy than fission. Cold fusion, accomplished without complex reactors, remains possible, though a long shot.

15. Unfortunately, solar collectors in orbit would be a tempting military target, meaning such a long-term energy solution might be practical only in a peaceful world.

CHAPTER 6: ARLINGTON

1. *Venture Impact: The Economic Importance of Venture Capitalism.* Arlington, Va.: National Venture Capital Association, 2008. This study is written by

Global Insight, the Waltham, Massachusetts, consulting firm that is the chronicler of the Sonic Boom.

2. The first Seagate hard drives also retailed for about $2,000, which inflates to $5,000 today. That's just for the hard drive. Today a full-featured desktop computer with TV-quality screen and blazing-fast printer retails for around $1,000. In 1981, I purchased one of the early IBM PCs, with slow-moving daisy-wheel printer, for $5,900, or about $15,000 in today's money. It was like buying a car! That 1981 PC had only a slight fraction of today's computer power, and of course no Internet access—in 1981, no one even knew what that meant.

3. "Economics and the Entrepreneur" by Carl Schramm. *Claremont Review of Books,* Spring 2008.

4. IBM's first laptop, in 1986, weighed twelve pounds.

5. Actually, press coverage was the part that was expertly timed; IPOs are scheduled well in advance, so investors have time to ponder the prospectus.

6. Whether Sirtris or any firm ever will perfect an antiaging drug was unknown at this writing.

7. Venture capitalists, and private equity firms, which are similar, also sometimes invest in struggling young firms whose initial backing came from somewhere else. In cases like these, there are complex negotiations about how much stock the new investors receive, because their entry dilutes the value of the equity of the original investors' stake. Generally, the longer it takes a new firm to get on its feet, the less the ground-floor investors see at the end—because every time new money is brought in, existing positions are diluted. This means that if you have invested in a start-up and you hear that the company is seeking a cash infusion, you groan. Your stake is about to become smaller.

8. Skype was a home run for the venture-capital firm Draper Fisher Jurvetson, which put about $18 million into the start-up in 2004 and saw the value of its stake climb more than twenty times in a single year, until eBay bought Skype in 2005.

9. *Worth* here refers to market capitalization, or the selling price of a company's stock times the number of shares in circulation. In 2000 the "market cap" of Alcoa was $34 billion.

10. The place where the San Francisco Forty Niners play was for a while 3Com Stadium, and for a while the place where the Baltimore Ravens play was PSINet Field. Don't rush out and try to buy something made by PSINet. After 3Com could no longer pay for the naming rights in San Francisco, another firm paid to have the stadium briefly called Monster Field. It turns there are two corporations named Monster, one which makes audio cables and one that is a job-search agency. Two corporations named Monster—no, I don't know what that says about capitalism. The Ravens' field was at this writing called M&T

Bank Stadium; I hope that by the time you read this the banking industry will still exist.

11. Telefonica's loss was greater than 100 percent, when "opportunity cost" is taken into account. Had Telefonica simply placed its $5.4 billion into conservative investments such as investment-grade bonds, four years later the company would have been holding $6.3 billion or so. In opportunity-cost terms, Telefonica started with $5.4 billion and managed to lose $6.2 billion. That's impressive! What you might have done with your money, instead of what you did, must always be factored in. In 1998, Daimler-Benz spent $36 billion to acquire Chrysler. A decade later, in 2007, Daimler-Benz "sold" its Chrysler division to a private equity firm called Cerberus—"sold" in quotes because Daimler-Benz in effect paid Cerberus $677 million to take Chrysler's pension obligations off Daimler's books. Had Daimler-Benz in 1998 simply placed its cash into conservatively managed investments, the amount would have risen to about $60 billion by 2007. Thus, in terms of opportunity cost—what Daimler might have done instead with the money it had—the company lost about $60 billion on Chrysler. Daimler's opportunity-cost loss exceeds the Enron bankruptcy, which wiped out about $50 billion.

12. Today's downsized, renamed CMGI is located in Waltham, Massachusetts, the subject of chapter 2.

13. Anytime an investment adviser or broker claims to have a "secret formula" for making money, slam down the phone. The investment adviser who claims a "secret formula" is invariably running a Ponzi scheme. There are no sure-fire secret formulas. Or if there were, the possessor would not offer to share the profits with you!

14. Funds registered as hedge funds are free from regulation and disclosure. Originally hedge funds were used to hedge—to buy overlapping positions that would reduce losses if a market went way up or way down. Today a "hedge fund" is any fund engaged in risky investment plays while exempt from federal oversight. Don't ever put money in a hedge fund unless you can afford to lose every cent.

15. Venture capitalists don't like to disclose much, and generally are not required to. In 2006, when Ned Lamont ran for the Democratic senatorial nomination in Connecticut, some financial details were released regarding his wife, Ann, a venture capitalist for Oak Investment Partners, a leading firm. Oak had just raised a $2.6 billion investment fund, among the largest ever assembled for venture purposes. According to *The New York Times*, Oak charged a 2 percent annual "carry" for its basic services, meaning if the $2.6 billion fund existed for five years, Oak would be paid $260 million merely for babysitting the money. If there are profits when the venture firm sells off its positions in new businesses

supported by the fund, Oak keeps 25 percent, according to the *Times;* if there are no profits, Oak is not penalized, other than in the sense that it might have difficulty attracting investors to the next fund. Suppose Oak makes bad decisions and the investors' money is lost; Oak still gets to keep the $260 million administrative fee. Suppose Oak makes good decisions, and the $2.6 billion doubles to $5.2 billion. Oak gets $1.3 billion (25 percent of the $5.2 billion), the investors get $3.9 billion, or about a 6 percent return over five years. Suppose Oak makes great decisions and the fund trebles to $7.8 billion; Oak gets almost $2 billion, a quarter of the final amount, while investors about $6 billion, almost a 20 percent return over five years. From such figures it is easy to see why *The New York Times* estimated that Ann Lamont and other senior officials of Oak earned about $15 million annually. From these estimates, it is also easy to see how the venture-fund managers make out almost no matter what happens, while investors come out ahead only on the occasional big money-maker such as YouTube. A venture firm that regularly lost money for investors eventually would go out of business, but its executives would still keep their bonuses.

16. Harry Rein, mentioned in the main text, attained a small fortune by backing CommerceOne, the late-1990s progenitor of "business-to-business" Web sites. CommerceOne had what sounded like a fabulous idea: thousands of businesses each year publish bid specifications for vendors, a process done in person and involving reams of paperwork. What if businesses could publish their needs on one central Web site, where any producer could place a competitive bid? CommerceOne offered to be a clearinghouse for business supplies sold to businesses. The firm went IPO in 1999 at $138 a share; soon shares were selling for $196 each; Rein and other venture capitalists behind the new enterprise raked in millions in profits. By 2004, CommerceOne was out of business, its shares were worthless and its investors had lost every farthing. But venture firms and other backers kept their gains. Rein did nothing wrong; CommerceOne had a legitimate idea that might have worked. Just bear in mind that any person who advises you to invest money may benefit from his own advice a lot more than you do.

17. The theoretical underpinning for lack of disclosure rules on venture capital, and also on hedge funds, is that these asset classes are sought out only by sophisticated investors who fully understand they may lose their money. Naïve grandmas don't buy into Kleiner Perkins or Carlyle Group funds. That's the theory, at least.

18. Sometimes an "angel" is a single rich person, sometimes a few well-off people who pool their resources outside the formal structure of an investing firm. Some entrepreneurs prefer to work with angels, because angels are the least

bureaucratic sources of financing, and may be more patient than venture firms, which sometimes face pressure to close out funds and distribute gains. But if you've got a personality clash with your angel, it's like working for a boss you hate.

19. I tried a box and they were delicious, though I still prefer my local fish store, where the premium crab cakes cost half as much and haven't been frozen. At least by mentioning my taste test, I made my order tax-deductible.

CHAPTER 7: CHIPPEWA FALLS

1. Owing perhaps to its amusing name, Chippewa Falls is sometimes mentioned in the movies. In the big-bucks Hollywood flick *Titanic,* the Leonardo Di-Caprio character says he is from Chippewa Falls and reminisces about learning to sail on its scenic Lake Wissota. That lake, indeed scenic, was formed as the reservoir of a hydroelectric dam—which was built five years after the *Titanic* sank.

2. Cray built the lab within walking distance of his Chippewa Falls home—which contained a sizeable bomb shelter, as this was the 1960s. Cray didn't want to live in a major city, because he feared big cities would be targets in a nuclear war.

3. *Rising Above the Gathering Storm* from the National Academy of Sciences. Washington, D.C.: National Academy Press, 2007.

4. Like many modern disclaimers, the Google disclaimer was in small type and all caps, both of which make text harder to read. I have no idea what I agreed to by clicking ACCEPT—perhaps I signed away all intellectual property that someday may be created by my heirs. Surely the ideal contemporary disclaimer would include the words PLEASE DO NOT READ THIS DISCLAIMER.

5. *Economic Report of the President 2008.* Washington, D.C.: Government Printing Office.

6. "Service Sector Growth in China and India" by Yanrui Wu, University of Western Australia.

7. Google "CIA World Factbook" to glean this sort of comparative information easily.

8. In the 1920s, automaking was the number-one U.S. economic sector, with more than 20 percent of GDP, while health care was about 1 percent. Now health care is nearly 16 percent of the economy, auto manufacturing below 3 percent.

9. *Productivity and American Leadership* by William Baumol and Susan Ann Blackman. Boston: MIT Press, 1991.

10. "No Country for Young Men" by Megan McArdle. *The Atlantic,* January 2008.

11. "Rising Health Costs Cut into Wages" by Michael Fletcher. *Washington Post,* March 24, 2008.

12. On Veterans' Administration health-care quality, see "The Best Care Anywhere" by Philip Longman. *Washington Monthly,* January 2005.

13. "Paying Doctors to Ignore Patients" by Peter Bach. *The New York Times,* July 24, 2008.

14. A cow used for milk "creates more value," in economic terms, than one slaughtered for meat, as a milk cow can feed many people for many years.

15. A standard question of both science and science fiction is whether radio and microwave (TV) signals that "leak" from Earth will attract space aliens here. Maybe, but the window in which this might happen appears brief, as the power levels used in communication are steadily declining. From about the late 1930s to the late 1990s, many wireless and microwave signals were powerful enough to penetrate the atmosphere and "leak" into space. Today, as the power-level needs of communication devices keep declining, fewer and fewer signals possess the oomph to reach space. Within a decade or two, Earth may fall silent from the standpoint of alien astronomers listening for artificial signals.

CHAPTER 8: CAMDEN

1. *Made in China* by Donald Sull. Cambridge, Mass.: Harvard Business School Press, 2005.

2. Congress was debating the number as this book went to press.

3. America's fiscal 2009 federal deficit is expected to be a breathtaking $1.8 trillion, three times the worst previous deficit. Raising taxes to 100 percent on those earning above $500,000 would produce about $1.3 trillion in a year, failing to wipe out a $1.8 trillion deficit. And of course 100 percent taxation would backfire by bringing economic activity to a halt. A realistic soak-the-affluent tax plan, such as raising the top-rate tax across the board from 36–39 percent to 50 percent, would increase federal revenue about $400 billion in a year—still not enough to close the deficit gap. Spending cuts simply must happen, especially in the big entitlement programs, Medicare and Social Security. Needless to say, every constituent and interest group wants spending increases, not cuts. The estimates in this note and the associated main text paragraph are from the Congressional Budget Office.

4. "Democrats for Rich Heirs" by Michael Kinsley. *Washington Post,* April 10, 2009. From the article: "Perusing the Forbes 400 list of America's richest people, it's striking how few of them made the list by building the proverbial better mousetrap. The most common route to gargantuan wealth remains inheritance."

5. Fewer than 1 percent of estates pay estate taxes, which provide only a tiny fraction of federal revenues.

6. Investors tend to remember the good guesses, forget the bad ones. Thus, if you had money in Churn Associates during a period when the fund went up, since one third of stock guesses are correct, you made money and told your friends, "Those brokers at Churn Associates are geniuses!" That statement reflects well on you, implying you are superclever for choosing the right broker. In the two thirds of instances in which you either lost money or did not gain as much as you might have with a routine investment such as an S&P index fund, you don't tell your friends, "I am a fool because I handed my money to Churn Associates." Investment managers rely on human-nature aspects like these for sales promotion. The economist Peter Bernstein, who died in 2009, documented the amusing truth that two thirds of Wall Street stockbrokers' investment choices do worse than simply holding an S&P index fund.

7. According to a *New York Times* report, the computer model that AIG used to predict the movements of credit-default swaps—the financial instruments whose collapse ended up costing U.S. taxpayers $172 billion—had no negative term for housing prices. The superhighly paid "experts" who wrote the model assumed it was literally impossible for housing prices to decline.

8. In 2008, Paul Krugman was awarded the Nobel for economics for an update on this theory. As a young economist, Krugman proposed an explanation of why two nations engaged in mutual trade could both benefit even if both were making roughly the same goods—the larger markets and increased competition would cause both to improve products and cut prices faster than would occur if they weren't engaged in trade. His analysis became one of the intellectual underpinnings of globalized economics, and has been proven correct by subsequent events.

9. Paul Ehrlich's 1968 bestseller *The Population Bomb,* for instance, predicted that "hundreds of millions of people" would starve to death in India during the 1970s as that country descended into total anarchy. Today commentators speak of the "Indian miracle"—a fast-growing economy, reasonably stable food production and democracy in a country with nearly a billion citizens.

10. Milton Friedman memorably said of *The Affluent Society,* "Many reformers— Galbraith is not alone in this—have as their basic objection to a free market that it frustrates them in achieving their reforms, because a free market enables people to have what they want, not what the reformers want people to have."

11. *Job Creation in America* by David Birch. New York: The Free Press, 1987.

12. "We Need to Recapitalize the Banks" by Edmund Phelps. *Wall Street Journal,* October 1, 2008.

13. Said by Hillary Clinton, John McCain, Joe Biden and Mitt Romney; perhaps by others.

14. The former Fed chair Alan Greenspan received a reported $8 million advance for his droning as-told-to *The Age of Turbulence,* which serves mainly to convince the reader that Alan Greenspan has an extremely high opinion of Alan Greenspan. Published in September 2007, the book predicts nothing about any coming problems in credit markets.

15. Science fiction has a long history of anticipating trends in society as well as science. The University of California at Irvine physicist Gregory Benford wrote a 1976 novel, *In the Ocean of Night,* in which a twenty-second-century spaceship is sent to investigate an artificial object discovered in another star system. The spaceship has no captain. There's a person who is roughly an officer administrator, who schedules meetings and duty hours and the like, but all major decisions are made via public debate among the thousand-person crew, followed by plebiscite. When I read this book thirty years ago I thought, "Come on, in important organizations there will always be someone in charge who gives orders." Today I am not so sure.

16. *The Moral Consequences of Economic Growth* by Benjamin Friedman. New York: Alfred A. Knopf, 2005.

17. *The Origin of Wealth* by Eric Beinhocker. Cambridge, Mass.: Harvard University Press, 2005.

CHAPTER 9: LOS ANGELES

1. Attend a concert of your civic symphony or a performance of your city's regional theater, visit the nearest art gallery, attend an opera staged by any decent-sized university—ten bucks says you'll be impressed. United States high culture is in better shape than commonly understood.

2. The soccer World Cup also draws millions of spectators to its qualifying rounds.

3. "Rutgers Football: A Game of Secrets" by Ted Sherman and Josh Margolin. *Star-Ledger,* December 7, 2008.

4. *Beyond the Classroom: Using Title IX to Measure the Return to High School Sports* by Betsey Stevenson. National Bureau of Economic Research, 2009.

5. A detailed argument that emphasis on sports is bad for higher education can be found in *Reclaiming the Game,* a 2005 book by William Bowen and Sarah Levine. Bowen and Levine focus mainly on elite institutions, such as the Ivy League schools and the members of the New England Small College Athletic Conference (Williams, Bowdoin and so on). The authors' core contention is that elite schools should not recruit athletes or grant admissions preferences

based on sports ability. My view is that since elite college admission would be highly sought after even if footballs and basketballs did not exist, college sports serves a positive role by helping to make very large numbers of high school graduates enthusiastic about attending the majority of colleges that are not elite.

6. Mandelbaum notes that baseball was the American sport of the nineteenth century because its pace fit the agrarian lifestyle—baseball can be played in a farm field and is relaxed and untimed, the competition continuing until whenever it is completed, just like farm labor. As long as someone brings a bat, ball and gloves, you can set up a baseball game. Football, by contrast, requires elaborate equipment and facilities, and is a timed sport—dominated by clock movements, much as is a factory.

7. According to the National Federation of State High School Associations, in 2008 about 1 million boys and 1,000 girls played varsity or junior-varsity high school football.

8. The United States was also first to establish a large system of schools to teach teachers, a reform that got petty tyrants and ignoramuses out of the classroom. "Normal school" was the old name for what are now called teachers' colleges, and teaching the teachers to act normal was part of the goal.

9. "U.S. Universities Rush to Set Up Outposts Abroad" by Tamar Lewin. *The New York Times,* February 10, 2008.

10. The center is an affiliate of the University of Maryland University College, the adult learning facility of the Maryland public university system. But "University of Maryland University College" looks so much like a typo that I've used the sponsor institution name.

11. "Measuring Up." National Center for Public Policy and Higher Education. San Jose, California, 2008

12. The rich don't care about the price and the poor get need-based aid, but in a nation where the median household income is about $50,000 annually, few average families have any hope of sending a child to an elite private school. A few colleges such as the Ivies, Bowdoin and Davidson have in recent years announced admirable plans that allow the children of the middle class to attend nearly free—but only if they qualify for academic admission. Since few high school graduates have the grades to qualify for elite colleges, the plans don't help most families.

13. "Transformation 101" by Kevin Carey. *Washington Monthly,* November–December 2008. Carey's article makes the important point that tuition costs are skyrocketing even though some aspects of education are growing cheaper—computer-aided learning actually does work for some subjects, and is far less expensive than traditional tutoring.

14. Most college endowments were down at this writing, owing to the soft stock market.

15. "One-Quarter of California High Schoolers Drop Out." *Los Angeles Times,* July 18, 2008.

16. "The Misplaced Math Student" by Tom Loveless. Brookings Institution, 2008.

17. The SAT is now just named the "SAT," letters that don't stand for anything, in the way that the KFC chicken company now claims KFC doesn't stand for anything—the "F" certainly doesn't stand for Fried! Once SAT meant Scholastic Aptitude Test, but critics complained that "aptitude" sounds like innate ability and thus is an elitist term. So the letters were changed to stand for Scholastic Assessment Test—but the idea of people who presume to sit in judgment of the learning of others using the phrase "assessment test" didn't go over. Now it's simply the SATs. Perhaps soon "D.C." won't mean District of Columbia, it will just mean a place called D.C.

18. "How to Raise Our IQ" by Nicholas Kristof. *The New York Times,* April 16, 2009.

CHAPTER 10: SÃO JOSÉ DOS CAMPOS

1. *The Post-American World* by Fareed Zakaria. New York: W. W. Norton, 2008.

2. I recommend attending the football games of your local high school or small college—they're a lot of fun, parking is easy and tickets are five dollars.

3. I am not thinking here of his dystopian novel *1984* but rather his 1937 book-length essay, *The Road to Wigan Pier.*

4. *World Values Survey 2008. Perspectives on Psychological Science,* July 2008.

5. Having devoted my last book, *The Progress Paradox,* to the conundrum that "life gets better while people feel worse," I won't repeat the details. Though if you want to be happy, you'd better buy that book!

6. *Preexisting* means, obviously, the same thing as *existing.* I have no idea why health insurers insist on this redundant term.

7. 2008 Annual Report, Organization for Economic Cooperation and Development, Paris.

8. I am suspicious of computer-based college courses. But almost everything done via the Internet has improved in quality, so perhaps Internet-based education likewise will improve.

9. State-law minimums for high school attendance should also be raised to eighteen years. A disturbingly high percentage of minority students, especially Latinos, leave the public school system at age sixteen or seventeen, never graduating from high school. Fully a quarter of Latino students in the Los Angeles County public school system drop out of high school within a few

months of turning sixteen. They do this because it is legal for them to leave after age sixteen—and because the age-sixteen minimum creates a psychological assumption of "I've done what the law requires." In the contemporary world, the law ought to require high school attendance through age eighteen.

10. "End the University as We Know It" by Mark Taylor. *The New York Times,* April 27, 2009.

11. *The Economic Impact of the Achievement Gap in America's Schools.* San Francisco: McKinsey & Company, 2009.

CHAPTER 11: YOUR TOWN

1. Your first reaction might be to say that if average life span extends into the nineties, society will be dragged down by pension costs. But if you'd told a nineteenth-century rationalist that today men and women typically enjoy active twenty- or even thirty-year retirements, your nineteenth-century interlocutor would have replied that society would be dragged down by pension costs. So far, life extension has been financially manageable for Western nations.

Index

impact of Title IX, 178
personal freedom, 14–15
and population dynamics, 24–25
role in economic growth,
    xiv–xv, 22
U.S., social progress toward, 17
in workforce, 55
Woodward, Susan, 119–20
work, merging with home, 197
    See also jobs
WorldCom, 43, 119, 122, 162

Xbox, 138
Xerox, 122

Yahoo, 116, 118
Yakutsk, Russia, 58
YouTube, 116

Zakaria, Fareed, 192
Zhang Ruimin, 150, 151, 152
Zink, 38, 41
Žižek, Slavoj, 152, 153

ABOUT THE AUTHOR

GREGG EASTERBROOK is the author of six previous books, including *The Progress Paradox: How Life Gets Better While People Feel Worse.* He is a contributing editor to *The Atlantic* and *The New Republic,* and a former Distinguished Fellow of the Fulbright Foundation. He lives near Washington, D.C., with his wife and three children.